The Life and Times of Dacoit Queen Putli Bai
and
Other Short Stories

About the Author

Born in Bhopal in April 1935, **Shri O.N Shrivastava,** MA (Political Science and English Literature) belongs to the family of Late Shri Diwan Daulat Rai, whose ancestors migrated to Bhopal from Lucknow in 1749 and then served the erstwhile Bhopal state for over 200 years, working in various high positions. Shri Shrivastava joined the Indian Police Service (IPS) in 1959 and then having worked for over 14 years in various assignments within Madhya Pradesh he opted for deputation to the Government of India in the Intelligence Bureau (IB), where he joined in 1974. He retired in 1993 after completing 35 years of service in the IPS – 20 years in the Intelligence Bureau – of which he spent 18 years working in the seven North Eastern States. In 1994, the Government of India appointed him as the Governor of Nagaland and Manipur – two most sensitive states in the North East – where he worked for almost six years.

Shri Shrivastava is an experienced police officer, and a capable administrator. As an intelligence officer for over twenty years he did master the rather difficult art of working with people. His three years in the dacoit-infested Bhind district from 1961 to 1963 and then 18 years in the North-Eastern States, provided him a unique opportunity, of studying from very close quarters, the problems created by the dacoits and separatists. The short novel 'The Life and Times of Putli Bai' is essentially an expression of his experiences in the dacoit – infested Bhind district. It brings into sharp focus the problems faced by the average citizen in trying to make a living in these areas. It also brings into open the desire, lying dormant in every dacoit's heart of being able to live a normal life. The story also very painstakingly describes the essential basic human feelings present in every policeman working in these areas – unable to find fulfilment due to the badly caste-ridden society and the machinations and conspiracies hatched by different gang-leaders – on a daily basis – for supremacy, ending up in inter-gang violence at regular intervals.

The twenty years spent by Shri Shrivastava in the Intelligence Bureau – the eighteen years spent by him in the seven North Eastern States and about six years spent by him as the Governor of the sensitive States of Nagaland and Manipur and his secret parlays with the top leaders of almost all the underground groups in the region had given him an insight which is revealing and which brings into focus the 'why' of many of these separatist organisations. Therefore, whenever his narration takes him into these areas, he experiences no difficulty in giving expression to the sub-terranian currents on the run in these areas – the unique culture of its people and the enduring phases of this region's history.

Shri Shrivastava has launched himself into writing just three years earlier. Since then his articles, write-ups and short stories have regularly appeared in newspapers and magazines. He has already published two books in Hindi namely 'Dasyurani Gudiya' and 'Shubh Dristhi' both containing one short novel and eight short stories each. The books have been well received.

'The life and Times of Dacoit Queen Putli Bai' is his first attempt at writing in English.

Shri Shrivastava was awarded the Padma Shri in 1990 for his outstanding work in the North East and J&K. In addition, he is the recipient of President's Police Medal, the Indian Police Medal, Police (Special Duty) Medal with 5 bars, the Eastern Star and about half a dozen other decorations. He is presently settled in Bhopal, leading a retired life and lending his shoulder to social issues.

The Life and Times of Dacoit Queen Putli Bai and Other Short Stories

O.N. Shrivastava

CONCEPT PUBLISHING COMPANY PVT. LTD
NEW DELHI-110059

ISBN-13: 978-81-8069-676-3

First Published 2010

Published and Printed by

Concept Publishing Company Pvt. Ltd.
Regd. Office:
A/15-16, Commercial Block, Mohan Garden
New Delhi-110059 (India)
Phones : 25351460, 25351794, *Fax* : 091-11-25357109
Email : publishing@conceptpub.com,
Website: www.conceptpub.com

Editorial Office:
H-13, Bali Nagar, New Delhi-110 015, India.

Cataloging in Publication Data-- *Courtesy:* D.K. Agencies (P) Ltd. <docinfo@dkagencies.com>

Shrivastava, O. N., 1935-
The life and times of Dacoit Queen Putli Bai and other short stories / O.N. Shrivastava.
p. cm.
ISBN 13: 9788180696763 ISBN 10: 818696766

1. Short stories, Indic (English). 2. Dacoits--India--Fiction. 3. Police--India--Fiction. I. Title.

DDC 823.914 22

In loving Memory of
all those
who encouraged me in my struggle in life
– in every possible way;
and
helped me achieve undreamt heights

Preface and Acknowledgement

Dear readers,

My MA in English literature notwithstanding, I frankly confess that I am no man of literature. My language therefore is not literary. I commenced writing at the ripe age of seventy when my vocabulary and its usage, like my habits, has become too well defined – has become too conditioned by the official life that I lived for more than forty five years. Readers therefore are likely to miss in my writings, serious literary content.

I, however, have tried to compensate my readers by using a language which I call the language of heart – more appropriately the language of love. Taking liberty I quote:

सब से मधुर बोली वही, सब से मधुर भाषा वही।
बोलें जो नयना बावरे – समझें जो सैयां सांवरे।।

(The sweetest of whisper is that – the sweetest of language is one – which is spoken by the eyes of one madly in love and is understood most easily by the beloved)

So the language of my writings is – the language of heart.

Stories and memories originate and flourish in a mix of facts and romance. The writer himself, also the readers, both are left wondering as to where the reality ended and romance/ fiction and fantasy took off. Stories need names, places and characters. My stories too have all these. They also move within the parameters set by places and timings. That should be the reason as to why some characters start appearing real from the very beginning – perhaps due to their emotional appeal. All stories have a core or an emotional content the spring of which is in real life or in some real event. My stories and my memoirs both follow the same content and form. My readers are however requested not to start searching for me amongst my characters. That would end in their's loosing focus on the characters which I have created for them.

I want to write ten books – six in Hindi and four in English. I have started writing at the late age of seventy and with this book I have completed just three – two in Hindi namely, 'Dasyurani Gudiya' and 'Shubh Drishti' and the present one in English. I am presently busy writing a short novel on the life and times of a singer named 'Ruhi Messey' who had just two expectations from her life – to be able to sing right through, and to be able to laugh through all ups and downs. We do need in our lives a few such islands where we can rest and laugh – 'in this world so full of care'. Who would therefore not want to meet Ruhi Messey, a characterful of songs, laughter and life.

This collection has eight short stories and one short novel. A few of these stories are essentially memoirs. Cover story 'The life and times of Dacoit Queen Putli Bai' is based on some true events and one true encounter. The story tries to re-live, the essential core of goodness lying dormant in the immense recesses of the heart of a singer turned dacoit. It also brings to life the futility of attempts for reformation of dacoits caught up in internecine gang rivalries in a caste-ridden society. The transistor radio recovered from the scene of encounter is a character in itself, relaying the life and aspirations of the Bandit Queen. Story 'Mother First' highlights the relationship between a father and a daughter – and story 'One Night in Dehradun Express' the relationship between a husband and wife – also men in general. Stories 'Bade Babu' and 'Raijore Das Babu' are based on true characters and bring into sharp focus the essential integrity, strength of character and dignity present amongst the lower rungs of administration. 'Jackie – a Mother' is also a real story based on the life and death of a street-dog named Jackie. It highlights the fierce maternal instinct present amongst animals – almost at par with humans. 'Rehana Kashmiri' highlights the struggle of a Kashmiri girl to settle down in life, decently, under the rigorous code of conduct set by a highly religious and orthodox society.

This book, like the earlier ones is the outcome of continuing encouragement – received by me from my wife Nini and children Tripti and Amit and my son-in-law Chetan and his parents. I am indeed indebted to them. I am indebted to my neighbour, thinker, writer Ghanshyam Saxena who encouraged me into bringing out this book. And finally I am so deeply indebted to Mrs. Tara Joshi, a writer and a literary figure in her own right, who liked the short novel Bandit Queen so much that she single handedly took over the responsibility of translating it from Hindi into English – and did so in her own hand, providing me the impetus for translating and writing other short stories. I would ever remain grateful to her.

And finally my sincere thanks to Shri Ashok Kumar Mittal ji, Proprietor, Concept Publishing Company Pvt. Ltd., New Delhi, for having agreed to take over the responsibility of publication of this book. To all those and to all my near and dear ones who kept on encouraging me – from time to time into continuing writing — I would never have enough words to thank them. May God keep all of them healthy and happy – ever and always.

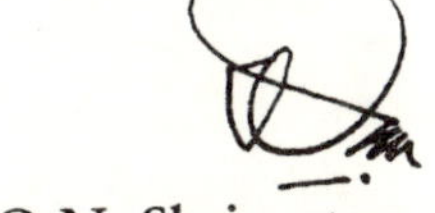

O.N. Shrivastava
'Green Gate', 8, Qutbi Plots,
Professors Colony, Bhopal-462 002 (MP)
Tel.: (0755) 2661710; Mobile: 9893061941
E-mail: onshriva15435@yahoo.com

Story Sequence

Love Eternal

मेरा उनका क्या दूँ परिचय
कई जन्मों के नाते हैं।
हर बार बदल कर यह काया
हम दोनों मिलने आते हैं।
धरती के इस आँगन में...

—महादेवी वर्मा

(How do I introduce 'one' to whom I had remained related in several lives, and to meet whom I had returned to this earth again and again ... wearing a new body each time)

* * * * *

The dead do not return to life – that is the truth eternal. However there may be a case where one came across someone, who resembled the one already dead – in totality. This may force one to sit up and introspect – only to realise in the end that the dead and the living can not be the same – would never embody the same emotions, experiences and expectations!

* * * * *

The year was 1950 and they studied together, in the Government Hamidia College, Bhopal – both doing their

Bachelor of Arts. She belonged to a family of Roman Catholics. Her father was the then Station Master of Bhopal railway station. They occupied a palatial house in the railway colony – a walking distance from the Station Bazaria (small market) – next to the railway station's entrance. She was extremely fair, slim and tall and blessed with large expressive eyes and smiling features. Her father owned (in British terms Lorded over) and supervised the humblest of the goings on within the parameters of Bhopal Railway Station – strictly. The father wielded a lot of clout and was therefore very rich. Her family was counted amongst the few affluent families of Bhopal. For her, therefore, money was no problem.

She was Prabhawati Clifton – colleagues simply called her Prabha. In her family her grandfather was the first convert and her mother the last – having converted just a month prior to her marriage. Her mother's marriage to her father was the culmination of a widely acclaimed and prolonged love affair. The father was an excellent hockey player – a wily centre-forward – and the mother was one dedicated hockey fan. The Bhopalis of those days used to fondly talk about this romance as the 'stick and ball' romance.

Prabha's father was recruited by the British in the then GIPR (Great Indian Peninsula Railway) as a loco-man. He however greased his way up the railway administration ending up as the Station Master of the then all important railway junction in Central India. His long association with the British did influence his likes/dislikes greatly. He liked everything that the Britishers liked – hated everything that they hated. He wanted his children to grow up in high and exclusive society mixing only with the British children – getting married into Anglo-Indian families – if not British. Prabha's mother however was forward looking, benevolent and free from any hang ups. She saw nothing wrong in her daughters – she had three of them; no boy – associating with the non-British, non-Anglo youngsters, from brown families. By 1950 as it is, there were hardly any British family left in Bhopal – just a dozen Anglo families. While the father drank away his days living in a dream world, the mother was pragmatic and practical. She understood that if she kept the choice restricted to British or Anglo boys only, her daughters might end up remaining unmarried. She therefore at times, encouraged her daughters associating with even average Bhopalis. Her father's strong opposition to Christian girls getting married into non-Christians families was however all the time at the back of her mind and she respected his wishes. She therefore frequently warned her daughters against getting too seriously involved with non-Christian boys – since such an affair was bound to end in frustration.

It has been said times and again that affairs of love respect no boundaries – particularly those set either by religion or society. In this case too it didn't!

Prabha was sixteen – at the most seventeen when she joined Hamidia College in BA Part One. Colleges those days sported an entirely different character. Hamidia College functioned from a regal building – Minto Hall – which had Italian marble for cladding and floors, Swiss crystals as door knobs, Swiss lamp shades and chandeliers, and Burma teak all the way for doors, windows and fixtures. It even had its own skating rink.

College education was not a craze those days and therefore the strength of the College was small – less than 300 – including about 70 girls. Bhopal was a small town and therefore everyone knew everyone else. Nothing happened within the college boundaries that ever remained confined within its four walls. Bhopalis were avid 'gap-baaz' (gossipers) known for embellishing, enlarging, adding salt and pepper to the smallest event happening within the college premises and circulating it far and wide. No affairs, not even flings or serious matters of heart therefore, ever remained under wrap.

Prabha was simple at heart. She never claimed any serious intellectual prowess. She conceded that she did reach BA – Part I, by just muddling through her examinations. She is believed to have told one of her serious boy friends that she just knew about 120 english words and that by using only that brief vocabulary she managed to clear all her examinations from class ninth to BA. Realisation of this shortcoming did put her perenially in search of just one student – year after year – class after class – with proven academic credentials on whose support, she could lean upon. And in Arun she found one such student!

Arun belonged to a Hindu family, with a recordable past – not a mentionable present. For seven generations his great grandparents worked as Ministers to the Nawabs amassing wealth and clout. In the last three generations, no one worked – yet everyone remained busy – quarrelling within and squandering the earnings of seven generations – a tall order successfully accomplished. Arun belonged to a generation struggling at subsistence level – with his father having remained unemployed for 20-25 years.

It is said that adversity brings out the best in a man. Arun proved this in totalily. He grew up in an environment of all round penury – in which no one ever thought of making academic excellence as a stepping stone to a life of fulfilment. Arun did! He believed that if he and his family has to get back on rails – he has to excel in studies through a life dedicated to toil and hard work. He exactly did that. He was not a topper in his struggling phase. But once he got on to his feet – he never looked back – topping every examination that he took. When he landed in BA – Part I, he was so sure of his academic excellence that he gave himself a little room by dedicating some of his time to games – even to befriending the fair sex. In his scheme of things there was no space for attempting things half-heartedly and therefore half way through his BA – Part I, he become an accomplished badminton player.

There is a Chinese saying: 'The mightiest of rivers have the humblest of origins.' Lao-Tzu has also said that the longest journey starts with the smallest step. The contents of these sayings apply emphatically to all aspects of life – most aptly to 'matters of love'.

Prabha and Arun studied in the same college – same class — spending over six hours together each day. Yet for quite many months they did not exchange even one word of love. It was Prabha who sometimes stopped Arun outside the classroom seeking clarifications either in economics or in english literature. She used to unhesitatingly confess that these subjects never sank into her head. Arun used to offer some on the spot guidance and the matters used to end there.

Arun was the one who should have taken the 'first step'. He was however hesitant not knowing how the 'first step' is taken – more importantly not knowing what it should be like.

Hesitation took a toll of five months and soon it was December 1950.

God certainly has his own calendar of events. Prabha admired Arun's brilliance– but said nothing – implicit or explicit. She admired Arun for his great talent, excellent memory and his newly acquired skills in badminton. Arun too found Prabha pretty, petite, smart – simply very – very attractive. However, whenever he came to the verge of taking that 'first step' – he felt frozen.

Yet it did happen one day – all of a sudden and quite unexpectedly! It was a chilly day in mid December. Both Prabha and Arun were standing next to each other on the skating rink – which also doubled up as a badminton court. Professor in-charge was fixing up badminton teams for the annual sports. He asked Arun: 'Would you want to participate in mixed doubles?'

'Of course' – Arun replied.

'Do you have a partner?'

'Of course sir – Prabha – who else!' He uttered these words alright but his heart sank into his knees. He did not have Prabha's OK! What if she said 'No'. Prabha's voice from behind, however, surprised him.

'If not Arun, then sir who else can be my partner?' Then turning towards Arun she said: 'I am with you Arun.' Then – laughingly added – 'for you only – ever and always'. And before her words could sink into Arun's head – she added:

'Always – yes – also in badminton – o.k. – cut!'

And the scene ended to everyone's satisfaction.

In the hurly – burly of the events no one noticed that that very crucial yet the smallest step towards the long journey has been taken.

The tournament started and was over within 3 days. Arun – Prabha's team lost in the 3rd of the five rounds to the finals. The team would not have lost in the third round – but for rank bad display by Prabha who that day was totally unfocussed. She realised it on the spot and as the cheering for the winning team died down – she came to Arun – took hold of his hand – and with tears in her eyes said:

'Arun you lost ... just because of me. You played so well today! You needed a better partner. I am so lazy – good for nothing. I made you loose...'.

She would have gone on but Arun hugged her, put his hand on her mouth and said:

'No more Prabha – we lost not because you played badly but because the opponents played better. For God sake don't curse yourself. You are such a good player.'

And he felt Prabha melting into his arms – unnoticeably.

The hug on the badminton court was noticed by a fairly large crowd – of boys and girls – some coming from orthodox burqa-donning families. The story was embellished and put in circulation salt and pepper added to it.

Soon enough everyone in Bhopal town was talking of one blossoming romance in the Hamidia College between Arun and Prabha – though in effect there were no such feelings at all between the two. Arun's mother was informed by one big well wisher of the family, of the 'badminton – court scandal' – as it soon came to be known. Arun's mother however preferred to ignore it. Once again it was the house owner who had brought this gossip home to Arun's mother, expecting serious retribution. Arun's mother simply asked – 'is it?' and for her the matter ended then and there.

The story evoked an altogether different reaction in Prabha's house. Her mother took the news in her stride – 'such things do happen in colleges'. Prabha's father was of course furious. He would perhaps not have bothered as much if Arun was a Christian. His daughter getting friendly with someone who did not even belong to his religion was not digestible to him. The mother intervened explaining that Arun was academically brilliant – a big help to Prabha in her studies – and that she saw nothing wrong or defamatory in what happened on the badminton court. Prabha's father had inherent faith in his wife's wisdom and therefore the matter ended there.

With passage of time Prabha and Arun came closer. Exchanging of books and notes is what everyone does in colleges. In Prabha and Arun's case too, one book or one note started getting exchanged – each day. Each exchanged book or note contained – hidden between its pages – one neatly written, carefully folded letter covering innocent developments around each other – written of course in the language of heart.

Such exchanges remained under wrap for a couple of months. However, the turn over of the letters being swift – everyone in the college gradually started knowing everything. Professors came to know of it – students too – also student's families. People started visiting Arun's house informing Arun's mother of the goings-on. They hoped to poison Arun's mother's ears that way. They did succeed too – though not very emphatically. One wintry evening Arun's mother asked Arun:

"Bete what is all this going on in your college? People are pestering me with all sorts of information".

'No Amma – nothing at all. I and Prabha are just two good friends! I don't know why people are so jealous?'

'I hear Prabha comes from a very affluent family'.

'Yes Amma'.

'Also understand that she is very pretty'.

'Yes Amma'.

'Understand, she is a Christian'.

'Yes – but that hardly matters?

Amma was silent for a few minutes, her eyes remaining glued to the floor. Then having organised her thoughts, she started speaking.

'Arun bete! You know that your father had been unwell – for quite sometime. If things go wrong, neither he, nor I would be able to help you out. Even otherwise, due to your father's illness my being any help to you remains a mute question'.

'Yes Amma –I know. I however promise you one thing ... nothing would go wrong between the two of us ... as a matter of fact there is nothing at all between the two of us'.

'Listen Bete – I trust you ... fully. My advise to you, however is ... You may love if you so desire, but never become possessive of whom you love. If you became possessive, you would soon start claiming – this one is mine – when in fact – no one or even nothing is yours. In Prabha's case, the status divide between you two is so wide that this affair cannot end in anything but disaster. That can be ruinous for your studies – over which you have staked everything!'

Arun realised in a fraction of a second the wisdom of every word that her mother has just uttered – the status gulf and the religious divide. He knew that Prabha's father would never agree to giving his daughter in marriage to Arun because of the precarious condition in which his family survived – due to father's prolonged illness and the need for Arun to stake everything upon academics – his only hope of being able to salvage the family's pride.

'Amma, listen – I understand every word of what you have just said. Your each word has sunk into my head. Have faith in your son ... nothing would ever happen which could become a source of worry to you. I enjoy being in Prabha's company. Allow me that freedom ... of being close to someone whose company I like. OK, Amma?'.

'Yes, Bete. I trust you. My blessings to you both'.

Amma got up from where she was sitting and ran her fingers through Arun's lush hair in a gesture of blessing. She did that frequently to Arun who enjoyed the feel of her fingers in his hair.

This happened in February 1951.

In March, shortly before examinations – Arun got laid up with malaria. Since his father was already in a private ward in Hamidia Hospital, the doctors agreed to have Arun as the second patient in the same room. Arun's mother occupied a camp-cot placed in one corner – looking after Arun's father.

One morning after Arun's admission into the hospital, Prabha walked into their room – a bouquet of flowers plucked from the college garden in her hand. She passed on the bouquet to Arun – and with just one wink and one big smile, she wished Arun, swift recovery. Then she walked over to Arun's mother, bent herself fully over her feet and rested her head there. And when she noticed Arun's mother's hesitation in allowing an unknown girl to touch her feet, she without lifting her eyes, implored:

'Amma – bless me like you have been blessing Arun. Allow me to share half of his wisdom – please, Amma!'

Arun's mother was nonplussed. In an effort to clear the air around them Arun told her mother: 'Amma this is Prabha. You have heard so much about her from others. Now you see her yourself.'

Amma caught hold of Prabha by her two shoulders lifted her up and gave her a seat next to herself on her camp cot. Then she started running her fingers through Prabha's short hair. Prabha was overtaken by Arun's mother's gesture and in one spontaneous reaction dropped her head into Arun's mother's lap and closed her eyes.

Arun's mother was quiet for a few seconds. Then in her inimitable affectionate voice, started speaking.

'Beti – in our families unmarried girls do not touch their mother's feet. It is the mothers who touch their feet – the only exception to the rule being the daughters-in-law, who are expected to touch mother-in-law's feet. I am sure, you are not aware of these customs. Don't even try to understand them. They are so complicated. I am comfortable the way you are. So just relax!'

No one knew what prompted Prabha, but in just one motion she covered her head with the end of her saree – bent really low and touched Amma's feet again.

Amma put her hand again over Prabha's head and blessed her.

'Long live – Beti. Be happy!'

Prabha, got up quickly and moved towards Arun's father. She thereafter busied herself in attending to him. She straightened his pillows, wiped tears from his eyes, straightened his covers – looked into the patient's history – brought out the medicines then due – and helped him with a glass of water. She even lifted his head slightly by putting her arm under his head so that he found gulping pills – easy.

She stayed in the hospital for one more hour. However during that period she paid no attention to Arun – just kept on looking after the father and chatting with Arun's mother. When she finally left – the two i.e. the father and mother were mighty impressed. As she was leaving they asked her to come again and invited her home as well.

The rancour and ill-will generated by months of whisper and malice by Arun's ill-wishers was wiped off in an hours time.

While still in hospital Amma once again asked Arun if he had any plans of getting married to Prabha to which Arun replied – 'not at all Amma'.

* * * * *

Arun's full recovery took one more week. Thereafter he left the hospital to appear in the examinations. Results were declared soon enough and they both passed – Arun in first division and Prabha in second. Summers arrived. Then came monsoons ending the scorching heat of summer. Colleges reopened and both Arun and Prabha joined the final year.

With parents consent, Arun started visiting Prabha's house – nearly every evening, for joint studies for the finals – also to help Prabha with her studies. No one objected. Everyone appeared happy.

That too became the talk of the town, with gossip-managers left counting the number of days to the marriage.

* * * *

It should have been December 1951 when the anxiously awaited Raj Kapur's movie 'Awara' came up for screening in Bharat Talkies. Bhopal still had just one college and the craze with students – both boys and girls – used to be – 'first day – first show'. On the very first day of the screening Arun went to Bharat Talkies, half an hour prior to the start of the first show and found 'House-full' boards on all windows. As he was planning to leave, he saw Prabha standing in the lobby accompanied by her two younger sisters. When Arun informed Prabha of the non-availability of tickets – she invited Arun to join her since she had one extra ticket. Prabha held four balcony tickets – seats no. 41, 42, 43, 44. She gave Arun the first choice to pick up anyone of the four tickets with eyes closed and Arun picked up 42 while Prabha picked up 41. Both were happy!

In the row behind Arun sat four persons – two men and two women from the family of Arun's land lord. The lights went off and the movie started and what a soul—stirring movie it was? The three sisters occasionally wanted to talk to each other or consult each other about some scene in the movie – and for doing that they including Prabha had to bend over Arun – so very close that Arun could hear their heartbeats. There was nothing serious in it. It was just innocent careless fun. However, the house owner's family sitting in the row behind, watched not the film but what was happening on the seats in front.

The movie ended with a thunderous applause and everyone returned home.

The land lord's family lost no time in meeting Arun's mother early next morning with a tale peppered solely by imagination – bordering on obscenity. Arun's mother was in serious discomfort. She never thought that Arun will ever cross the limits of decency and that too in a public place.

Arun returned from the college in the afternoon to an angry mother, who straightaway confronted him with the gossip passed on to her by the landlord's family. Arun allowed her mother to spend herself fully and intervened only when she started crying. He explained to her truthfully as to how he came in possession of that one seat in between the three girls. He also explained to her mother as to how the girls wanted to pass comments amongst themselves on the on-screen happenings and since they couldn't have talked loudly they bent low over him to get closer to each other. It was all innocent fun with no obscenity involved – by any stretch of imagination.

Amma had implicit faith in Arun. Having heard his explanation, she quietened down. She ended the conversation by reiterating that he should not do anything that could mar the family's reputation and that since she saw no possibility of Prabha becoming her daughter-in-law, it may well be right for Arun not to do anything which might harm Prabha's reputation too.

The matter ended there – harmony at home – yet one more scandal brewing outside – something for the people of the town to gossip about.

Soon enough it was one more year – 1952.

* * * * *

Final exams were scheduled from March 15. Everyone therefore got busy with preparations. Meetings between Prabha and Arun became less frequent; though the two kept on meeting almost every evening at Prabha's residence – for joint study sessions. When it was a week to examinations the two decided, by mutual consent, to put an end to joint-study.

The final joint study session came to an end on the evening of March 7 and as Arun was preparing to leave Prabha's room, Prabha advanced towards him and collapsed into his arms. Arun was caught unawares. With difficulty he managed to put Prabha back into her chair. He offered her a glass of drinking water which she quickly gulped. Arun took a seat next to her and requested her not to feel weak, since they would keep on meeting each other, during the summer break and after.

Prabha paid no heed to what Arun was saying. She just sat quietly – head resting on the table top. Four-five minutes would have gone by that way. As she raised her head to speak, her face was soaked in tears. She said:

'Arun, it is unlikely that we would meet henceforth. Why? I give you a letter which you read in the quiet comfort of your home. I am so grateful to you for having helped me out with my studies. I am such a dullard. If I become a graduate, it would only be because of you. I would owe it to you ever – Arun! You are such a wonderful person! Which girl would not want to be around you? I am so thankful to God that he brought us together, even if it was for a very brief period. I would cherish forever these carefree days – spent by us in each other's company. I would never forget the protection of your arms on the badminton court. How reassuring it was? I would ever cherish the feel of that hug – always and ever".

She has in between got up from her chair and had started moving towards the door with Arun in tow. As Arun was about to walk out of the main entrance she caught him in a very tight embrace, rested her head against his heart and quietly slipped in his hand a neatly folded letter. Then saying 'bye Arun – God be with you' – she turned around and in one go entered her bedroom!

Arun cycled back furiously towards his home. He was wondering all the time as to what makes Prabha say – we would not meet again? Why? Is it a diktat from her parents? Is it because his utility for the family is over? Why this sudden twist in the tale?

Back home he rushed into one empty room and switched on the reading light. He thereafter very carefully opened Prabha's letter – with trembling hands and anxious mind.

'My dear Arun,

What I tell you today is something that I could not have summoned enough strengh to tell you in person. Excuse me. You would call me a coward. Yes, I am!

My father would never have agreed to my marrying a non-Christian – my mother perhaps would have! But in this one matter her voice was not material because of her own background.

I don't know till today – what you thought of our relationship? You never told me. But I was aware of its futility from day one.

Love never is a decision which one takes consciously. At least I did not! To me it was a wild storm pushing me from the back and I blindly, though hesitatingly allowed myself to be blown over.

Arun you are a wonderful person. If I got mesmerised by you it was more your fault than mine. You are made that way and no girl could have resisted you. I was lucky that of all the girls in the college, much much prettier and better endowed than me, you decided to come closer to me. It was on the badminton court that I realised that I have fallen in love with you. That bond kept on growing stronger with each passing day.

The decision now is – of course taken with my consent, that I marry Vijay Daniels! He is fair and attractive. He is a talented guitar player, an equally good hockey player. He has recently been commissioned into the Indian Army as a Second Lieutenant. Our marriage is fixed for April 15 in the Railway Station Church. Do come Arun. Don't know when I would see you again!

Hearing all this would leave you heart-broken. Don't! Our affair was doomed to end with my marrying someone else. You would then be wondering as to what this love of mine was all about? Yes I loved you with all my heart – and all my soul – and even when I get married to Vijay, I would keep on wearing in my hair, vermilion of your love – life after life – till Divinity united us. So don't grieve – don't feel upset. Bye! Bye!!

Yours eternally

Prabha'

Arun remembered his mother's words: 'Prabha ... you may love her if you so desire. However, never become possessive of one whom you love. In your case the status and religion divide is such that I don't see your affair culminating in anything ... but disaster'.

He quickly went over to his mother and finding her alone showed her Prabha's letter. Her mother went through the contents carefully – word to word. It should have been good thirty minutes when she finished reading that letter. Thereafter she carefully folded it back and returned it to Arun.

'Don't grieve Arun. I am sure Prabha had just been practical. She knew the futility of prolonging this affair. You go and attend her marriage ... with all your heart and wish her a very long and happy married life – after all you loved her so much. Go bete! And also do your examination well!'

Arun sat for some more time with her mother and then quickly got up and returned to his room. It took him a day to absorb the full impact of these sudden developments. But then going over what her mother had told her it became easier for him to absorb the shock.

He appeared in his exams – with all his might – and when the results were declared he found his place amongst the first ten in the first division. Prabha too worked hard and was happy to get a high second division.

She got married on April 15 – with all fanfare. Her father was delighted – her mother was sad. Arun attended the wedding, joined the festivities and wished the two – all the best.

Prabha and Vijay's send off at the Bhopal Railway Station was a grand affair. Arun was there too. As Punjab Mail steamed out of the railway platform Arun found Prabha's eyes glued on to him – tearful. Arun held back his tears till he was safely out of the railway station.

Arun thought that with Prabha getting married and gone she was now out of his life ... that his two-year long affair with her had come to an end. Has it?

* * * * *

Arun continued his studies in the same college for two more years, completing his Masters in 1954. Then he appeared in the All India Services Examinations and got into the IPS. Doing various postings in his home cadre (Madhya Pradesh), after the outbreak of hostilities on the Indo-China border, he volunteered in 1963 — for a posting to Nagaland. He joined there in October 1963 as Commanding Officer of a Madhya Pradesh Police Battalion.

Army officers do get posted to all odd places. Arun therefore lost touch with either Vijay Daniel or Prabha. However in 1964, Arun learnt from an army officer that Vijay is now a Major and is due to join an Infantry Bn. in Mokokchung-Nagaland. Mokokchung those days was a non-family station for army officers. Therefore, chances of Prabha accompanying Vijay to Mokokchung were nil. Arun didn't want any re-run of 1950-52 – the memories themselves being so painful. He therefore decided to keep off from both Prabha and Vijay.

Arun remained in Nagaland from 1963 to 1967. The left over of 1963 and the first nine months of 1964 went by without any news of either Prabha or Vijay. However, in October 1964, just a week short of Puja holidays, a situation report (sitrep) from Mokokchung Brigade Headquarters alarmed Arun. The sitrep mentioned of an Army Jonga travelling between Guwahati in Assam and Mokokchung in Nagaland having met with an accident on Burra Pahar and having rolled down about 150 feet into the Brahmaputra, killing all its six occupants including the driver and one batman. Those dead included wife of Maj. Vijay Daniel's and two other ladies who were travelling unauthorisedly to Mokokchung for joining their husbands, in Puja celebrations.

Arun was heart broken! Tears rolled down uncontrolably as memories flashed past. What a way to go? What an age to die? RIP Prabha: Born 1933 – Died 1964 – Age 31 years.

And Arun decided not to remember this episode any more and to efface Prabha's memory from his mind and heart!

* * * * *

Arun retired from the Indian Police Service in 1993 – after a service of nearly 36 years – 26 years spent on postings in the North East. In recognition of his work in this region, the Government of India posted him in August 1994 as Governor of one of the North Eastern States. He joined his posting soon after.

A day prior to his swearing-in, Arun decided to get a message for the people of his state – recorded by the local Doordarshan staff. The message was meant for telecast over the local Doordarshan network – also for relay by the local AIR transmitters. The recording was scheduled for 5 p.m. a day prior to his swearing in.

Arun reached his office two minutes to five all dressed-up for the telecast. The Doordarshan staff had already laid the cables, set the cameras and positioned the recording equipment as they have been doing – Governors after Governors. Bang at five the Doordarshan staff walked in.

And there awaited the biggest surprise of Arun's life. As the young girl – in-charge of the DD Camera team walked into his room, Arun missed couple of heartbeats. Isn't she the same? Yes she is! She looks to be the same! Same large expressive eyes concealing God knows what secrets – same fair complexion – same height, nose, and smile – same dark straight hair! For a few minutes Arun was spell bound. For a few seconds he slipped into his long-lost dream world. Then he pinched himself back to reality. Was it Prabha standing in front of him? Has she come back to life?

Arun returned to reality with a start as he heard the girl wishing him a warm welcome to the State and a very good evening. Same Prabha's voice – same Prabha's accent! Yes! How did she come to possess all this? In order to clear the fog which had enveloped his mind, Arun asked: 'Ma'am, how should I address you? .

'Your Excellency I am Shanti Bora - you remember Shanta of Santa Claus!'

Shanti had her Identity Card (I. Card) dangling from her neck. Arun felt bold enough to ask.

'Can I have a look at your I. Card – Shanti?'

'Of course, Your Excellency! 'And in a second Shanti's I. Card was in Arun's hands – Ms. Shanti Bora, Father's name Arun Bora – Born October 1964 in a tea garden belonging to the Tatas – situated bang on Burra Pahar in Assam – photograph identical to that of Prabha's – identical to the one which Arun had preserved and has always kept with him.

Arun was wonderstruck! Here is a girl – Prabha's twin – born approximately the same month as Prabha died – in the same area Burra Pahar where Prabha met with her fatal accident – and to Arun, of all the persons. Is it just a coincidence? Is it that Prabha didn't die and is living – and now standing in front of me? Is it Prabha born again – her second birth?

Shanti's very affectionate voice shook Arun again out of his reverie. 'Your Excellency – all set for recording'.

'Oh – my speech?'

'Excellency – it is on your table'.

With that the cameras started rolling – the recording started – came to an end in just five minutes – all very professionally done. Arun got up and shook hands with the DD staff – Shanti's hand the last. She held on to Shanti's hand a little longer than usual, exchanging pleasantries. Shanti left the room as swiftly as she had come in – unmindful of the goings on, in Arun's heart.

Arun's struggle was unique. His heart told him that it was Prabha's soul resting in Shanti's body. It got freed from Prabha's body on the day of accident and found a safe heaven in Shanti's. Other facts too supported the calling of his heart. Mind however refused to believe that such a thing could ever happen.

* * * * *

Arun had vowed 30 years earlier that he would efface Prabha's memory from his life. He could not! At least twice a month, during his normal tours he would go over Burra Pahar where on one pretext or other, he would stop his convoy exactly at the spot of Prabha's accident. He would also get down from his car would gaze into Brahmaputra hoping to see Prabha coming back to him. Then he would remember his vow – would shake his head off in an effort to ward off Prabha's memory.

It was not unusual for Arun to get drawn towards Shanti Bora! It was her advent which had generated fresh hopes in his heart. He would argue: 'If Prabha's soul rested in Shanti, then it would have already told her of theirs having been together, forty years earlier – in 1950-52 – living memorable days, in each other's company.' Arun would peep into Shanti's eyes trying to find if they treasured any of those memories? He was invariably in for disappointment since startled Shanti would close her eyes and walk away – like a frightened doe. She was affectionate, freedom loving and an excellent girl – almost like Prabha. But she was no Prabha! She could not have been— since the 'dead do not come back to life!'

Yes, she possessed most of Prabha's endearing qualities – which were music to Arun's heart. She also appeared touched – to a great extent, by Arun's warmth and therefore never missed any of Arun's many engagements. She would invariably seat herself in the front row – in the segment reserved for 'Press & TV'. She would invariably be there well before Arun's arrival and as he would get on to the dais, their eyes would meet, would exchange one glance, sometimes a wink, ending in a 'namastey' – with folded hands. Distance would intervene, yet that 'namastey' would bring the two together – close enough!

Arun stayed on in his post for about six years. Then it was time for him to leave. Shanti came again to record Arun's farewell message – again a very professional work done. Arun wanted to watch reactions on her face as he read out his farewell message. But Shanti begged Arun's excuse and waited outside till the recording was over.

And finally it was time to leave. Shanti had been covering the goings on right from the sunrise. As Arun was getting ready to get into his car he saw Shanti standing all by herself in the centre of the big lawn – TV camera hanging on her shoulder. He broke steps and walked up to her.

'Bye, bye Shanti'.

'Sir, please come again – next time as an ordinary person – to be with us. We would love that. We would never forget you.' And Arun noticed tears filling up her large expressive eyes.

And what did Arun do? He caught her in a tight hug, like he had caught Prabha forty years ago – on the badminton court. And the next minute he was heading towards his car – one hand resting all the while on Shanti's shoulders.

'Bye, bye Shanti I would never forget you. Not any one of

you. I would keep on coming to you as often as possible. So don't grieve. Don't loose heart. We would certainly meet – soon.'

And the car was out of the Raj Bhavan compound leaving everyone behind – Shanti behind – Prabha behind!

Three months later, it was the New Years day – time for exchanging greetings and good wishes. Arun was surprised by a New Year Card from Shanti:

Dear Sir,

You are someone for whom I could not control my tears, when you left us – that too for a wonderful man who never even invited me for a cup of tea. A 'namastey' from the dais to me – standing alone in the audience will ever remain fresh in my mind. On December 12th I covered one of your favourite programmes – and I was missing you all along. You were so nice to me. I pray to God that people like you come to us again and again. Sir you were one person who conquered many hearts here. Everyone felt for you when you left us.

Please come again.

Shanti

× × ×

Shanti, however, was no Prabha. The dead are dead – are gone – and no one who is dead ever comes back to life – never ever. She was just Shanti. Her being born in Burra Pahar – where Prabha died, would have been just an accident. Hers being born around the time when Prabha died; her inheriting Prabha's physical feature etc. too would have been an accident. When Arun was leaving the Raj Bhavan Shanti cried, almost like Prabha cried when she was leaving Bhopal Railway

Station. But she didn't possess Prabha's heart! Prabha was Prabha and her heart died the day her car rolled down Burra Pahar into Brahmaputra river. Yes on quite many occasions Shanti reacted like Prabha. This, however, could not have happened since she possessed Prabha's heart – which she did not. This would have happened since Arun continued to behave in a manner identical to how he used to behave with Prabha – invoking identical reactions!

* * * * *

Then what finally happened to the characters in this rather long story. Arun died a bachelor at the ripe age of 82 carrying secrets – young and old, entombed in his heart. And Shanti? She got married to her dream prince and is now the mother of two – a boy and a girl – same features as Shanti's – same features as Prabha's. Prabha was survived by her daughter – mother's look alike who migrated to USA at a very young age of seventeen. No news of her. And Prabha:

R.I.P. Prabha
Born: 1933
Died: 1964

"To live in the hearts of those
one leaves behind
is not to die".

Rehana Kashmiri

She was born in Srinagar's Lal chowk and her name was Rehana. Her father, worked as a low-paid artisan in a carpet weaving factory and supported a family of fifteen – from that one small income. Rehana was second among sisters and third amongst brothers and sisters. In her family she had one sister and two brothers older and four sisters and five brothers younger to her. If mother and father were to be added to this motely crowd – then by Gods grace the total strength was fifteen in all. If the houses situated bang on Lal Chowk were left out, then Rehana's house was fifth in one of the narrow side lanes.

Rehana's elder brother Javed joined an electrical shop in his locality, at the age of twelve and within one year acquired proficiency in various types of electrical repairs. In two-three years time, he became such a famous electrician that in 1985 when one of the Commandants of the CRPF battalion posted in Lal Chowk needed the services of an electrician he recruited Javed in his Bn. – as a contract employee. In 2-3 years time when the Battalion moved to Delhi, Javed too shifted along with his Battalion to Jharoda Kalan on the outskirts of Delhi. In Delhi Javed came in contact with a powerful politician from J & K, who using his political clout got Javed a permanent government job in Vigyan Bhavan as an electrician. In his new job Javed started earning about four thousand rupees a month, which became a vital financial support to the family.

Then came 1989 and Kashmir Valley started getting soaked in blood. Violence commenced with explosions in five empty buses of J&K State Transport. But in two months time, the entire valley was on fire. Srinagar town started witnessing violent incidents on a daily basis. Not a single day passed without sounds of gunfire or of explosions being heard in the town. Call them extremists or separatists or terrorists or mujahideens – give them any name – the dimensions of violence became so grave that even people who had lived in the valley for many generations – started trembling with fear. Pandits were the first targets of violence – also of psychological warfare unleashed by the extremists. Many were murdered. Several dwellings owned by them were burnt down. Several women from Pandit families disappeared – never to return. These incidents led to an exodus of Kashmiri Pandits to places outside the valley. Local administration gradually became irrelevant. For many months it was only the writ of the undergrounds, that ran in the valley. No one came to the help of the fleeing Pandits – not even those who were then in power – not even those who assumed power in 1990 – not even neighbours who are always taken as poles to lean upon in distress. Not even a word of sympathy was uttered in support of the fleeing Pandits – even by the administration.

The scenario was something like this when the Central Government asked me to take over additional responsibility of the Kashmir Valley.

For me, Kashmir was entirely a new subject. I was unaware of the nuances of the problem. I wanted to visit Kashmir Valley for about a month as an ordinary tourist, to get first hand knowledge of the expectations of the people from the Central Government. My proposal met with stiff resistance at all levels. Therefore in disgust, I took a month's leave and landed in Srinagar. I spent that entire month in small hotels, in cheap house-boats and in moving around in cheap

Shikaras. This visit provided me a unique opportunity of understanding the Kashmir problem, in consultation with the men on the street. During that one month – whosoever became my friend – remains a friend till date!

Soon enough that one month was over and it was time for me to return to Delhi. I hired a taxi from the house-boat itself which dropped me uneventfully at Srinagar airport. At the airport I got myself checked in and took a seat in the lounge awaiting the departure announcement. I should have dozed off a bit when I heard someone calling. "Bai (Bhai) Saheb – Bai Saheb". I opened my eyes and found the house-boat owner standing next to me.

'Bai Saheb – we want to trouble you a bit. This one is my brother. (He said pointing to the person standing next to him). Bai Saheb – his son Javed is working in Delhi. His sister Rehana also stays with him. My wife prepared some 'Rishta' (a Kashmiri dish) this morning. We want to send the same through you in one tiffin carrier – alongwith some Kashmiri Kehwa (Kashmiri drink) and some walnuts to Javed! Can you take this much trouble for the children? They will collect this bag from your bungalow in Delhi.'

And before I could think and react, my 'Bai Saheb' has already thrust the two shopping bags – into my hands. I could see from outside that one shopping bag contained one small tiffin-carrier and some walnuts – the other one about two dozen apples. Showing the shopping bag containing the apples to my new-found 'Bai Saheb', I asked:

'Bai Saheb – what is this? You only wanted to send Rishta, Kehwa and walnuts through me?'

'The apples are for 'Babi' (Bhabhi) Jaan! Sir, we have already rung up Javed and either he or Rehana will come and collect the bag from your house. No trouble for you, Sir!'

'Which Babi jaan?'

'Sir, for our Babi jaan! Your children too should be able to enjoy Srinagar apples'.

And without pretensions I took both the bags from my Bai-Jaan!

Srinagar valley was witnessing waves after waves of violence day in and day out. Yet human relationships had not deteriorated to an extent that humans start suspecting humans. Some semblance of security check was in place – but not of the type that one witnesses today. My co-travellers waiting for the flight in the lounge were not happy at my having accepted packets from a stranger. Some of then even warned me. I thought, what harm have I done to anyone in Kashmir valley, that he would try to kill me – get me blown off. What would anyone gain by getting me killed?

My heart won against my head and ignoring the warnings of my co-travellers, I kept the two bags with me under my seat.

It was half an hour and the flight was ready for departure. With the two bags in hand I entered the aircraft alongwith my co-passengers. Then shoving the two bags under my seat, I took out my half-finished novel and got busy with its characters. It should have been 4-5 minutes when an army officer accompanied by 2-3 jawans came up to me and asked:

'Sir, did you accept two bags at the Srinagar airport from a Kashmiri – whom you don't really know'.

'Yes – and no – not from a stranger'.

'Who is he then?'

'He is my brother – 'Bai' from 'Srinagar'.

'Sir, we want to take the bags out of the plane for checking'.

'Any suspicions against the two of them?'

'Not really. But sir, it is a question of security of about 200 passengers'.

'OK. You can take the bags to wherever you want – screen them and if nothing objectionable was found, please return them to me – here itself'- I said handing over the two bags to the officer.

The two officers with the two bags in hand, left the aircraft literally on the run. From my window I could see the bags being taken to a spot, well away from the aircraft – away from the terminal building. It should have been good ten minutes when I saw the two officers re-enter the aircraft – the two bags in hand. Handing over the bags to me – in a very apologetic tone, they said.

'Sir, we are extremely sorry for the inconvenience caused. Co-passengers were feeling scared'.

I gave no answer. No sooner the checking team got out of the aircraft, the air hostess closed the door. In another five minutes, we were airborne – destination Delhi.

* * * * *

In Palam, as I was getting out of the airport, the two bags in hand, a co-passenger came close enough and remarked.

'Sir, the bags might contain time-bombs! Please be watchful'. And having said so he disappeared – through the exit gate.

I was in a state of confusion. So many people, making the same assertion. May be there is a bomb in those bags. Gathering my wits I summoned a taxi and left for my residence. Reaching home, as a mater of abundant precaution, I left the two bags in my garage.

Next day, at usual time I left for office. Around 12 O'clock when I was busy with my work I received a call from my residence: my wife informing me that one young Kashmiri girl Rehana has come to collect some bags brought by me from Srinagar. I told my wife that the two bags were lying in our garage – that the one containing apples is for us and the other one which has a steel tiffin-carrier in it is to be handed over to Rehana. I also asked my wife to take Rehana's address and telephone number – on a piece of paper.

When I returned home in the evening, I found the slip left behind by Rehana – lying on my table. She lived in some unknown locality of Najafgarh town – about 30 kms. from New Delhi. In order to be able to identify that Rehana was the girl from Kashmir – my wife had added the word 'kashmiri' – as an extension to her name.

That is how Rehana became Rehana Kashmiri.

* * * * *

In just a couple of months violence became the most dominating feature of Srinagar valley. Bomb explosions, firings and deaths – from both sides, became daily routine. The Chief Minister was removed. The Governor was replaced. President's rule was imposed in the state. The problems of the valley however kept on multiplying, by the day!

'Dard badhta hi gaya, jyun, jyun dawa ki' (The pain multiplied with every round of medication).

It was either March or April 1990 when Vigyan Bhavan in New Delhi caught fire. It should have been two in the afternoon when the fire was first noticed. By about three thirty the entire building was reduced to ashes. The Committee Room in which the fire was first noticed was that day hosting an important conference on national security. All important security experts and security specialists were present in the committee room. The fire was first noticed in one corner of the ceiling which everyone thought was due to short-circuiting. To begin with, it appeared to be a minor fireworks display with sparks cascading from the ceiling. However, within few minutes the entire ceiling, was on fire.

Senior police officers present in the meeting felt that the fire could be quickly and easily brought under control by getting the power supply to the committee room switched off. Senior officers of Delhi Police present in the meeting ran helter and skelter trying to locate the electrician on duty. However, the individual who had the knowledge and the keys of the switch boards and who was supposed to have been on duty at that moment was not located – neither in the duty room – nor in the canteen, nor anywhere else. Half an hour's search produced no results. The current was not switched off. Gradually the entire electrical wiring in the building caught fire. By about six in the evening, when the fire-brigade finally succeeded in bringing the fire under control, the entire Vigyan Bhavan minus its R.C.C. structure was gone – consumed by flames.

Government of India ordered an enquiry by a Committee of serving and retired officers, to find out the causes of fire and to rule out arson and sabotage. Staff which was supposed to be on duty and was found absent was placed under suspension and a departmental enquiry ordered.

Government continued to function as before – at the same pace as it is used to prior to the Vigyan Bhavan fire!

* * * * *

In the mouth of May on a hot summer day – Rehana appeared in the courtyard of my ground floor flat in Tilak Marg. My wife rang me up in office informing me of her arrival. Since I was tied up in an important meeting, I requested my wife to ascertain from Rehana the reason for her visit. My wife lost no time in telling me that due to very high level of violence in Srinagar town, Rehana was finding it difficult to continue her studies there and therefore her father has sent her to Delhi to be with her brother Javed and to continue her studies here. She has already cleared Class IX in Srinagar and is now seeking my assistance in getting admission to Class X.

Prior to Rehana's arrival, two other children – of Pandits from Srinagar, had similarly shifted to Delhi and I had helped them in getting admissions. All schools in Delhi were aware of the law and order situation in Srinagar valley and were willing to help children shifting from there. And in doing so they were even willing to go to the extent of increasing the number of seats, if that became necessary.

In the above context, I asked my wife to ask Rehana to come over after two days and to take her to the Principal of Bal Bharati Air Force School. I also told my wife that in between I would have talked to the Principal and fixed up Rehana's admission. When my wife told Rehana of the likelihood of her admission in Bal Bharati Air Force School, she was overjoyed.

Exactly two days later and exactly at 10 O'clock Rehana was at our door. Without wasting any time my wife drove her to the Bal Bharti school for a meeting with the Principal. However when the duo reached there the principal was out – attending a meeting in the Secretariat. She returned at 12 O'clock and my wife got a chance to meet her. My wife apprised the Principal of the prevailing law and order situation in Srinagar. She also put across her request for Rehana's admission in Class X – on special consideration. Consultations with the class teacher took some time. However, by one O'clock Rehana was duly admitted to the Bal Bharati Air Force School. In order to keep track of the fact that Rehana had been admitted, on special law and order consideration, the Principal added 'Kashmiri' after Rehana's name. The school office too while issuing her admission slip recorded her name as 'Rehana Kashmiri'.

That is how Rehana became 'Rehana Kashmiri' in official records.

* * * * *

I had not met Rehana so far. She used to visit my Tilak Marg residence sometimes, while returning from school. My children used to be home by then. My wife used to serve lunch to all of them together – and Rehana appeared happy.

Then one day Rehana came and complained: 'Aunty ji – I am finding it difficult to get the better of school Hindi. My teacher consequently is very unhappy with me. Can Uncle ji get me an exemption from appearing in Hindi examination – by talking to the Principal?' When I returned home that night my wife updated me with Rehana's request. I assured my wife that I would talk to the Principal, first thing next morning. However, the requirement totally slipped off my mind due to some pressing problems that day. I also thought that may be with the passage of time and with little extra effort Rehana would succeed in getting over her Hindi handicap.

It was August – should have been around fifteenth, when one afternoon she again landed in my house. She was continuously crying. My wife rang me up in my office.

I however, failed to make out head or tail of Rehana's problem. Regarding her Hindi handicap I asked my wife to tell her that I would certainly get it sorted out by talking to the Principal. But Rehana's crying did not stop. I got her on the telephone for ascertaining as to what caused her so much discomfeiture. Sobs and tears however made it inpossible for me to make any thing out of her words.

I therefore advised her to write down her problem on a piece of paper assuring her that I will follow up no sooner I returned home. I pacified her – asked her to have patience – reassured her that her problems would soon be over. I returned home in the evening to find the following letter left behind by her.

'Bai Saheb rakhi doh osuk aamat ba osus na gairai tami khatir cho mein baro ofsos.

Mainai Khandrani saut karat kat baat. Mayati gayab dil khuyesh. Khudai karan aiye tahit sehat-mand.

Bai Saheb chekar tath Bal-Bharati Hindi khatir Principal sauth kauth. Hal kya dara aav?

Myon Bai Javed chu bekasur. Dilli police aas hek jaankari diath.

Chaun Lakat Beni

Rehana'.

Next morning, taking help from my Kashmiri staff I got the letter translated into English. Translation ran somewhat as follows:

"On the Raksha Bandhan day I came to your residence with the Rakhi. Could not find you home. I was disappointed.

I met Bhabi Jan and was delighted. May Allah keep both of you safe and happy!

Regarding my problems with Hindi you might have talked to the Principal by now. What result?

My brother Javed is innocent. Can you pass on the correct information to Delhi Police?

Your younger sister

Rehana"

Rehana's problems with Hindi were not difficult to sort out. I rang up the Principal who assured me that she would work out a solution soon by talking to the teacher concerned. The Principal wanted Rehana to meet her and the Hindi teacher within the next two days giving my reference. The principal ended up by saying that Rehana's problems with Hindi be treated as over since they were now the School's responsibility. I conveyed the details of this conversation to my wife who in turn conveyed the contents to Rehana, the next day.

I, however, could not get the hang out of Rehana's other problem. What problems her brother Javed is having with the Delhi Police? He is a government employee. He would always be carrying his identity card. Having failed to understand Javed's problem with Delhi police I decided to meet Rehana in person and I therefore requested my wife to invite Rehana to lunch, coming Sunday:

* * * * *

Sunday morning. It was getting to be ten when I first saw Rehana. She rang the door-bell and I was the one who went outside to open the door for her.

I recognised her instantaneously – age about 15 years, 5'2" tall, complexion like that of an apple – long and high Kashmiri nose – large deep set blue eyes surrounded by arched shapely eyebrows – straight black hair tied in a single pleat with one loose bunch of hair flying free – partly covering the left eye – heavier than usual in shoulders and upper body-wrapped in printed shalwar-kameez – ordinary sleepers in her feet two gold rings in each ear and one Sathya Sai Baba locket in the neck. In brief an attractive young girl.

She spontaneously bent down trying to touch my feet. I stopped her midway caught hold of her by her arms and hugged her.

'What are you doing Rehana? You are my younger sister'.

Rehana was speechless. Her head resting on my shoulder she started sobbing and shedding tears.

'What is wrong Rehana? You are with your elder brother for the first time. Then why all these tears? Stop crying. Today my children are home. Let us sit together, eat together and laugh together!'

Bhai jaan how do I laugh? Nothing is right with me. Everything is so topsy-turvy. My elders are worried in Srinagar for me and for Javed. My heart is glued on to my parents, my brothers and sisters and to their welfare. Now Javed is in Delhi Police's custody for the last two days. Don't know how is he? Is in what condition? We all are so worried!

'Why is Javed in Delhi Police's custody?'

My children and wife had arrived in the meanwhile and taken seats arround us.

'Bhai jaan police suspects that Javed had a hand in Vigyan Bhavan fire'.

'Did Police give you any reasons for their suspicion?'

'Yes, Bhai jaan ... Javed was on duty at the switch boards when the fire broke out. He was however absent from duty around the time of fire. He remained absent continuously for two more days thereafter'.

'And how does Javed explain his absence? Where was he?'

'Bhai jaan, he says that he had gone to the Ram Manohar Lohia Hospital during lunch break. He had gone there to enquire about the welfare of the Minister's daughter who had been admitted to the hospital, a week earlier. This was the same Minister who had got him the Vigyan Bhavan job. He had hoped that the going and coming would not take him more than half an hour. However on reaching the hospital he found the girl in a precarious condition – in coma – with three doctors in attendance. The Minister too was present along with his family. It was 3 O'clock by the time she regained consciousness. As he was getting ready to return to Vigyan Bhavan he got the information that the building had caught fire. He became immensely nervous. The Minister and his family members wanted him to return to Vigyan Bhavan. He however, was so nervous that he waited in the hospital for it to get dark and when he thought that no one would notice his movements, he left for South Avenue and hid himself in the Minister's house'.

'What was the need for Javed to go into hiding? Absence from duty was simple dereliction of duty. He could have at the most been dismissed from service. It would not have become a cognizable offence. Why such foolishness?'

'Yes, Bhai jaan – if he had come back to senses in time, none of us would be facing this problem. But he remained in hiding in the Minister's servant's quarter for two days. It was only on the third day and that too when the Minister became really angry and threatened to hand him over to the police, that he agreed to return to Vigyan Bhavan. And when he did finally report, the authorities straightaway placed him under suspension. This too was O.K. We were ready to go through one more phase of his joblessness. But now this police case! Bhai jaan – you now please find some way out.'

Having said all this, Rehana became quiet. My wife had in between served tea and everyone got busy having tea and biscuits – Rehana too. I was once again on the horns of a dilemma. What to do now?

'Since Javed is in police custody – does that mean you are staying alone?'

'No Bhai jaan – my father has arrived from Srinagar and is staying with me'.

'And who is looking after your brothers and sisters in Srinagar'.

'Bhai jaan, my mother! One of my uncle too has joined her'.

'When did you last meet Javed?'

'Bhai jaan, day-before morning — when the police came to pick him up'.

'O.K. Rehana – now you leave your worries to me. Today is Sunday. All offices are closed. All the same I would try to locate Javed. If I could, I would meet him today itself. It would be better to get his side of the story first, before proceeding any further in the matter. Then I will talk to senior officials in Delhi Police. You don't worry. Your brother will get justice. ... Eat something with my children before you leave.'

Getting in touch with Delhi Police took half-an-hour. And when the contact did eventually materialise it remained infructuous. I therefore decided to meet the Commissioner of Police (C.P.) and got an appointment with him at his residence rather promptly – 2 O'clock the same afternoon.

Meeting with the C.P. proved fruitful. To begin with, he too had no knowledge of any such arrest. But when he put his

Crime Branch on to the job, he got the information that yes such a person is in fact with them. On my seeking a meeting with the arrested individual – the C.P. too became curious and decided to come along.

We were soon in the Police Station and Javed was in front of us. He appeared generally O.K. except that he gave an impression of having not slept for two nights. When I mentioned Rehana to him he started crying like a child. 'Poor girl has been left alone! No one around to protect her. Is weak-hearted! Might commit suicide out of fear.' On being told that at present she is in the company of my wife and children and that 'Abba' (father) has arrived from Srinagar and is staying with her – he quietened down.

Once he felt little reassured, I asked him to tell us his side of the story. He told us all what Rehana had already told us. He mentioned that he is madly in love with the Minister's daughter – that it has been one sided love so far. That she was admitted to the R.M.L. Hospital and I desperately wanted to meet her. I decided to visit her during lunch hour – without taking anyone's permission. I was hoping that I would be able to cycle to the hospital and be back before the lunch hour got over and that no one would come to know of my absence. When I reached the hospital, I found her in coma. I became very nervous. Lost all control over my senses! I started believing that she is already dead. When I got ready to return to Vigyan Bhavan, I found a whole lot of patients being brought in ambulances from there. Through them I came to know that the Vigyan Bhavan has caught fire and has been reduced to ashes. Sense of fear and guilt got the better of me. I started believing that if I returned to Vigyan Bhavan they would shoot me down. Scared, I ran into the servant's quarter of the Minister's bungalow and went into hiding. After two days – when the Minister assured me that he would look after my interests and that I need not worry, I reported back to office.'

I enquired if he had any witnesses who will be willing to testify to his presence in the hospital, at the time of fire in Vigyan Bhavan.

He said: 'Yes, there were at least three doctors attending to the Minister's daughter. They had all seen me. On their instructions I held the drip bottle in my hand 3-4 times and changed the oxygen cylinder once. I don't even remember how many times I should have handed them over syringes and medicines?'

I advised the police officers accompanying the C.P. to get Javed's statement recorded – also verified. I also requested them to get in touch with the J&K Police and find out if Javed had at any time in the past, harboured pro-separatist tendencies or if he had while in Srinagar maintained contacts with the separatists. I also told them that in my opinion it was necessary to contact the Minister and take down his statement too. I ended making two more requests to the C.P. – one, that the above requirements be got completed expeditiously and two, that if the statements pointed to the suspect being innocent, he should be promptly let off. I ended up by adding that Javed not being on duty at the designated hour was a serious dereliction of duty and he should be made to face a departmental enquiry for that. Explaining to Javed that he might be required to wait out for 2-3 more days, we came out of the police station. C.P. was to meet someone in office and therefore I returned to my residence alone.

Rehana was waiting at my residence. I made her aware of the details of our meeting with Javed – also the developments regarding the investigation. I told her that if nothing suspicious was found then Javed would be let off in 2-3 days time. Rehana felt reassured and straightaway took a bus home.

Police completed necessary enquiries within two days and

finding nothing suspicious against Javed, they let him off. He returned home and his father left for Srinagar.

* * * * *

Within a week of the fire in Vigyan Bhavan, the Central Government had ordered the Constitution of an Enquiry Committee, for going into the causes of fire. Senior retired officers of the CPWD, also of the electricity department were its members. The Committee was to submit its report within two months. They did so in just one and a half month. In Committee's opinion the cause of fire was 'circuit overload' leading to electrical wires catching fire – due to overheating. The report freed Javed from any suspicion.

The departmental enquiry against Javed – for serious dereliction of duty – continued for over a year. The charges having been found proved – he was dismissed from service. Javed however stayed back in Delhi for one more year, looking after Rehana. Everyone needs a good electrician. Javed sustained himself in Delhi by catering to the ad hoc needs of the house owners – for maintenance of their electrical fittings.

Rehana in between appeared in the 12th Board examination of the CBSE. Her visits to my residence nearly dried up. I took it that she is very busy with her studies and is therefore not finding time to keep up with her social contacts. When I met her next she was awaiting the results of her 12th examination. That day too was a Sunday and I was home. Her sudden appearance outside my door surprised me. It had been two years since I had last seen her. She had grown from fifteen to seventeen and higher education and interaction with Delhi society had given her a lot of confidence and poise. She has ceased to be the innocent – looking shy girl that she was two years earlier and had become a pretty young girl – full of confidence. No sooner she was inside, she bent down and touched my wife's feet. Then throwing her shoulder bag on to the table she collapsed into one of the sofas.

'What brings you here Rehana? Where have you been all these days?' I asked.

'Bhai jaan, I am awaiting my Board results'.

'What do you propose to do next?'

'Bhai jaan, I want to do B.Com. (Hons.) from Shri Ram College!'

'How would you get admission there? Their cut-off generally remains 95% and above'.

'Bhai jaan, I too have done my papers very well. I am expecting well above 95%. However, if I fell short by 5-10 marks – my Bhai jaan is here in Delhi and what is there that he cannot get done?'

I had seen Rehana at an age when she just used to mumble. It was a revelation seeing her exude confidence in every word that she spoke. I prayed to God that He always kept her as cheerful, as today.

I was about to raise some more questions when my wife intervened to announce that the lunch has been served and is getting cold. Catching hold of Rehana by her hand I made her take a seat next to my wife and I took a seat right opposite her.

On the table, I got an opportunity to scrutinise Rehana. Golden rings in her ears – were there earlier too. Golden chain with Sai Baba Locket – had been with her before. Two gold chains around her neck – they were not there earlier. A diamond studded platinum ring on her ring finger. This and an Omega watch on her wrist – were recent acquisitions.

Rehana is yet to clear her Board Exam. How did she come in possession of all this jewellery? How?

Keeping myself well within the norms of social behaviour, I enquired:

'Rehana bete (my daughter) where is Javed? What is he doing?'

'Bhai jaan, he is here in Delhi. Is working as an electrician. Takes private calls. Earns enough to sustain the two of us – modestly'.

'Rehana has your father got a new job lately? Has there been a big increase in his income?'

'Not at all Bhai Jaan! But why are you asking all these questions?'

Saying bye to hesitation, I shot a direct question:

'Rehana bete – because I see a diamond ring on your finger'.

'O Bhai jaan – this ring! This ring has been given to me by Shankar's mummy.'

'But bete – who is Shankar' – my wife asked.

'Aunty ji – Shankar is my friend from Bal Bharati. He was ahead of me by one year. Is presently doing management in Bangalore.'

'But Rehana who is he and why did his mother give you such costly presents – a ring, a watch and two chains?'

'Bhai jaan, we are madly in love with each other – going to get married'.

'Then what is the delay Rehana?'

'Bhai jaan we will get married no sooner Shankar completed his MBA'.

'But Rehana – you still have not told us – who is this Shankar?'

'Oh-ho-Bhai jaan! He is the only son of Group Captain Raghavan. They live in this colony itself.

'Oh – you mean our Raghavan. He is a very good friend of mine. Congratulations Rehana – mubarak'.

My wife had in the meanwhile got up from her chair. In one single motion she hugged Rehana and putting her right hand over her head – blessed her. Rehana touched her feet once again.

'Rehana – where would you get married?'

'That is the problem – Bhai jaan. However, if there was any serious difficulty then we would rush to a temple and get married. No one can stop us?'

'But why do you need to go to a temple for getting married? Our house is here. We are ready to host your marriage – marriage of our second daughter. Why not? You also are like our daughter. However, is there any problem? Are the parents not willing?'

'Yes – Bhai jaan'.

'Oh Rehana – Raghavans are my very good friends. I will come along with you and make them agree. Let me see, how they don't agree?'

'Bhai jaan – please. Shankar's parents have no objection at all. They have been treating me as their own daughter – I don't know for how long. That is why Shankar's mother has given me all these gifts.'

'Then where is the problem! Your parents?'

'Yes, Bhai Jaan – my mother may perhaps agree – if I left

her with no choice. But my 'Abba' (father) ... he is a battle axe in this matter. He would never agree.'

'Then, what Rehana?'

'Bhai jaan even then no one can stop us.'

'Our blessings with you Rehana. Let us know if we can be any help.'

'OK, Bhai jaan – I will keep you in mind.'

And the conversation came to an abrupt end. On my insistence, we all visited Gymkhana Club where an impromptu celebration was organised. Cake was cut. There were so many wanting to wish Rehana all the best in her love ... that a queue formed up.

My mother used to say that celebrations should follow – not precede happy events. Holding celebrations prior to an auspicious event can sometimes mar the future of that event.

We returned home from Gymkhana happily. Rehana took a bus home.

* * * * *

It was the last week of June – more that a month since we had last met Rehana. Children from neighbourhood came and informed us that the CBSE result were out. We checked up and found Rehana amongst first divisioners. All of us were delighted. We thought of conveying her our good wishes. However, this had to wait till she rang us up or visited us.

It was getting 7 O'clock in the evening. I had returned form office and sat down to a cup of tea, when the telephone rang:

'Hello – Bhai jaan'.

'Rehana – dili mubarakbad – heartiest congratulation. What is your percentage?'

'Bhai Jaan – 95%'.

'Heartiest congratulations from all of us. May God take you places in life. May you find a place amongst the stars. May you shine so much that you become a symbol of pride for your family – your society'.

I would have gone on but Rehana interrupted me.

'Bhai jaan, I have to return home just now. Can I meet you tomorrow?'

'Why not, Rehana. But please come before ten thirty. Many congratulations once again'.

'Bhai jaan – I take your leave. I would be at your door, before nine tomorrow'.

* * * * *

My wife thought that Rehana is visiting us first time after such illustrious success. Therefore, she should not be welcomed empty-handed. She rushed to Khan Market and in between pulling down of shutters, she managed to buy a shalwar suit for Rehana – shalwar in red colour with a matching kurta and dupata in Sanghaneri print. Rehana will look very pretty wearing these – she thought.

Next morning, we didn't have to wait at all. It was not even nine and Rehana was at our door. We rushed outside, welcomed her – and prayed for her. My wife blessed her by keeping her hand on Rehana's head and by hugging and kissing her.

And when I lifted her chin to see her face, I was startled. Her face was bathed in tears.

'What happened Rehana? Is it the admission in Shri Ram College that worries you? With 95% they would roll out a red carpet for you. And then I am there na!'

'No Bhai jaan, my problem is different. Javed has passed on the information about Shankar and me, to 'Abba', who is now frightfully angry. He has ordered that I should return to Srinagar, forthwith. His orders are that I would not remain in Delhi for a day more and that I can continue my studies – if at all – in Srinagar. He is arriving here tonight to fetch me.'

'Don't worry Rehana. When he has arrived please tell him about your plans. Also explain to him your strong feelings in the matter. He will surely understand. After all he is your father. How can he ignore the dreams of his own child? You must explain the matters to him properly. I am sure he would agree.'

'And if he does not agree?'

'Then we both are here. We would meet him. We would pursue your dreams with him. We will make him agree.'

She appeared reassured. My wife brought out a chocolate and put a piece in her mouth. She didn't say 'no'. Then handing over the shalwar suit to her she wished her a long and happy life. As she was about to move out I stopped her once again and told her:

'Bete (child) ... there is nothing to worry. Your responsibility is just to tell your father that the two of us wanted to meet him. Thereafter, you tell us so that we could come over to your place. We will apprise your father of your bright future. We would tell him that if you joined Shri Ram College, your future would be assured and you will be able to touch unimaginable heights. I am confident that he would finally agree. After all he is your father – your biggest well-wisher.'

'Bhai – jaan if you say so?'

And she was ready to leave. Then suddenly, God knows what came to her? She returned to my wife with the shalwar suit in her hand – hugged her and started crying uncontrollably. My wife pacified her – encouraged her to take life as it came. As she was about to step out of our house – she raised her hands in prayer and prayed.

'Bhabhi jaan and Bhai jaan – I pray to God that if and when I am reborn – I should be reborn as your daughter and should be able to find and get Shankar. I am willing to wait many many lives for my prayer to be fulfilled!'

I was moved to tears. I advanced from the place where I was standing – put my hand on Rehana's head and blessed her:

'Bete – my daughter! May God protect you.'

'Bye bye Bhai jaan – bye-bye Bhabhi jaan' – and Rehana was gone.

* * * * *

Fifteen days went by waiting for Rehana's call. I sometimes thought that may be – in the interest of her bright future Rehana's father had given up the idea of Rehana's shift to Srinagar – that Rehana is still in Delhi trying for her admission in Shri Ram College.

Then on a very sultry day in July – should be any date between eleventh and fifteenth, I got Rehana's call in my office. It should have been around four in the afternoon. Noises on the telephone alarmed me. Noise of a railway engine, noises of hawkers – familiar railway platform noises.

'Where are you Rehana?' I asked.

'On the platform of New Delhi Railway Station. In a short while we will be leaving for Pathankot. Avoiding my father's gaze, I have come to telephone you!'

'But Rehana – did you convey my request to him for a meeting?'

'Yes Bhai Jaan – many times. He says that you are all mixed up with each other.'

'And what about your marriage... with Shankar?'

According to Abba – 'only over my (Rehana's) dead body!'

'Never loose heart Rehana. Apprise your mother of your sentiments ... of your future and your dreams. She is a woman. She would understand you. I have faith in God. Man may turn cruel – women would not – never where their own children are involved.'

Rehana once again repeated what she has said as she was moving out of my house – last time:

'Bhai jaan – if you say so! I respect you so much.'

'Never loose courage. If you ever felt that my coming there would help – ring me up. I will come and explain things to your father – your mother.'

'Bhai jaan...' and before she could say anything further the line was disconnected.

* * * * *

Two months went by and no news of Rehana. No call. May be gradually things have got sorted out.

Then came September 11. Srinagar valley witnessed many incidents of violence – Srinagar town just one.

On the morning of September 12, the coloured photograph of a girl – published by the Times of India on its front page – took my breath away. Same shalwar suit which my wife had presented her a few months earlier! Same Omega watch on her wrist – same diamond-studded ring on her finger – given by Shankar's parents – same two golden chains and one Sai Baba locket around her neck – same one bunch of loose hair stuck to her cheek between eye and ear – right arm fully extended – lying limp on the road left arm partly resting on her own body – only the wrist touching the road. right fist loosely closed – fingers of the left fully open – eyes slightly closed creating an impression of someone in deep slumber. No sign of injury – no trace of blood anywhere on her dead body!

So said Rehana good bye to this world – taking with her all her dreams closeted in the labyrinth of her eyes – leaving behind all that this world gave her – on one narrow footpath of Lal Chowk.

If she was to go at such a tender age – then why all that 'hai-touba' – why that torture of admission to Bal Bharati – travails of not being able to know Hindi well – the bone-breaking effort behind securing 95% - the struggle for getting admission in Shri Ram College – dreams of marriage with Shankar and of a happy life thereafter – to what avail! Why – God?

* * * * *

The coverage of the incident, by the newspapers, ran as follows:

On September 11, around 7 O'clock in the morning – when one BSF patrol was passing through Lal Chowk, the terrorists lobbed two hand grenades towards them – from inside a nearby house. The grenades exploded after hitting the ground. Twenty-three people were injured in this incident including nine BSF jawans. Rehana, a college student also died in the explosion. She had come to the bus stop to see her youngest brother off to school. At the time of incident, she was waiting for the bus, along with her brother. According to the post-mortem report the cause of Rehana's death was a bullet fired from very close range – going through her heart.'

* * * * *

It was fifteen days past Rehana's death. I was going through spells of agony and stress. Not knowing what to do, my wife suggested that I pay a visit to Srinagar and offer condolences to Rehana's family – also offer prayers at Rehana's grave. I thought – Rehana is gone! How going to Srinagar or offering prayers at her grave would be any help. Rehana has gone with unrealised worldly ambitions and unfulfilled dreams. I was in this state of uncertainty when the receipt of an envelope with Srinagar post office's stamp, alarmed me. Opening the envelope I found a letter written by Rehana on August 15, presumably her last, containing just five sentences. The letter was written in a hurry making her otherwise extremely cursive handwriting almost illegible.

'Bhai jaan – respects. I am under great pressure not to go to Delhi and I cannot survive without going there. My insistence on going to Delhi has become a source of threat – to my life. I have been repeatedly threatened. Now I have no choice – but to leave everything in God's hands – in whose sense of justice I have started having serious doubts. I am getting this letter posted through a friend of mine. Hope it would reach you safe and in time. Respects Bhabhi jaan –

Respects Bhai jaan. Now allow me to leave! If I did not meet you in this life – then I will await living under your love and protection in my next life.

Your daughter – Rehana.'

Rehana's letter raised many suspicions. My heart wanted me to take the matters to legal and logical conclusion. But when it came to me that Rehana is gone and nothing that I do will bring her back to life – my mind decided to let Rehana rest in peace in her grave – protected in totality – from the cruelties of society and religions, safe from the struggles of existence – sleeping away one long, carefree and innocent sleep...!!! Rest in peace – Rehana!

This is how came to an end, the short story of one sublime affection of an innocent sister for her brother – leaving everyone heart-broken!

You too would be distressed having come to know of this very tragic end of a brief but innocent life. Whom should one blame? You decide!

* * * * *

Group Captain Raghavan died within one year of Rehana's death – due to a massive heart attack. Shankar completed his MBA gloriously and was last reported working on a high post with the IBM. He is still unmarried!

* * * * *

Mother First

'Jai Papa'

'Jai Bachche'

And the day used to get going.

For about ten minutes Sonia would run her fingers through her father's hair – more or less a daily routine. Her mother would say – 'Sonia from now on itself, is a mother!' Whenever she saw her father lazing in bed, she would take his head in her lap and would start running her fingers through his hair, and the morning would go by peacefully. Her mother prayed; 'let each morning pass this way – peacefully.' She found it difficult to imagine what bitterness each new morning would bring for her.

Sonia used to think: 'My mother is unwell. She has gone to Calcutta for treatment – leaving everything in Papa's hands. I am the eldest of the three. I should be able to look after my two younger brothers. I should also be able to look after my Papa. The large retinue of servants is no good! On their own they don't remember their responsibilities. They have to be reminded all the time. Mother while leaving for Calcutta told us: 'Children, look after yourself and each other. My heart would always remain involved with all of you. The better you behave, the earlier I will return – fully cured.' But why my mother is so unwell? Why is she suffering so much? She can't run with us. She can't get up or sit down on her own. Why? That day when the three of us insisted that she played badminton, she did get on to the court but remained stationary. Once when she tried to strike the shuttle she screamed with pain. How can I help in lessening her pain? This time she has gone to Calcutta for treatment. Oh God, please return her fully cured. Oh God! kindly listen to me. In future I would do nothing that was wrong. I would never be lazy – never. I will get ready every day – on time. I will help my brothers too, in getting ready. Help them with tiffin – time table – studies.'

'Sona ... Sona'. She heard her father shouting.

Sonia's chain of thoughts was shattered – also shattered were her resolves!

'Sona – not got up so far? What is wrong with you? It is already 8 O'clock' – shouted Papa. And as he turned to go away he found Sonia sitting in her bed. Reason enough for another sermon!

'Sona, you are really lazy. In bed still? What are you dreaming? You people are really having a great time. If your mother was here she would have thrown you out of your bed by now. There is no one now to supervise you people. So enjoy every minute of your freedom? Are you not ashamed? You are so young – yet you get up so late. By this time you should have been out of your bathroom. Peep into neighbour's houses. There – girls of your age not only look after themselves but also look after their brothers and sisters – cook food and still find enough time for studies. Here you are – spending time like a Dutchess....!'

Papa would have gone on with his lecture. However somewhere in between Sonia got up and ran into her bathroom. In a fit of depression she started brushing her teeth. All pious resolutions of the morning evaporated into thin air. She started thinking – 'I am good for nothing. I would never be able to achieve anything – nothing would ever get done by me properly'.

And cursing herself she got busy in taking her bath. Before getting out of her bathroom she heard Papa shouting again:

'Gone to sleep inside? ... or what? You really are very lazy Sona – Who takes so much time in the bathroom?'

Inside her bathroom Sonia was unaware of what was happening to her two brothers. As she got out, she started helping her younger brother in getting ready for the school ... the elder brother – scared out of his wits, was getting ready on his own. She knew that it would now be the turn of the 'ayah' to get a scolding. Which also meant that the two brothers would get ready soon, since they didn't like their 'ayah' being scolded.

No sooner Sonia got ready it was time for her papa to leave for office. Wishing good bye to papa, as he left for office, was her daily routine. On a day when Papa was in good mood, he would answer 'bye-bye bete'. However, generally the car would roll out of the porch, her bye-bye remaining unacknowledged.

The fear that Papa would get angry and would give a shouting to everyone, was all–pervading. Even the humblest of daily activity was not free from this fear. Shouting was more frequent when 'Ma' was present in the house. These days the frequency of shouting was a bit less. Sonia however, has taken it for granted that nothing would ever get done by her that would meet Papa's spontaneous approval.

* * * * *

When Papa returned from office, he invariably found children home. His entry into the porch was a signal for the commencement of activity – every one rushing and running. Papa used to curse himself: 'What a torture? Not even a moment's respite. All the time something to do – someone or other on his head!' Then the shouting routine used to get triggered off. 'You people have not removed your school uniforms? How lazy are you all! Not taken your milk? Come on drink ... immediately!'

* * * * *

And it was on one such day – when all daily chores have already been done that papa called Sonia and asked: 'Why don't you go out for a walk? Why do you remain sitting and lazing at home? You have already started behaving like an old woman! Old and recluse! Sitting down with a magazine. Vendor delivered the paper and you picked it up. Whether Papa has read it or not is none of your concern.'

Papa's logic startled Sonia. She got up from her chair in the verandah, leaving the newspaper half-read, and walked out with a very heavy heart. Papa got the newspaper and that quietened him.

What should she play – thought Sonia? Time in the school passes so smoothly – so cheerfully. Back home every minute is such a torture. She started thinking no one from amongst her school friends lives close by. No one in the vicinity belongs to her age group. 'Ma' used to tell Papa to teach Sonia playing tennis. It Papa really wanted he could have taught me by now. 'Ma' cannot. Come – let me ask Papa whether he would like to play badminton with me?'

Sonia's eyes brightened up with hope. Yes, this can prove to be a wonderful idea. If Papa played badminton with me the evening will pass – effortlessly. She started feeling light in her feet. With lot of expectations in her heart and literally on the run, she reached where Papa was sitting reading newspaper, and innocently asked:

'Papa will you play badminton with me?'

Papa should have been focussed on some very important news about the affairs of the nation. Taking his eyes off the newspaper therefore was an effort. He answered: 'No bete – I won't play'.

Papa's reply smothered Sonia's enthusiasm – to some extent. Denial of simple requests can be so disappointing – so frustrating. Sonia's innocent heart couldn't accept denial. She found it impossible to subdue her enthusiasm. Putting all her strength behind every word and in very a meek and humble tone she asked:

'Papa – please – come on. Let us play.'

And it appeared as if she has touched a high voltage live wire. She was startled. She heard her Papa say:

'Why are you harassing me? You do not want me to read the newspaper. Have I not told you once – I won't play. Then why are you after my blood?'

Then suddenly in his usual fit of anger Papa threw the newspaper on the floor and screamed:

'Come on – let us play badminton. How have you suddenly become such an ardent badminton player? Now come on. You have no consideration for others' comfort. You think of something and you must have it. I am not your servant ... that I would do whatever and whenever you want. Now come on – we will play. I would not read newspaper – O.K. It is your order, so now come on ...'.

Sonia was aghast – lost! This sudden turn of events confounded her. She never intended to make her Papa angry. On the contrary she thought that playing a game would relax Papa – would make him happy. Good intentions notwithstanding, she ended up making him angry. She was on the verge of tears. She was unable to move her feet. Papa returned to his harshest possible language and said:

'Now come on, let us play What has glued you to the ground? I am ready to carry out your command'.

But how can Sonia play now? Her enthusiasm lay buried nine fathoms deep. Her feet have become unmovable.

Papa was brimming with rage. He waited just a few moments and then seeing no effect of his command on Sonia, he became really wild. Angrily, he caught hold of Sonia's arm and shoving the badminton racquet into her hand, he started dragging her towards the badminton court.

Sonia started crying – loudly. She never wanted to make her Papa angry. She had thought that Papa would be happy playing badminton. She did however miss out one simple point – that Papa was busy reading newspaper and talking badminton to him at that moment was not the in thing.

Shedding tears profusely Sonia uttered 'Sorry – Papa'.

Word 'sorry' quietened Papa a bit. He thought Sonia is gradually getting back on track. This smothered his anger. He thought – how very strict the parents need to be – to bring children under control.' Then pulling Sonia towards him, he said:

'Come on. Now wash your face. And in future do not pester anyone like this. I too return from office – dead tired. You either play yourself or ride a cycle – or just walk. There are hundreds of ways to keep one-self entertained. Anyway, now you go inside, wash your face and hands properly and come. We will go out for a drive. Call your brothers too'.

Sonia stealthily crept inside – avoiding the gaze of the ayahs, servants and her two brothers!

* * *

How tender and confused a girl can be at age twelve, Sonia's father never knew? He never had time for going into these simple things. He was one amongst ten brothers – no sister. He therefore got no opportunity to understand girls – or women. Having completed his Masters in Agriculture, he got a job as a Manager in a tea garden in Assam. He came from an affluent family and manager's job made him twice as rich. He succeeded in assimilating within the four walls of his house considerable wealth and all items of personal comfort and enjoyment. He just needed to move a finger and he got whatever he wanted. There was no dearth of servants, ayahs and bearers in his house. If there was any dark spot in this otherwise colourful setting, it was his wife – Sonia's mother who always remained sick. Her ten year long struggle with arthritis had made her irritable, obstinate and short-tempered. Husband and wife used to quarrel often. There were serious differences between the two on almost all matters. When they quarrelled they quarrelled in a manner that the entire household listened. Even the children listened to their mutual bickerings and hot exchanges. In course of time, Sonia learnt to accept these fights as a part of her daily routine. All the same, she prayed to God daily to prevent these fights, since it spoiled the peace of mind of each and everyone in the house.

Mother too scolded Sonia. Yet her scolding was invariably corrective – never unbearable. Sonia sometimes thought: She was not happy in this house. This time she would ask her mother to put her in some hostel. She loves her Papa dearly. But she could never make out as to why he was always angry with her. Ma gets angry too, off and on. She too is full of lecturing. None of this would be there if she stayed in a hostel, with friends. 'I would not stay here – would not stay in this house – would walk away to a hostel.'

On the spur of the moment the twelve year old decided to walk out of her home into an unknown world, called a hostel.

Having so decided – prior to going to bed she quietly pulled out one hand-bag and put two sets of clothings into it. She also put one comb, one pocket mirror, one pen belonging to her father's tea company, a few inland letters, one torch and one handkerchief in it. She took out her mother's wrist watch and tied it on her wrist.

It was past midnight and when everyone was fast asleep, she got up and got ready to leave. She first offered prayers before the deity of her house. Then she sat down writing a small note:

"Papa, I am not happy in this house. I love you immensely. But I am somehow so foolish and so uncouth that I never do anything right. Even when I am desperately wanting to please you, I commit some silly mistake and make you angry.

When mother returns from Calcutta – Papa, please tell her all this because leaving this house is such a pain. I am constantly crying because I love you so much, I love my mother and I love my brothers so much, I cannot tell you.

Your daughter

Sonia.

As she finished, sobs and tears overtook her. She even found it difficult to put on her shoes – she fumbled with laces.

Sonia's innocent heart overflowed with love for everyone. Yet her father's style of living, and his lack of concern for the feelings and sentiments of his children – did create an environment in which Sonia found it impossible to continue living under the same roof.

Prior to getting out of her house, Sonia first glanced towards her Papa and then towards her two younger brothers – all in deep sleep – Papa snoring away. And quite unsure of herself she stepped on to the dusty-track, trodden upon by countless human beings – surviving under whose footsteps and bearing whose weight and the weight of all their agonies – the track had become really really old!

* * * * *

Stealthily, Sonia came out of her room and on to the upper verandah. The chowkidar was there but he too was fast asleep. She peeped into the bird's cage. Both the birds were spending their night peacefully. On Sonia's approach they flapped their wings a few times and then quietened down again. Neighbour's cat was not far away waiting for her prey! But the cage was strong and therefore the birds were safe.

Rabbits too made some movement. They got on to the grill and stood up with their feet against the wire-netting. Sonia touched them with her hands and then moved on.

Dark night! Hand bag in one hand and torch in another. Sonia gradually climbed down the few steps to wilderness – descending one step at a time. She had no fears. She nurtured no malice or anger against anyone. It was one innocent heart, dented badly by the blows of cruel destiny advancing to a destination – unknown. She was quite clear in her mind of the 'why' of her decision – a very risky decision taken at a very tender age.

Getting out of her garden gate she looked first towards her left and then towards her right. Which direction she should proceed? On the left is the city and its gruelling population. On the right are lonely fields – tea gardens. She felt scared. After all at home she would not even get into the bathroom if it was dark. While going to sleep an open window scared her. Today, how that same Sonia would walk alone on this totally dark street? In two minds, she walked over to the lamp post outside her house and leaned against it. She looked behind and noticed, rising in front of her, the very same staircase over which she should have gone up and down, hundreds of times. Sprawled in front of her was the very same bungalow where she was born – twelve years ago. First one room, then behind that another room – and another and her Papa and two brothers sleeping there. Today she is leaving that very house which she always called her own. Once out of its boundary, that very house would become inaccessible to her – for ever.

The delicate strings of her heart – started playing together – in a chorus. She felt dizzy. She left her bag on the ground and with difficulty straightened herself. Then she started thinking:

'It is OK. I can go. But where? Wherever I go I would be alone. Here the two brothers would get up in the morning and search for me and not finding me, they will start crying – no end. I too would not be able to see them again – see my two brothers whom I was the second one to see after they were born – next only to my mother. I would also never see my Papa – and Ma! Oh, I had totally forgotten my mother. When Ma comes to know that 'Soni' has disappeared – she would die crying! No. She would certainly cry for some time but then would quieten down and after some years I would have been forgotten by all of them'.

'But I should have at least met Ma once – prior to leaving like this?'

And Sonia's tender-heart started become unsure. Serious doubts started assailing her mind about the wisdom of her decision. She started seeing through her mind's eye – firstly, the face of her mother in tears, then the faces of her two brothers running around the house, searching for her, then the face of her Papa. 'Papa shouts at me frequently. But if he did not find me here he would be so disappointed with himself. Who will run fingers through his hair every morning. After all he feels so good when I run my fingers through his hair'.

'Ma shouts, but repents soon enough by crying. How can I hurt a mother who is so considerate? She loves me most. She has told me so so many times and in as many words that if she was alive, she was alive only for me'.

'And those two younger brothers. Both of them would search for me in every nook and corner of the house. They will turn every thing in the house upside down searching for their Jijji (sister). Who would console them. The two ayahs are no good. Papa too is not much help. He does not know how to look after children. The youngest brother even refuses to drink milk from anyone else's hands. He would not only go hungry but would cry his heart out.

Sonia's tender heart started admonishing herself. How can she leave everyone and go, particularly when her mother while leaving for her treatment had specifically handed over the care of the two younger brothers to her. She is ready to withstand Papa's shouting and endure all troubles – still look after everyone. Ma is not home. Is lying in a Nursing Home in Calcutta. She would be thinking that even if she is not home, so what – her Soni is there making up for all shortcomings. Oh God if I also left what will happen to everyone?

She can withstand any distress but can't see her brothers, in tears. Her heart started sinking. Her eyes got filled up and thinking of her mother she started crying.

Then guided by some unknown force she ran back towards her house. Taking two, sometimes even three steps in one go, she climbed up the stairs and rushed into her room. There she threw herself in between the two brothers and lying face down started sobbing.

Every mother in this universe can bow her head in salutation to the sense of motherhood displayed by Sonia – at such a tender age.

* * * * *

Papa turned in his bed and since there had been some noise in the room, he looked around. He saw Sonia in her brother's bed and asked: 'What is the matter Sonia?'

Calming her voice Sonia answered: 'Nothing Papa. I am taking the younger brother to the bathroom or else he will wet his bed'.

And Papa turned his head instantly to the other side and went back to sleep.

He could never know that his very own flesh and blood – his innocent daughter – how aggrieved is she – how much is she suffering? And more importantly just a few minutes earlier what a great tragedy was going to get enacted, under this very roof.

* * * * *

Next day, Papa received a telegram from Calcutta informing him that 'Ma' passed away on the operation table! She bid good bye to this world handing over her motherhood into the tender hands and heart of Sonia!

And Sonia became a mother even before she could become a teenager.

* * * * *

A Night in Dehradun Express

People knew her by many names, but I knew her only as Vimla ji.

That fateful night, when I accidentally came face to face with her in a first class compartment of the Dehradun Express, I was astounded. It should have been eighteen years since we parted company, sure of just one thing – we were unlikely to meet again! Knowing her was at best a relationship between two students of one University – the relationship having come to an end with my abrupt departure from the Banaras Hindu University (B.H.U.). Even in the University I was not close to her. For that matter no one would have been sure of having been close to her since she had set her heart on one 'somebody' and she remained lost in that one dream, day in and day out. Everyone who met her returned with one impression that Vimala ji lived in a world of her own. Probably that was one plain and simple truth too.

Yet in the B.H.U there was not even one student who could have laid his hand on his heart and claimed that he has remained unaffected by Vimlajis' charm. In appearance she was at best ordinary. Her charm lay in her captivating voice. Once she started talking, the sound of her voice was such that it could bring down the most diehard misogynist. That is why everyone in the university lived under her charm. Softness and richness of voice and total command over Hindustani classical vocal music was of an order that won her admirers, everywhere. There was no programme in the University in which Vimlaji was not asked to sing, again and again, and the applause and clapping did not go on for many minutes.

This was one facet of Vimlaji's personality that fascinated me most and today I have no hesitation in confessing that I was one of her very ardent admirers. Yet when everyone tried to get closer to her, I remained satisfied with remaining her admirer – only from a distance. Then when getting news of my father's sudden demise in Indore, circumstances forced me to leave the University – abruptly, I left Banaras leaving Vimlaji's memories - behind. I was confident that Vimlaji and my admiration for her had become history and that I am unlikely to see her again – in this life.

Four years after my departure from the BHU, I heard that Vimlaji did her post-graduation in English and then married the 'prince charming of her dreams'. I was also told that her husband came from an affluent family of zamindars from UP and that he had just then returned for USA, doing his Doctorate in Agriculture. I also heard that he was an extremely well-educated handsome young man who had on return to India taken up a job with a big tea plantation in Assam. And the day I heard all this, my story, in which Vimlaji was my 'princess charming' – came to an abrupt end – at least so I thought!

In the years gone by, whenever Vimlaji returned to my mind I thought of her as a contented and happy housewife. After all what else would a woman want from her marriage? Vimlaji's husband Mahendra was well educated – smart, handsome and rich – worked as a Manager in a big tea plantation pocketing at least twenty thousand per month as salary. They were blessed with two children – a boy and a girl – both receiving education in reputed schools in North India. And specifically for those reasons, I dreamt of Vimilaji as a happy and contended married woman. Why shouldn't she be happy? After all Mahendra was 'that very deity', lost in whom, Vimlaji spent her entire college life. Any women would be happy marrying a man of her choice. That was the picture engraved in my mind – of Vimlaji and of her married life.

And therefore when I chanced into her, after over eighteen years, in the first class compartment of a train, I was astonished! She should not have been old – just 37-38 years! Yet her head had more grey than black hair. Cheeks had sunk and dark circles had appeared around her eyes. Could this have been the result of her marriage. 'Impossible' – I told myself! Yes she looked slightly taller than what I had seen her last. Her physical appearance had otherwise not undergone any major change.

Finding her all alone – that too in a first class compartment, many memories from the University days flashed past my mind.

What should one call that but 'Destiny' – there was no one else in that compartment – but for the two of us. I thought her husband might have walked on to the platform and would be getting in soon. If he didn't, then it would be unwise to stay on in the compartment – all alone with Vimlaji. It might cause her avoidable embrassment. But what wrong if I stayed on? It is also possible that she might not be remembering me at all. After all eighteen years have gone by between those days and today. Let me therefore stay on. Once her husband turns up, I would get a chance to have a glimpse of their blessed married life. After all I have not yet been able to totally erase the memories of Vimlaji and of our university days – from my mind.

I was lost in these thoughts when I heard Vimla ji, saying – 'please be seated – where is your baggage'? and I jumped up.

'Namastey. I thought I have been forgotten. We are due to reach Dehradun early morning. I have therefore brought no baggage, except this briefcase.'

Vimlaji has recognised me and therefore come what may, I cannot change compartments. I would be required to observe normal courtesies too. Ten hour's journey still remains. I would need to keep my emotions under check?

Vimlaji was sitting motionless and quiet in one corner of her berth. With each passing minute, expressions on her face were becoming graver. My gaze was fixed upon her. I was trying to re-locate her smiling face from the university days, in her looks. I am not aware how much time would have gone by like this. But when the guard blew his whistle and the train started moving, I woke up from my trance. Vimlaji's husband has still not boarded. I could not hold myself back and asked:

'Vimlaji! The train has started moving and your husband has not returned?'

'He won't'.

What sort of an answer? I couldn't make head or tail out of it. Is it that this lady is not Vimlaji. But that is impossible. She surely is Vimlaji. Same face – same features and same voice. Everything same – except for the missing carefree smile of the college days.

'You are Vimlaji? Isn't it?' I asked.

'Yes'. Again the briefest possible reply.

'You recognise me Vimlaji – don't you?'

'Yes we studied together in the University.'

A sigh of relief ... at least Vimlaji has not forgotten me.

The train should have in the meanwhile covered a lot of distance. Outside the compartment it was pitch dark. We would probably reach Dehradun next morning by about 10 O'clock. However, sitting silent like this is not courteous. I must start a conversation. After all Vimlaji is not an unknown entity. In the university. I used to go round boasting that we two, i.e. me and Vimlaji had known each other in several births – had been together in many past lives. How can then one stay quiet today?

But why Vimlaji is so quiet? What sort of transformation is this? In the University, once she started talking she never stopped – gave no one else a chance to speak.

'Vimlaji where are you going?'

'Dehradun'.

'Your husband didn't come along'. I asked.

'No'.

'Where is he these days?'

'At home'. Vimlaji replied unenthusiastically.

'How are your children?'

She was perhaps not ready for this question. Therefore she answered but after a lot of hesitation.

'They are home these days. They are happy'.

Vimlaji thereafter took a deep breath. She perhaps thought that the conversation has come to an end and there would be no more questions. And that is exactly what happened. Finding her in no mood to talk, I too became quiet. I wanted to keep the conversation going. But what can I talk to her? If she was unmarried – like she was in the University – I would have asked her hundreds of questions – even about her boy friends. The problem today is that she is married – and is hesitant to carry on a conversation. However it would still be bad manners to be in the company of an old acquaintance and to not talk. I would have to take the responsibility of keeping the conversation going. But what if Vimlaji took an offence to my talking? I was still in the process of evaluating the pros and cons when the soft-sweet voice of Vimlaji startled me:

'How are you engaged these days?'

Same half-singing half-ringing voice that in an instant took the weight off my mind.

'Yes, Vimlaji. I write for some newspapers and periodicals. I also spend a little time writing short stories.'

'Oh – did you get married?'

'Not so far' – was my very simple reply.

Vimlaji once again relapsed into silence. I didn't know, whether my being unmarried did create any problem for her. I wanted her to continue talking and therefore I started feeling cheesed off. Why doesn't she talk? In the University once she started talking she would forget that there were some subjects on which girls never talked to boys. But why is she quiet today. Anyway, I am the man here and it is my responsibility to keep her entertained. Gathering my wits I asked:

'Vimlaji, – while we were in the university – you used to remain lost in some very secret somebody's thoughts. Do you remember?'

'Yes – of course'.

I heaved a sign of relief. At least I have found a subject of mutual interest.

'I was told that having finished your post-graduation you married your prince-charming – the deity of your dreams.'

'Yeah – yes.' My question startled Vimlaji.

'Then you would certainly be a very contented and happily married woman – having married someone whom you adored during your university days?'

My question extinguished Vimlaji in entirety.

I was watching her attentively. I did so in the past too. However, while in the University Vimlaji was known to be a girl totally at peace with herself, today she created an impression of being a lady in distress. Some sort of storm was raging inside her. Some thoughts troubled her. Her face was becoming graver. She was face-to-face with some terrible agony. Vimlaji is not happy with her present – became obvious from her looks. But what troubled her?

When I raised the question of her's being happy in her married life, I had no malicious intent – no jealousy either with her or with her husband – no ill-will towards anyone. The impossibility of my having been able to share Vimlaji's life notwithstanding, I did adore her – nurtured sneaking love for her. Today that old flame might have been extinguished – yet that sneaking admiration for her remained, hidden in some secret crevice of my heart.

I was lost in these thoughts when Vimlaji's stern voice – harsh and angry alarmed me.

'How do these things concern you – Anuj? I am happy – I am unhappy in my married life – is none of your business. If you believe that you had some say in my affairs – you are mistaken. You were no more than a co-student – those days. Even today you are no more than a University colleague of mine. Don't harass me by asking such questions. I can travel quietly – on my own. I need no support from you or from anyone else. Mahendra is next to Divinity for me. I am happy with him. Please don't bother yourself about us.'

Vimlaji finished all this in one breath and then relapsed into silence. Her face became red with anger. I reclined a bit in my seat and into the shadows to ensure that Vimlaji got no clear view of my face. I was not expecting such humiliation from Vimlaji. My motivation in asking that question was neither ill-will nor greed. It was one plain and simple desire to keep the conversation going.

After that rather offensive exchange Vimlaji uttered no single word. I too decided to remain quiet. Events of the University days flashed past my mind. Times were when she used to tell me – 'keep on talking – don't stop please – you are so interesting'. I had never expected such harsh words – as a reaction to what I thought was simply a day to day question. My heart refused to accept, that I deserved such harsh words or that Vimlaji could become so heartless.

What could have brought this 'sea change' in her ... sea change between Vimlaji of the university days and today.

I gradually reckoned that this could be the outcome of her troubled existence and that 18 years latter, her pride in decision-making is preventing her from acknowledging that 'she went wrong while taking the most important decision in her life' – or that she couldn't see through the glamorous exterior of her prince charming Mahendra.'

Vimlaji's pride in herself and her firm speak enhanced her stature in my mind. I knew very well that no women in Vimlaji's position – would ever concede – that too in front of a colleague from the University, that she committed a blunder while taking a decision, in a matter so vital to a woman. She would certainly not concede so in front of someone who believed that he was Vimlaji's favourite. With a heart badly bruised and gravely humiliated, I thought, that in uttering words that ' – Mahendra is next to God for her and that she is happy in entirety with him' – how much pain would Vimlaji have endured and what a big untruth she would have been compelled to say? How much torture she would have endured? Perhaps she noticed some glimpse of ridicule in my question and therefore became so harsh. My heart all the same was refusing to accept that Vimlaji could change – so much.

I was not able to see Vimlaji's face. She had moved her head towards the window grill. I was therefore in no position to know what was going on in her mind. On my part, I was finding it impossible to gather enough strength to restart the conversation.

Sinking and surfacing in these thoughts, I don't know when I went to sleep.

* * * * *

It should have been past midnight when the touch of a woman's hand, startled me. The train was racing at full speed. I looked around and found no one else in the compartment except Vimlaji and me. I had no idea as to when had Vimlaji changed into her night clothings. When I woke up I saw her in a black velvet dressing gown tightly belted on the waist. Her hair were thrown loose over her shoulders. In the dim light of the compartment I noticed grave dark shadows around her eyes.

'Angry with me' asked Vimlaji.

'Not at all'.

'Then I want to tell you a few things. Please get up and sit down. I have very little time left with me!.'

'But Vimlaji – it should have been just an hour or two ago when you asked me not to talk.'

'Excuse me for that. I don't know what went wrong and why did I utter those very harsh words. Please forget them. I am so sorry.'

I had in between straightened myself and taken seat on my berth while Vimlaji stood next to me. She resumed the conversation:

'You wanted to know if I was a contended and happy married woman ... having married my dream prince.'

'Yes Vimlaji – I did! But I am ashamed.' Please excuse me. I did cross my limits! Don't know why? I am so sorry about all that.'

'No, not at all. There is nothing to feel sorry about? You did no wrong in asking me that question. You have all the rights since you are an old colleague of mine and my well wisher. If anyone should regret it should be me. I am so very sorry Anuj.'

When I mentioned it to her that she should not be tiring herself by standing on the floor of a moving train – she came and sat next to me – on my berth. Sitting next to me and close enough I found Vimlaji visibly tired. It should have been just a few minutes when she started speaking again:

'Listen Anuj – I am deeply distressed at having not answered your question. That is why I took this unusual step of waking you up. My apologies. I have now decided to bare my heart to you – to tell you everything – though this would require going back many years – to some point during our university days'.

'But Vimlaji I am not keen to know all that. I only pray that Got kept you happy – wherever you were and whatever you are'.

'Okay – Okay – but now it is not possible for me to hide anything from you. I have nurtured these secrets for eighteen long years. Today I have found you! It is perhaps God's wish that I bare my heart to you – tell you everything – hide nothing.

You will have to sit up and listen to all that I have to say. Are you not my own? Don't I know this from our University days!'

'Vimlaji, digging past can make one miserable and I don't want you to go through any further torture. You were always known for your intellect. Please don't force me into listening to your story.'

Vimlaji was not ready to hear a 'no' – from me. Her pride re-surfaced and her face turned red with anger. She started speaking again – but in a very terse voice.'

'I took you as my own – as my genuine well-wisher from the past. Therefore, I decided to bare my heart to you – to tell you everything. And now you don't want to hear – that too after I have vowed to myself that I will tell you everything.'

There was a very brief pause after which she started speaking again – this time in a tone displaying extreme impatience.

'No Anuj you have no choice. You will have to hear me out. Understand? You have no choice.'

And having said all this she fixed her gaze upon me ... seeking my approval. I was on the horns of a dilemma. I knew that right from her University days, Vimlaji was used to ordering. Her tone therefore did not surprise me. However, even before I could decide what next – I saw Vimlaji moving towards and closer to me. It should have been a fraction of a second when I found her hand in mine and her head in my lap. She lay so close to me that I started hearing her heart-beats – even her breathing.

You may call it my weakness – but the fact is that I never could say 'no' to Vimlaji ... fearing that it might displease her. I knew very well that saying 'no' in such tender moments might hurt her ego – and she might never want to see my face again. I therefore sat transfixed – oscillating between hesitation and fear. Then suddenly in one moment of expectation I raised my eyes towards Vimlaji and found her gazing expectantly at me – her entire personality having become an expression of pain, suffering and longing. I found it impossible to remain a mute spectator anymore. Then too my lips uttered no words – but my eyes gave the approval. And then forgetting the world and its norms, and breaking all societal barriers, we became one in flesh and blood – spending about half an hour that way. And with love-making out of way, Vimlaji became a bit relaxed. She drew a deep breath, pulled her dressing gown from under me – straightened her clothes retouched her hair with her fingers and then moved towards her own berth taking her seat by the side of the window. I noticed her trying to organise her thoughts ... perhaps thinking, where to start.

Five minutes went by and no one spoke. Then with her gaze still fixed upon me, Vimlaji started speaking:

'You know, my elder sister Nirmala. When her marriage negotiations were on, her would-be-husband Kailash used to visit our house occasionally, accompanied by his younger brother Mahendra – who was then doing his Masters in Allahabad University. That is how I came to know Mahendra. What should I tell you about Mahendra's looks and the ease with which he carried himself amongst girls? If he started a conversation he never ended it unless he has made each and every one of us laugh. His attraction was multi-faceted and my universe was child-like.

In the University, the normal topic of conversation amongst girls used to be just boys or future husbands. That innocent world of ours thrived on dreams and fantasies. It is not true that each of us waited for our prince charming – from the land of fairies, descending upon this planet riding a horse. But the husband of our dreams was never less than one prince charming. Today I am not able to say what was the spell that bound me to Mahendra – to such an extent that I started believing that he alone was my prince charming ... and I could marry no one else. My dream world comprised only Mahendra – just Mahendra. No one on this planet could have been handsomer, endowed with better qualities or better behaved, than Mahendra.'

'I offered my innocent youth on to Mahendra's feet. He became my deity, my object of worship and I became his most dedicated worshipper. When I think of those days, I realise that I took Mahendra as my husband because he had cast a spell over me and won my heart in the first meeting itself. It was in the first meeting itself that I established him as 'the deity' in the sanctum-santorum of my heart. In my life I was perhaps destined to be or was even fond of becoming a worshipper even before becoming a lover. I was ready to sacrifice my entire being on the feet of the 'deity' who was going to be my husband. Mahendra was my deity – my God. His willingness to accept me as his wife left me with no doubt that as a husband too he would behave no lesser than a God. What hopes...?'

Vimlaji took a little break before beginning again. A sigh escaped her lips – unconsciously! She closed her eyes and relaxed her head a little. I thought she was trying to get over her feeling of hurt and extreme pain. Seeing her in this condition I started feeling agitated. My heart wanted her to stop there itself. I wanted to share her sufferings even if those moments of sharing were going to last only till day break. But then it came to me that making her speak out her tale of woe can go a long way in relieving her distress. I therefore, pulled myself forward in a gesture encouraging her to continue.

'Are you listening to me? Isn't it,' asked Vimlaji without opening her eyes. She was not willing to risk scattering away her recollections.

'In due course of time Mahendra's elder brother got married to my elder sister. Mahendra was a part of that big 'barat' (marriage party) which came for the marriage. Whenever we came face to face with each other we exchanged glances and we smiled and I soon enough surrendered my innocent youth at Mahendra's feet. I can remember even now as to, how a powerful current used to surge through my body – whenever Mahendra set his gaze upon me. I was so enamoured and so sure of him that one day I collected all my 'sahelis' (girl colleagues) at my place and made them have a secret glimpse of my 'aradhya' (object of worship).

'Then another day as I was standing in front of my window a voice alarmed me! 'namastey Vimla – what are you looking at?' I turned around to find Mahendra standing there – smiling away. I had not known till then as to how one reacts to such advances. I started sweating from top to toe. We were in front of each other and I was speechless. There was no one around. We two were alone in that room. Shame and anxiety made me run towards the door. However as I was about to get out, Mahendra caught hold of my hand – 'answer my namastey at least' – said Mahendra – smoothly, still holding on to my hand.

'Mahendra's touch sent a shiver through my body. I thought I was going to faint. I perhaps would have, had not the band playing loud music outside, suddenly stopped playing. That gave me a brief space to regain my wits. It was the very first time in my life that I had been caught in a situation like this and that too without knowing how to get out of it. Today I can not say how did that happen? Like a robot, I brought my two hands together, pronounced a very crispy 'namastey' and ran out through the nearest door. Having taken eight-ten steps I turned round to see what was happening behind me and I found Mahendra smiling – that very naughty smile.

After this episode. I met Mahendra many a times. We kept on coming closer to each other. I started secretly addressing him as my 'Ishwar (God)'. I started talking to him in his absence – started worshipping him in the privacy of my life. I however never knew why Mahendra's presence always made me speechless. What he thought of me or what were his feelings towards me – I could never know. Yes, whenever he found me alone he cought hold of my hand, pressed my toe with his feet or hugged me passionately – and I thought that he liked me so much that he was unable to spend even one single day, without touching me. I could have tried to analyse and find the secret meanings behind these advances – but I didn't. I neither had the knowledge nor the experience nor even the desire to go deeper into them. I was overwhelmed by the yearnings of my heart which had already accepted Mahendra as my prince charming – my Ishwar (God) – one who could do no wrong'.

'Subjects like love or marriage never cropped up during our conversations. Whenever we were in each other's company, I was generally quiet. He spoke a little and every word that he spoke became a treasure.

'I started dreaming that once we were married we will have a small house. I will live in it like a newly-wedded girl. I would be respectful towards visitors and will keep my eyes glued to the ground ... all the time. I will talk slowly and in measured tones. I will take care of Mahendra's clothes and will look after all his needs. We shall convert our small house into a heaven, where only love and sweet words would rule. I shall live like his princess – also like his devotee. I certainly dreamt more about looking after Mahendra and catering to his needs than anything else. What were Mahendra's expectations from marriage – I don't know – even today? Yet, I remember that after marriage he once casually mentioned it to me that he yearned for a companion who was pretty, modern, smart and fashionable – in sum a total socialite who could become an asset in his tea-garden job. He detested the idea of having a wife who behaved like a villager and brought the smell of muck from her village into his house'.

'Before marriage, I never got an inkling of his expectations from me. In my case, my dreams of married life would have been fulfilled by converting a small thatch roof in a way side village – into my home.'

I was watching Vimlaji's face intently. For the first time I saw her trying to open her eyes. I couldn't make out what was it that she wanted to say, yet saying which was such a torture. Her face became an embodiment of suffering – of pain and her gesture of constantly closing and opening her eyes became indicative of a volcano building up inside her – ready to burst out any moment, into flames.

Our train came to a halt at some wayside railway station and then after a few minutes – started moving again. Vimlaji sat unmoved during the halt. As the train picked up speed – she started speaking again:

'Soon after doing his M.Sc. Mahendra started preparing for studies in the USA – for doing his doctorate. Prior to his departure for the USA he visited Banaras and suggested that the two of us go out to watch a movie. My parents saw no difficulty. Here was an opportunity when if I could free myself from the restrictions imposed upon an unmarried girl talking freely to her would-be-husband, I would have cleared many doubts. Yet I remained tongue-tied – weighed down by social mores and the teachings of the elderly.'

'We had just got on to the cycle rickshaw when Mahendra told me: 'Vimla – I am going to the USA for two years. Hope you would not forget me.' I sat dumb-struck. Mahendra started speaking again: 'Vimla I wanted to tell you so many things, but could never find an opportunity. Now I leave India for two years and leave with a fear that I might loose you.'

'Silence ensued ....! We both were silent. My heart started shedding tears – silently. It was my good fortune that before I started crying – we were outside the cinema hall. I failed to articulate my feelings. I failed to gather enough strength to tell him that forgetting him was out of question – not only in this life but in many lives hereafter.'

'Sitting inside the cinema hall my heart, in its plain childishness decided to accept Mahendra as its one and only God – as the prince charming – as my worthy husband – not only in this one life but in all lives hereafter. This perhaps was an innocent reaction to Mahendra's one sentence: 'I am going to USA for two years. Hope you would not forget me'. How naïve, how impulsive and immature, how trusting – was I. Such vital decisions should not have been taken in moments of doting, madness, impulsiveness and senselessness. Yet I did that! This perhaps is the real nature of a woman – call it her weakness – may be her failing too. She stakes her entire life – all dreams and her entire future without as much as a second thought, on just three words of love! I love you!'

'Truly speaking, even today, I have no regrets over that decision of mine. I believe – and sincerely too, that if destiny had written 'perish' against my name, I would have faced the same ordeals – same sufferings, even if I had married anyone else.'

'Anyway, no point now in going over all those things.'

'We sat through the movie without uttering one single word. We still talked volumes in the language of love. We did many things in the language of silence! It was not Mahendra who was sitting next to me. It was some one Divine who had descended upon this earth in the form of a lover. I was dreaming all the time of a small house in wilderness – surrounded by green fields – children and a small happy family. Mahendra's eyes were all the time glued on to my face. He would sometime take my hand into his – sometimes leave my hand in his lap – sometimes he would re-arrange my hair. I tried several times to see Mahendra from the corners of my eyes, but failed.'

'Intense faith in him as an individual, overwhelming respect for him mixed with a bit of superstition should have been the reason for my inability to see the dark spots in his personality ... a common failing with women – who blinded by a few sweet words of love, fail to identify and separate truth from the 'put up show' and substance from the mask or shell.'

Vimlaji put a stop here to her monologue and for the first time opened her eyes ... and as she did so, tears started rolling down her cheeks and on to her dressing gown. Don't know for how long had she kept these tears captive inside her closed eyes. I felt agitated – worried! I had in my life witnessed many heart-wrenching scenes. I can, therefore, safely say that the tears shed by Vimlaji were not tears of pain, agony or regret. Those very eyes of Vimlaji which had dreamt a million dreams of one happy and blissful married life did become her medium of returning all those very dreams to this world in the form of tears.

My one big weakness – I get easily moved by tears more so in women's eyes. Sitting there in that first class compartment, I knew very well that there was hardly anything that I could do to help Vimlaji out. I therefore wanted to run away from in front of her, even at the risk of being dubbed a coward. I knew very well that it was impossible for me to be any help in relieving her distress. Yet I also thought that encouraging her to speak out her long tale of woe might help her in making her feel lighter. And that way, I thought I would, be discharging my duty towards one of my University colleagues.

Vimlaji closed her eyes again and started speaking:

'Mahendra left for USA and I utilised the interregnum to do my MA. My parents wanted me to study music as well. Honouring their wish I worked hard and within that limited period of two years. I obtained Doctorate in Music too. There was no moment when Mahendra was off my radar. Whenever I saw a handsome young man on the street, I thought it was Mahendra. It appeared as if Mahendra has become an extension of my own body. Anyway, why should I bother you with these petty details. They neither have any end, nor any meaning left in them!'

Travelling backwards in terms of time, I wondered how Destiny can transform a girl, who always laughed like a mountain stream, who always talked in tones produced by bangles striking against each other – into such a wreck.

'You would have seen that famous movie 'Parineeta' – did you? When I was watching that movie with Mahendra I saw him all the time in the role of Ashok Kumar and myself in the role of Meena Kumari. That is one reason why I liked that movie, immensely. Even today I have not been able to forget its thrill – the thrill of mine being Meena Kumari and more importantly of his being Ashok Kumar.'

Thereafter, there was a mad scramble of thoughts in Vimlaji's mind. She wanted to re-arrange them in a logical sequence. It should have been about half a minute when she started speaking again:

'One winter morning, in the University, I received by post an envelope from Mahendra. I opened it and read it ... very expectantly. My heart did a jig going through its contents. I still remember some of them. He had written – 'I am yours –

only yours! My love with you is not momentary. It is indivisible, perpetual, immortal. The day I was born – I was born for you – only you. You are my Lakshmi, my owner, my protector, my co-traveller in the journey of life! You are my destiny and destination! You are my only object of worship. You are my everything! To get you I can put any thing in my life at stake – to keep you happy I can make any sacrifice.'

'I took the letter to my elder sister. She was overjoyed. On her part she had already decided, quite sometime back, that she would get the two of us married no sooner Mahendra returned from the USA. There were no limits to what my heart had already started planning. I had already started seeing everything green, in my married life'.

'That letter is still safe with me. It is my one precious possession. It represents some fleeting moments of immense pleasure in an otherwise long-drawn story of a very painful existence. When I think of the contents of that letter today, I laugh at myself and upon my childishness. I had gone through that letter many a times after my marriage. What a role reversal? From my being everything for him, he became everything for me – my owner, my protector, my Divinity and my Deity. He wrote that he was willing to pay even the biggest price for my happiness. 'What a joke it was – upon my life? What ridicule?'

At this stage it appeared to me that Vimlaji has exhausted herself. When she re-opened her eyes tears started rolling down her cheeks – almost like a stream and she made no efforts to either stop them or hide them. Seeing her in this condition, my heart started sinking – even missing heart beats. I was in no position to console her and Vimlaji was gradually becoming 'suffering personified'. She sat quiet for a long time – emotions choking her throat. She also appeared tired of talking.

I looked at my watch – it was past two. We were still 7-8 hours away from Dehradun. I prayed to God imploring strength for being able to hear Vimlaji out. The train stopped once again at some way-side railway station. Vimlaji sat unmoved – pain and suffering writ large all over her face. As the train moved out of the station, she started speaking again:

'No sooner Mahendra returned from the USA, the elders from the two families met and fixed up the date of our marriage. There were no problems. Mahendra's parents made some demands but my elder sister intervened and got them settled – in consultation with the two families. Renowned Pandits from Banaras tallied the two horoscopes and predicted peace and harmony, happiness and joy, love and just milk and honey in our married life'.

At this juncture Vimlaji let go an audible sigh saying 'it was not just Mahendra, but even the Gods were playing a cruel joke with me!'

'Shortly before our marriage my elder sister took ill and we two were told to visit Shimla for looking after her. Myself and Mahendra started visiting hospital together. The desolate foot-tracks and that very caring and thoughtful behaviour of Mahendra – are some moments that I cherish even today. I call myself fortunate – even if it is for memory's sake, the otherwise cruel Divinity did give me at least some moments to cherish ... some islands of joy.'

'Under the cool shade of the marriage mandap (pandal), the Pandits (priests) recited holy mantras, lit up sacred fire, the musicians played shehnai – ladies sang auspicious songs, Mahendra looked towards the skies – and with stars and fire in the havan-kund as witness, gave a word to all assembled that he would work for making me happy, would work for one peaceful and blessed married life for the two of us.'

'We went round the sacred fire seven times and in just those few moments I was a married woman.'

* * * * *

'Time is not static ... it moves and moves really fast. Very soon it was time for me to leave my home and hearth, my brothers and sisters and to move towards my new home – a home for living out my dreams. Everyone who came to see us off shed copious tears. I too was inconsolable and cried and cried. Then the marriage party, with me in company, reached the railway station. A first class coupe (with four berths) had been reserved for us. My elder sister being the only woman in the marriage party was given a berth in the same compartment as the two of us. The remaining one berth was reserved for my Jija (my sister's husband). When I heard of my elder sister being in the same compartment as us I was disappointed!'

'The train started moving out of the railway station and with that started churning the wheels of destiny. I kept gazing at the railway platform fast disappearing from my view, along with all my family members and well-wishers who had come to see me off – to wish us all the best, now and for ever. I kept on watching the city of my birth disappear from my view alongwith all memories of childhood and youth and the love and affection showered by the members of my family and friends.'

'This is how came to an end, my relationship with the place of my birth'.

'The presence of my sister and her husband in our compartment, blanketed the possibility of any conversation between the two of us. It however, left me free to indulge without let or hinderance – in my hobby of day-dreaming. I do not remember how much time would have gone by like this. I am also not aware what Mahendra thought of the whole situation.'

'My sister's husband got down at the next railway station and when he did not return to the compartment even after the train had moved out, Didi took out a bed-sheet from her suitcase and hung it between the two berths in such a manner that neither of us could see each other. And that is how I entered my married life.'

It is difficult to say how many tears Vimlaji would have shed while narrating all this. She was crying all the time. Her throat was getting choked, off and on. Her voice was coming out in whispers. In my life I have never seen a woman in such distress. Seeing her crying so uncontrolably – time started hanging heavily upon me. My courage and confidence started deserting me. I started feeling that I too would start crying.

Vimlaji was sitting unmoved in her seat – her gaze fixed upon infinity, eyes wide open – tears gradually drying up! I started feeling that I would not be able to stand this tale of woe any longer. My head started reeling. I started praying for a stoppage, so that I could get down and inhale some fresh air. It was sheer cowardice – but I have no hesitation in acknowledging it even today. In my heart of hearts I wanted to be some help to Vimlaji ... in mitigating her distress. I was, however, aware of the societal norms under which we both, namely Vimlaji and me lived, which made any long-term rescue effort impossible ... notwithstanding that Vimlaji was a lady whom I once adored and loved and dreamt of making her my life-partner. She was sitting there right in front of me crying, and I was feeling so helpless.

In between sobs she started speaking again:

'That day too the train ran like this – taking me, my Mahendra and our dreams with it. I wanted to have a good look at him but gave up realising that now I have become his wife and there should be no hurry. The spirit underlying the institution of marriage and its new found excitement made me feel shy and I forced myself into controlling my emotions!'

'Then came the next stop where even Didi left the compartment – leaving the two of us alone. I started feeling more shy and more nervous. My heart started pounding taking me to the verge of unconsciousness. I started questioning myself – what next?

'Vimla' called Mahendra.

'Yes' – my heart echoed with pleasure! How endearing was that one word.

'Vimla, oh... please show me your face!'

'Perhaps all husbands, after their marriage, start the game of love this way. Mahendra's words touched my heart. How endearing was he and how magical were his words. How much of request was dissolved in those words. My ghunghat (veil) still covered my face. I was feeling shy and nervous and therefore could not lift my veil and show my face. All the same deep inside me, my heart rejoiced – racing on merrily, with new found happiness. Every moment of that exclusiveness was golden.'

'Vimla – that 'nath' (nose ring) that you are putting on looks pretty on your face! Let me see it, please.'

'His every word was one declaration of immense love – yet with impatience too lurking behind. I was living and rejoicing the thought of me and Mahendra becoming one and therefore had neither the time nor felt any need for going into the sentiments behind Mahendra's request. I was airborne with pleasure. I was finding it difficult to believe my good fortune. In those moments of joy, it didn't occur to me that in compliance with Mahendra's request – I needed to lift my ghunghat (veil) and show him my nose ring. For me every moment was precious and I wanted to treasure it for my life. Inside my veil I was smiling all the time with pleasure. I took a side-glance and found Mahendra watching me intently. Call it pride or shying – I did not lift my ghunghat – did not lift my veil!'

When Mahendra spoke again – just third time after our marriage – he sounded not only impatient but irritated.

'Why don't you show me your nose-ring? Don't you want to?'

'I was startled. What is happening? Why Mahendra is getting angry.'

My heart missed a few heart-beats, but I quietened myself. I told myself – can my Mahendra ever be angry – that too with me? Perhaps I am being a little eccentric. Mahendra has always been fond of playing pranks! Today also he is just doing that? Knowingly he is trying to tease me. If seeing my face was the issue, he could have by now thrown away my veil and lifted me in his arms. Who was there to see and disturb us? No one.'

'I waited expectantly for a few minutes and when I checked through my ghunghat, I found Mahendra walking away from my berth to his own. I thought, he has become really angry? What is there to get angry about? These are plain and simple love games. All girls, and all boys, when very young, play them! Does anyone take offence to them?'

'Having taken his seat on the berth opposite to mine and having reflected on the situation for a while, Mahendra spoke in a voice which was cut and dry.'

'O.K. If you don't want to show me your face, so be it. I won't ask again!'.

'Lightning struck me with its full fury. Mahendra's tone reflected injured pride – mixed with a bit of anger. I decided that I should not be sitting quiet any longer. Feeling shy and holding oneself back might spoil the game, forever. I had never seen Mahendra so injured and so angry. He can not! My heart once again intervened to say – mad girl – Mahendra is not angry, he is just trying to tease you. Why he shouldn't – after all he too has discovered a companion – to love – a companion to tease!'

'Making myself as humble, as accommodative and as pleasing as possible – in measured words, I said:

'Mahendra – I have now become yours. Now not only my soul but also my body is yours. If you so desire, why don't you come to me, remove my ghunghat (veil) and see me, see my face, my nose ring and everything you wanted to see!'

'I do not know how Mahendra interpreted my words. I would have perhaps continued but I found him intervening in a tone – distinctively harsh.'

'What is there for a request or prayer? First time in my life – and first time between the two of us, I made what I consider to be a simple request and you didn't comply. Very first time in our married life a very simple request of mine had been ignored by you. I never dreamt of such a situation. Anyway, I am not going to make any request to you again. I believed that I have married a modern girl and as your husband I have an absolute right to see your face. Let me see, how long you won't?'

'I became quite worried. After all this fault-finding and admonishing, how could one remove her ghunghat and show her face? But if I did not, he will think that I am challenging him. But is Mahendra really angry? Till today – he had not spoken even one harsh word to me. I used to think that he did not know how to get angry. May be this was one unknown angle to the start of our married life. My heart refused to believe that Mahendra can really become angry with me. I took it just one of his many ways of teasing his young wife.'

'Mahendra moved in his seat a little. Then he got up and I thought that the drama which he wanted to enact would now get over. He will now come to me. After all how playful is Mahendra? He makes everything so interesting!'

'My heart started beating faster. I could not understand his anger. I thought he is going to come to me now – any moment. He would lift my veil and will give a start to our new life. These were the very moments for which we have waited for so long. Are we not going to become one today?'

'Time ticked by but Mahendra did not come. Is he feeling shy? He is a man, so what? Taking the first step on the path of love is not an easy task – even man might hesitate. And why not?'

'Several minutes went by and the touch which I was waiting for and for which I was so impatient did not come my way. It occurred to me that if I did not act now – decisively, the entire situation might get messed up. I told myself that it has now become my duty to lift my ghunghat and to end the impasse. Summoning courage I therefore pulled my ghunghat up. I believed that no sooner I had lifted my veil, Mahendra would come running to me – would lift me in his arms, would love me and would end our eternal thirst for each other.'

'But what is this? Mahendra threw a fleeting glance towards me and turned his head towards the window. What has happened to him? My God! What is all this? Does anyone remain so angry and for so long?'

'Gathering my wits and in a very endearing voice I called "Mahendra".

'Yes'. was his reply – without even as much as looking at me.

'Mahendra you wanted to see my nose-ring. Isn't it?'

'Not at all! Why are you harassing me?' And Mahendra's answer stunned me. I was left speechless. This facet of Mahendra's personality which I had so far taken as playfulness was in reality anger and it had found expression in those few words, to which I did not know how to react. I did not know why he has become so angry with me? What have I done which he though was so wrong? This is not what my Mahendra used to be! If I had erred I can apologise. He loved me so much all these days. How can he remain angry today? Today is the day when we are about to start a new life. Nothing should go wrong on this day.'

'Mahendra – you seem to have become angry'.

'Not at all', Mahendra replied.

'Pardon me Mahendra. Really I should not have been so hesitant – so shy! Mahendra please.'

'Mahendra remained frozen in his seat – didn't utter even one word.'

'Are you really angry with me Mahendra? I give you a solemn assurance – you excuse me today – just only once – I would never let you get angry with me again! Mahendra – please.'

'I had earnestly hoped that my apology would end the unpleasantness – that Mahendra would laugh and setting aside this unfortunate episode the two of us would move in the direction of becoming one! After all, were we not madly in love with each other till the other day?'

'Mahendra, however did not utter one single word. On the contrary, he turned his back towards me and went to sleep. I struggled hard to find out as to what was it that had offended him to so badly – that too on a night like this when tens of sins are forgotten and hundred of faults are overlooked. Today was our first night when he was in front of me not as a lover but as my husband! Oh! How should I beg pardon ... I thought?'

'And impulsively I got up from my berth ... went to where Mahendra was sleeping and catching hold of his two feet, I implored:'

'Mahendra – please pardon me. At least say something. You are everything for me from today – my life – my happiness. Please excuse me for once!'

'It did not however occur to me that Mahendra has changed. He was not the Mahendra of the days gone by. He had become my husband and has ceased to be my worshipper of yore. Raising the pitch of his voice – he shouted:

'Stop harassing me. Go and sit down on your seat. Don't you hear?'

'And my patience with Mahendra got exhausted. I went into a fit and still clinging on to Mahendra's feet, I collapsed on to the floor. Oh God! What is all this? Where is my deity? Is this the harsh truth – the reality behind all dreams and man-made plans. I didn't know when, but tears started rolling down my eyes. I kissed Mahendra's feet. After all he was my God next to God! Big tear drops running out of my eyes landed onto my hands – on to his feet. He was alarmed. But he pulled his feet away.'

'I thought, Mahendra would at least have some value for my tears. If even as late as at this juncture he had picked me up and held me close to his heart, I would have forgotten all my pain and all my tears. After all he was my husband. Yet my tears kept on wetting his feet and he remained unmoved! I failed to understand as to how could he suddenly become so heartless and so harsh.'

'And as if Mahendra has vowed not to speak he did not utter a single word ... far from lifting me up and holding me close to his heart. I kept on sitting on the compartment floor shedding tears, on to his feet. Even my tears failed to move him.'

'My crime – just that I did not turn out to be a modern girl matching his expectations ... out of shyness, did not lift my ghunghat (veil) and uncover my face when he ordered. But how even so many tears were not enough to wipe out that small failing?'

'So Mahendra has really changed - I thought. He completed playing the part of a lover faultlessly, before marriage. Now he has ceased to be a lover – has become a husband. Prior to marriage he had no rights over me. Therefore, he was 'lover incarnate' whenever he appeared before me. Today having acquired exclusive rights over me, he has stopped respecting my dreams and started treating me as his personal property. He comes from an affluent family – rolling in wealth. Today I have just become one more piece of his vast property.'

'My heart did not revolt. It could not have revolted. After all I had worshipped him all these days as my God next to God. If my God has become angry, it becomes my duty and my religion, to win him back. He is my Lord - Lord of my heart – of my body. I should do only what he wants me to do. Being angry doesn't mean that he has become bad or an unwanted person... . I thought.'

'I kept on shedding tears, but Mahendra did not get up or tell me – Vimla don't cry. I kept on apologising in as many ways as I could think of. But I failed to move him.'

'Is marriage the biggest defeat in a woman's life? At least that had been my experience. It was the first time in my life that tears rolled out of my eyes uncontrolably – due to unbearable pain – that too on my wedding night – on the very first night of the start of our new life. My tears were so intense that they could have melted even a stone. But they failed to move Mahendra. He perhaps was priding himself in having humbled me. This perhaps was his way of making his title – over his newly acquired property, known to his newly wedded wife. Perhaps it was through the medium of my tears that his manhood and his ego was feeling satiated. Certainly in his mind he would have held women in low esteem. That is why turning my womanly pride into dust would have been so satisfying for him. As far as I am concerned, this was the first and the biggest defeat of my life which too was handed over to me by my Destiny – selectively – through the medium of my lover – my husband – on the very first night of my marriage itself. Oh God – if this is the start of my married life, what can I look forward to, in future.'

'The simple and straight forward manner in which I had staked everything in my life, upon a dream – blinded by teen-age love – stood shattered. I knew fully well that I had started on a journey of tears and reprimands and that there would be no going back. I had become just a woman and that too because of my body. For man – perhaps woman becomes just a body after marriage...her tears or the cries of her heart and soul, just become something to be ridiculed...!'

'And in this emotional upheaval I lost count of time. I forgot how much time has elapsed since I started crying – wetting Mahendra's feet with my tears. But this night which had started on a dramatic high had to end also on another dramatic high. The train started slowing down and stopped at some big railway station. Noise from outside filled the compartment. One could see day-break from the edges of the windows. Fateful night was just getting over – my wedding night! Suddenly my sister's husband entered the compartment and in quick realisation I pulled my ghunghat once again over my face. I also moved back to my seat and since I desperately wanted to hide the impressions of the night...my ghunghat came in handy.'

'My ghunghat which was my very worst enemy sometime back – having led to the unfolding of one great tragedy – became my best friend towards the end, having helped me draw a veil around my tears and my tragedy'.

'My sister's husband threw one sinister glance at me and smiled. He believed that the two of us had spent the night making love like lovers possessed by the Love God – Kama Deva!'

* * * * *

'And after a few hours I was in my in-laws house – my new house.'

'After the events of a long tragic night the benevolent God, for once helped me out with a room – all to my self – to sit back and cry in total freedom. And I cried and cried to my heart's content – wetted the entire ghunghat' ... tears had already washed away the bridal make up.'

'My elder sister entered the room and saw me but said nothing. She perhaps thought that all girls cry leaving their parent's house – I have cried a little more.'

'Fact remains that I have continued crying ever since and my tears have never ceased! I thank them since they have never refused to take care of a heart in agony.'

'Having spent herself fully – Vimlaji relapsed into a long bout of silence. I did not know how to react to her tale of woe. It was a moment of trial for me. If it was I and not Mahendra in front of Vimlaji, I would not have allowed her to shed even one of those many tears. What happened was a mockery – not only of love but also of that very sacred institution of marriage. I could have met Mahendra that very day and would have made him realise his follies and make amends. What happened was neither love nor even an assertion of genuine manhood.

Faced with societal restrictions I had no choice but to surrender to circumstances – Vimlaji had surrendered on the first night itself.

God the Great – either don't give dreams to innocent girls like Vimlaji or also give them courage and at least a bit of opportunity to realise at least part of those dreams. And if realisation of even part of those dreams is not possible – then at least don't allow those dreams to be crushed in the cruel manner in which Vimlaji's dreams were crushed. Agreed, that blinded by love Vimlaji failed to see through the mask and failed to identify the real nature and below the surface predilections of Mahendra. But such a small mistake should not have entitled her to such harsh punishment ad nauseum. Destiny however, has always subjected the trusting and the pure to such ridicule.

The train stopped again within 10-15 minutes at a small, dark, way side railway station. Sudden stoppage startled Vimlaji. Her eyes were now open but were sans tears. Perhaps she had already emptied her entire life's treasure of tears in just one night. She sighed and asked: 'How long to Dehradun'.

'Six more hours' – I answered.

'Oh, then we have lots of time! I still have so much to tell you.'

Vimlaji's reply sent me reeling. My God what more I still have to listen? No – no – I can't hear anymore. But how will I ask Vimlaji not to proceed any further. Howsoever I may want, I am in no position to help her – to relieve her distress. And if I can't help her then what right I have to continue listening to her story. Her sufferings tortured my soul. I was feeling suffocated. May be if I got down and inhaled some fresh morning air, I would feel better.

'Vimlaji, I just want to get on to the platform .... Shall be back shortly'.

'Ok.' Said Vimlaji, eyeing me curiously.

I got down promptly to a nearly dark platform and went behind a tea-stall. There was still a bit of time to day break. Many questions started tormenting me. Perhaps I have lost my normal mental balance. After all she is the same Vimlaji whom I adored in the University and whom I loved. What fate? Today she is shedding tears in front of me and I am in no position to even console her. I would not be able to see her in this condition anymore. My manhood would not be ready to accept such a big defeat.

And the engine blew its whistle! ... once, twice...

Vimlaji was telling me that she still has lots to say. Oh God, if the beginning is so tearful – what the end is going to be like. No, I do not have the strength to listen to her any more. Let me go inside and beg her pardon. But if I re-entered the compartment it would become impossible for me to leave her. No, I won't get in now. Don't know why she wants to tell me all those things? Don't know with what tragic intent, she has proceeded on this very tragic journey. If I did not return to the compartment she would take me to be a coward. Let her think so. After all faced with societal restrictions everyone becomes weak.

Train started moving...slowly. No, I won't get into the train – nor I would look up towards the compartment. But Vimlaji might search for me on the platform. Perhaps this might be the last opportunity for me to see her. Let me turn and see her – may be for the last time?

I could not hold myself back. From behind the tea stall I looked up at the moving train. True enough, Vimlaji was there in the compartment's open door – same black dressing gown, same open hair – same tearful eyes. She perhaps didn't see me standing behind the tea stall. The train kept on advancing and in a few moments disappeared from my view – the train and with it Vimlaji.

When I recovered, I started wondering what would have happened to Vimlaji? Many imponderables – many doubts started assailing my mind. It was not difficult for me to find out what would have happened to her. But I had no courage left to find more – more than what she had already told me!

* * * * *

Three days later a news item in one of the local dailies startled me. It was written:

"The lady who was taken out day before, in an unconscious condition from the first class compartment of Dehradun Express, passed away this morning in the Intensive Care Unit of a local hospital. Hospital sources revealed that overdose of sleeping pills was the likely cause of her death. Doctors believe that of the fifty sleeping pills that the lady was carrying with her, she would have consumed at least thirty in one go. From the woman's hand bag a slip was recovered with name 'Anuj' inscribed on it. Police is finding it difficult to proceed further since nothing besides the name is found written on the slip. A suicide note written in a trembling hand has also been recovered from the deceased's dressing gown. In the brief suicide note the lady has declared that she alone and no one else was responsible for her death. The note bore her signature as Vimlaji. The husband who is a manager in a tea garden in Assam, has identified and taken over his wife's body and has left for Banaras for cremation.

* * * * *

There was never any doubt that the end of Vimlaji's story would be tragic. But no one could have dreamt that her story would come to an end so tragically inside a railway train and that too as a consequence of an overdose of sleeping pills. But, if one looked back, suffering, misery and misfortune too got seeded into her life in a similar manner – in a moving train – in a first class compartment – on a similar dark night – her wedding night!

It was that very seedling which having gradually grown into a tree was contaminating Vimlaji's life. It should, therefore, be no surprise, that such a life of suffering came to an end in an identical manner – in a train – in a first class compartment – and on a similar dark night.

An unpardonable feeling of guilt chased me through out my life. Had I stayed on in the compartment for 2-3 more hours – had I listened sympathetically to her remaining tale of woe – had I allowed her to unload herself of her sufferings – she would perhaps be living today? I am another one, guilty of Vimlaji's tragedy – other one being Mahendra.

* * * * *

Several years later: I am standing once again on the platform of that very small way-side railway station. It is already day break – it however is still half an hour to sun rise. Dehradun Express has just passed in front of me in great speed – its first class bogies too. It appeared for sometime that Vimlaji would appear again – her head outside the first class compartment door – her hair flying in the air – that I would once again be able to see her in her black dressing gown !!! Not seen! It has been several years – every year on that fateful date and fateful time I park myself behind that very tea stall, on the same platform of the same small way-side railway station and await the arrival of Dehradun Express. Is it sense of guilt or feeling of remorse or penance that brings me here – I cannot say!

* * * * *

Raijore Das Babu (Das Babu – The Servant of the People)

'Raijore Das Babu' or 'Janta's Das Babu', is the story of one very ordinary individual, born during British days, in a very small tea garden in Sibsagar district of Assam. It also is the story of a government servant who has now been forgotten by everyone, including those who used to throng his residence right from day-break and in doing whose work and in sorting out whose financial problems, he spent his entire service – also the better part of his life. This short story, based on his exemplary character is also my humble tribute to him.

* * * * *

Das Babu's real name was Paritosh Bhattacharya. No one can say with certainty whether he was an Assamese or a Bengali. His ancestors are believed to have migrated into Assam three generations earlier from the then Sylhet district – now in Bangladesh. They came to work with the British in their tea gardens. However, over a period of time they assimilated themselves fully into the Assamese society by adopting Assamese language, Assamese food habits and culture also by forgetting what they had brought with them from Sylhet. Till such time India was not partitioned, they used to visit their village in Sylhet district, once a year on what they used to call their annual pilgrimage. These visits also catered to looking after their land and property situated in their village. The partition of the Country and the creation of East Pakistan jolted these arrangements. By the time Paritosh Da touched the age of understanding, this schedule of annual visits to Sylhet had almost broken down. On the contrary people started importing from East Pakistan gory tales of atrocities, perpetrated upon the minorities by the people of their locality – supported by the local Government. Paritosh Da therefore nurtured a sense of animosity towards the government of East Pakistan – also towards the peoplé of his native district. His ancestors left behind a big house and twenty seven acres of land in their ancestral village which all was encroached upon, occupied and usurped by the religious fundamentalists. Such of the youngsters who tried to raise their voice against forcible conversions – were either put behind bars on accusation of being Indian agents, or forced to flee to India. That is why Paritosh Da nurtured rabid anti-Pak sentiments, both in mind and heart. People of Assam were his extended family and he essentially lived for them.

Paritosh Da's parents and grand parents worked dedicatedly for the British, from 1885 to 1951, in their tea plantations in Assam. Even after retirement they lived under the care and protection of the British. Aroma of tea leaves was their life-sustaining force, their only intoxication. They therefore developed no links with the world outside their tea garden. Paritosh Da's father was offered a job by a British tea planter the very day he passed his BA examination from Calcutta University in first division. He started as an ordinary clerk and ended as a section officer. He earned voluminous commendations from the British planters on every post that he held – by dint of sheer hard and dedicated work. Paritosh Das's mother belonged to an average Assamese family. She came from a very small village in Barpeta district of Assam. In Paritosh Da's mother's family, parents preferred government jobs over tea garden jobs – for their children. Specifically because of this, the day Paritosh Da passed his BA examination from Cotton College, Guwahati, his mother ran around and got him a job in the Assam Treasury Service.

I met Paritosh Da for the first time in 1966. Paritosh Da was then the Section Officer in Guwahati Treasury and I was Commanding the 14th Battalian of the Madhya Pradesh Special Armed Force in Nagaland. In 1963, when Nagaland was still a district within Assam, 14 Jawans belonging to this Battalion were killed in an ambush by the Naga undergrounds. The Assam Government promptly sanctioned ex-gratia of rupees five thousand to each of those killed. However, in December, 1963 Nagaland separated from Assam and became a full-fledged state. Consequently the ex-gratia sanction remained 'not drawn', mainly due to red-tapism between the bureaucrats of the two states. In 1966, when I came to know of this pendency, I was dismayed. Five thousand rupees in 1966 were big money, for the family of a jawan who invariably came from a very poor background. I therefore, decided to work towards getting that money drawn from the Assam Treasury and to get it disbursed to the next of kin of the deceased. I met Paritosh Da in this connection.

Consultations with my staff revealed that there were two options for getting this money drawn speedily – one, if the ex-gratia could be drawn from Assam and not Nagaland, and two that it would help if I went personally and met the Treasury Officials in Guwahati – soliciting their assistance. It was in pursuance of the aforesaid suggestion that one fine morning I landed in Guwahati, along with the relevant papers and bills.

Two days of running around, trying to enlist the support of senior officers in Assam Treasury, brought me face to face with the reality that Guwahati Treasury was an impregnable fort which could only be accessed with the help of a sympathetic insider. I located Paritosh Da during my hunt for such a sympathetic insider. Well-wishers hovering around the Treasury had told me that my work would get done in no time – if I managed to get across to Paritosh Da.

Finding Paritosh Da was however not easy. People who needed his help used to throng his residence in Cheni Kuti right from day break. He used to remain surrounded by the needy – both men and women – throughout the day. When I saw him for the first time, it dawned upon me that the poor and the resourceless needed him more than I. Therefore, I decided to wait on. Then on the second day, by a stroke of good luck I found him alone. I explained to him very briefly the case of the deceased policemen – showed him the sanction order and handed him over the bills and the enclosures. He took a few minutes to understand the papers. Then he removed his spects, rubbed his eyes, looked at me – then looked at the papers again and then in a very humble voice and in perfect English he told me:

'Sir, you don't worry. You come day after. Your pay order would be ready. After all the policemen laid down their lives for the Country!'

And I showered him with thanks – more thanks – and many more thanks!

When I reached the Treasury the day after, I found him surrounded as usual by the needy. No sooner he saw me, he signalled to some body and it should have been just about two minutes when the original pay order was in my hands. For thanking him, I ran short of words. As I was about to leave, I went close to him and asked:

'Paritosh Da are you a reincarnation of some God?'

His answer was simple – straight from heart:

'Na baba Na! Moye to upekshito raijore kalyane kurmi! (I work for the welfare of the resourceless and poor). 'Raijore' in Assamese means of and for the public.

And I reiterated – with glee:

'No Paritosh Da – you are Das Babu! You are Raijore Das Babu! (Servant of the people)'.

As luck would have it, there were about 8-10 persons surrounding me and Paritosh Da. As they heard me addressing Paritosh Da as Das Babu, they all joined me and in unison started shouting 'Raijore Das Babu – Raijore Das Babu'. Gradually more and more people started addressing him as Raijore Das Babu and in one year's time Paritosh Da had become, for all practical purposes Das Babu. If after one year one wanted to visit Paritosh Da's place, he only had to tell the rickshaw puller that he wanted to be taken to Das Babu's residence and there was no chance of a mistake.

That is the 'how' and 'why' of Paritosh Da becoming Das Babu – or more appropriately Raijore Das Babu.

After 1966 there was no occasion when I needed Das Babu's help. All the same it was impossible to forget such a fine human being – so honest and so dedicated to the service of the poor, the needy and resourceless. Therefore, whenever I visited Guwahati and had some time at hand I made a bee line to his residence. Das Babu and his wife both welcomed me with an open heart. Das Babu was issueless. He had become a staunch devotee of Param Guru Sankara Dewa from his very childhood. It could either have been his strong devotion to Guru Sankara Dewa, or plain and simple faith in Divinity that made him dedicate himself totally to his work and to honesty, not only in action but also in heart, soul and words. He had promised to himself that at least five of his actions everyday would be for removing the distress of the poor, the needy and the resourceless. Yet, he used to spend his entire day doing that. It had become known all over Assam that if you could just meet Das Babu, at least some of your sufferings would get alleviated.

It could have been either his dedication to Shrimant Sankara Dewa, or it could have been his being childless that made him decide that soon after his retirement he would launch himself in entirety – into the service of the poor and needy. Therefore, after retirement in 1984 he made a bee-line for Shrimant Sankara Dewa's village Bugduba in Nowgang District of Assam. There having selected a picturesque spot on the confluence of rivers Brahmaputra and Kiling he set up a thatch house for himself and from there busied himself in the service of the poor. He started his mission by ferrying medicines for the needy from the city and teaching poor children. However, he gradually started running all sorts of errands for everybody. The poor used to visit his dwelling house with requests. As the times changed and a new crop of politicians and their 'chamchas' (hangers on) as also their mafiasco appeared on the scene, they started handing out threats for getting their jobs done. They threatened Das Babu that the land on which he had his house was an encroachment and that they would get the house demolished if he didn't behave – that one word to the administration was enough to get him thrown out of his land. Das Babu therefore was left with no option but to conform to the dictates of the evil-doers. In the beginning making such compromises was difficult. However as time passed, Das Babu learnt to live with such constraints and threats.

Days piled into months and months into years. Very soon it was two years to the date of his arrival in Bugduba. Das Babu crossed sixty and old age started taking its toll. He, however, didn't loose heart and kept on, courageously – lost in Shrimant Sankara Dewa and in the service of the poor.

In 1987, on a wintry day I came to know that Das Babu's health has deteriorated noticeably and that his struggle with a couple of diseases had left him very weak. I therefore decided to visit Bugduba. And one fine meaning, leaving Guwahati at seven I reached Bugduba by about 9 O'clock.

I met Das Babu under the shadow of his thatch roof house. No sooner he saw me, he started crying. He had retired only about two years earlier but started looking as if he had retired ten years ago. He would have been at the most sixty plus. But started looking seventy plus. Eyes had sunk into their sockets and the eye sight had become very weak. Teeth are always unfaithful! They come last and are always the first to go. Didn't know when and where they all left, leaving Das Babu toothless. Face had became lifeless and lost in wrinkles. Once he had stabilised, I enquired about his health – and then about the activities of unsocial elements who under the patronage of local politicians – had started harassing him – no end.

Health problems were essentially asthma-centric. In the past too, he had suffered from bouts of asthama, once or twice every month. However, some pills and some precautions used to put him back on his feet. Now he lived in a house made out of bamboo roof, bamboo walls and mud floor. There was no protection against wind and dampness. I felt that if he continued to live under such conditions, even God would find it difficult to save him. Therefore I decided to take him to Guwahati and get him admitted to M.M. Choudhury Hospital. I also decided to bear the entire cost of his treatment. The duo was hesitant to shift to Guwahati – 'why should they put the burden of such costly treatment upon me. There is an ayurvedic practitioner in Bugduba itself. His treatment is dirt cheap. It might take a little longer, but he would get well with his treatment.' When I faked a little anger, they agreed to come to Guwahati with me. Leaving the house in somebody's charge was a problem. I told them not to worry since there was nothing in the house that anyone would want to steal? Putting a lock on the main entrance I left the key with the local police outpost.

And the four of us left for Guwahati, in my jeep!

Das Babu was admitted to the hospital, in the afternoon. I requested the doctors for 'special care' and they spared no efforts. Fifteen days and he was fully cured – eager like children to return home. As he was getting ready to leave, I met him in the hospital. I had never seen him laughing so much. As he was getting ready to move into the mini bus which was to take him to Bugduba, he suddenly rushed towards me – embraced me and started crying like children. I pacified him. He expressed a desire to possess a boat in which he could provide free lift to the poor in crossing the river. I gave him rupees five thousand and asked him to buy one locally.

When I had got Das Babu admitted into the Hospital, I had known that his treatment would require 15-20 days of hospitalisation. Therefore taking advantage of the available time and with generous help from His Excellency, the Governor of Assam, I got his roof re-done with C.G.I. sheets and his floor plastered with cement.

During the course of his stay in the Hospital, some priests from the local 'Navagraha' temple – earlier acquaintances of Das Babu, met him in his ward and advised him to wear one nine carat 'Moonga' (coral) in a silver ring. They recommended that coral would help in protecting his health. I had overheard this conversation. Therefore without telling Das Babu, I got the recommended ring made in a jeweller's shop in Fancy Bazar. I had asked the silver smith to engrave 'P.B.' – Das Babu's original name on the inside of the ring. I was carrying this ring with me when I had gone to bid him good bye in the hospital!

Enroute I got a chance to check the ring. I was shocked to find that the silversmith had erroneously engraved P.C.B. in place of P.B. – assuming that Das Babu's real name should have been Paritosh Chandra Bhattacharya. Since nothing could have been done – I decided to keep on going to the Hospital and also to present the ring to Das Babu.

When I presented the ring to him, he lost no time in noticing the mistake. He however accepted the ring gracefully and put it on his finger in my presence. He also thanked me profusely. Praying to God that he brought us together again and again, he along with his wife got into the mini bus and the mini bus left for Bugduba. Both of them were extremely happy – were laughing all the time. I drew a lot of satisfaction seeing them that way.

Das Babu would have reached his house in about three and a half hours time. I could never know what his reactions were seeing his hut totally transformed.... I had stayed behind in Guwahati.

Then five years went by.

I was retiring in April 1993. Therefore in late 1992, I decided to visit Assam for meeting everyone with whom I had rubbed shoulders for over twenty long years – during my six postings in the North East. And when I reached Guwahati it came to me that I may as well visit Bugduba also – I would be able to ascertain Das Babu's welfare, and would also be able to touch the soil of Bugduba where Shrimant Sankara Dewa was born. I thought – I may not come this side again!

As I reached the bank of Kiling river, I was startled. I wondered whether I have taken the wrong road! I turned around to check my bearings. I was on the right road. A river was flowing on my left – it was in fact Kiling. Brahmaputra was flowing in front. Then what happened to Das Babu? What happened to his hut? Where did his hut disappear? And from where, this huge mansion – three storied tall has appeared? Who owns it? It couldn't be Das Babu's! He could put up only a thatch hut – with difficulty. How can an honest man go beyond a thatch hut? Enquiries revealed that one very influential P.A. (Personal Assistant) of an influential Minister did set his eyes upon that hillock on which Das Babu's thatch hut was situated. Thereafter what was Das Babu – no more than a fly! Nobody could tell what happened to Das Babu or his hut. However, when I made enquires in the Treasury, where about two decades earlier Das Babu worked, I was told that Das Babu's pension has not been drawn for over two years! Then what?

I requested the police and they made enquiries in the neighbouring villages. Some people said that Das Babu could not take increasing threats from the local mafia, and therefore returned to Bangladesh. In the context of Das Babu's bitter animosity towards that country, I found it difficult to buy this story. Some others informed me, that on a day when both Das Babu and his wife had gone to neighbouring Nowgong for some pathological tests, the local rowdies instigated by the honourable PA of the most honourable Minister, did set fire to the house and also to his boat, tied in the river. By the time Das Babu returned – not only the house but also his boat had been reduced to ashes. Das Babu's wife died of shock on the spot and Das Babu unable to withstand the emptiness of life after his wife's death, became a Sadhu. These people also added that Das Babu now runs a small hermitage in Nemati Ghat near Jorhat and continues with his mission of serving the poor. The story appeared plausible but knowing Das Babu, my heart refused to believe that he would have run away, under threat.

I met the local superintendent of police – an IPS officer. He could not add much to whatever was already known. He, however, mentioned that two days after the incident of arson against Das Babu's house and boat – two dead bodies – one of a man and another of a woman – were recovered by the fishermen – downstream – near Pandu Bridge on Brahmaputra – just outside Guwahati town. He suspected that these two dead bodies – which were in totally petrified condition, and whose hands were found tied behind their backs with iron wires, could have been those of Das Babu and his wife. The dead bodies essentially were bones, bulk of the body and clothing having been eaten away by the alligators, crocodiles and fish. Since nothing of significance, which could help in the identification, was recovered from the dead bodies, a case of unnatural death was registered in Jalukbari police station and after due inquest and investigation a final report was sent to the Court.

My heart refused to believe that Das Babu is no more. Whatever enquiries were possible – I got them made and having felt defeated, I returned to Guwahati and then on to Delhi.

Everyone who is born would die one day. One can have no regrets! However, if the God Almighty wanted to recall a soul so honest, so sacrificing, so duty conscious and so selfless, – no harm? But, he should not have been summoned in such darkness, in such anonymity, without a word of sympathy having been uttered, without tears of gratitude having been shed by his well-wishers! Destiny however, is known to play such cruel jokes with the poor and the honest!

* * * * *

That day as my plane took off from Guwahati airport, it came to me that as far as I am concerned the story of Das Babu had come to an end. I looked down from the aircraft window and saw the mighty Brahmaputra – flowing as ever. Tears rolled down my eyes – in humble homage!

And Brahmaputra kept on flowing – with the same serenity as it did in 1966 when I first met a living God ... Das Babu!

<u>December 1999:</u> Having finished my five years tenure in Manipur Raj Bhawan, I was returning to Bhopal via Guwahati.

I had known that it would now not be possible for me to return to the North East on a posting.

Since I was travelling from Kohima by road – S.P. Kamrup, joined me with his escort near Nowgong. It was three hours drive to Guwahati and we were together in one car. As we were crossing the bridge over Kiling river on the National Highway – I remembered Das Babu. I was stopping in Guwahati for a night prior to boarding the flight for Delhi the next afternoon. On my request, SP Kamrup agreed to get the unnatural death case diary retrieved from record and to get it submitted for my perusal the next morning, at Jalukbari Police Station. I had agreed that enroute to Guwahati airport I would stop over at Jalukbari Police Station for about fifteen minutes and have a cup of tea with the staff.

I reached the police station next morning in time and found the concerned case diary and a cup of tea on the table. Perusal of the case diary took no time – it just ran into three pages. The contents were no help. Soon after one head constable brought out a match-box in which the silver ring recovered from one of the two dead bodies was kept. I opened the match-box and saw the ring which had a spot for fixing a stone but the stone was missing. Out of curiosity I started rubbing the inside of the ring with my nail. Slowly some alphabets – in English – appeared. I scratched the ring a little further and lo and behold – there were those three alphabets – "P.C.B."!

* * * * *

No human life, not even that of the most hardened criminal, should end the way the life of an angel like Das Babu – ended! With Das Babu's death came to an end the joke that Divinity had perpetrated upon him – for so long. The game however did not end without one final bliss. Das Babu had decided to dedicate his last breath to the service of humanity! He did exactly so – by offering even his last mortal remains as morsels – to hungry fish and crocodiles.

* * * * *

It is not true that I do not believe in God. I believe in him with all my heart. I agree that God is a power which provides rhythm to the music of the universe – converts those notes into music. It is the power which divides the energy sources of this world into good and evil and creates the world as we live in today. Such a power cannot be human. It has to be Divine. However, in giving life to such a power – angels like Das Babu should also have some role. It is true that Das Babu was not superstitious. But he was a believer in good deeds. He didn't wear charms around his neck or arms. He spent no time worshipping Gods and Goddesses. He observed no fasts. I also don't! But he used each and every second of the Divine gift of life in the service of humanity – particularly of the poor. Then what sort of reward is this for those very good deeds. Does the life and struggle of Das Babu – more importantly his end – and does the evil perpetrated by the rich and those in power upon dedicated angels like Das Babu, not raise questions about the existence of God and his sense of justice?

* * * * *

Jackie—A Mother

Neighbours on their morning walk would have noticed Jackie's dead body, lying sprawled next to the garbage dump. However, in the context of the superstition attached to viewing a dead body - first thing in the morning, they would have preferred to ignore, what is believed to be an inauspicious sight. I came to know of Jackie's death through children waiting for the Delhi Public School bus. They had strolled towards the garbage dump and noticed the dead body.

"Uncle ji, Uncle ji – Jackie is dead! Her body is lying next to the garbage dump!"

"My God! I have allowed Jackie to die!" I cursed myself.

* * * * *

Everyone in my colony would have seen Jackie – some time or other. She roamed in the Professors Colony (my colony) accompanied by about half a dozen mongrels – without a worry in the world. Residents were generally apprehensive of the pack, which looked well fed and healthy – even menacing; ever ready to prove its exclusive right over the Colony. On her part, Jackie was unbelievably docile – even friendly with children. She allowed them not only to play with her, pull her tail – her ears, even punch her – without as much as a growl.

* * * * *

__*Day one*__ – Jan 17th 2003: I did not know her by her name till one evening excited voices drew me inside the Environment Park located in front of my house. About half a dozen children – youngest one Aakash just two years old – held in his hands two beautiful pups – not more than a day old – snowy fur, tightly shut eyes – letting out barely audible noises. The culvert under which Jackie had hidden them had a clearance of just about 10 inches, making human intrusion a near impossibility. Yet the 2-year old Aakash had already accomplished this feat by bringing the pups from under the culvert.

Security of the newborn pups being vital I asked the chidren: "Why did you pick them up? Who is their mother? Where is she?"

My questioning unnerved the children and the blame game started. "Uncle ji Uncle ji – on instructions from this one – no, no it was Aakash who wanted to play with the pups. Jackie is outside... she can't get in... we have chained the garden gate".

Night was at hand. Sensing that the pups needed immediate security, I asked the children to put them back forthwith under the culvert. Aakash complied with my instructions promptly. It should have been just a few seconds when I saw him, pups in hand, collapse on all fours and disappear under the culvert: reappear from the other side – empty handed. I had hoped that Jackie now would have no difficulty in locating her pups – in feeding them and protecting them. I had also hoped that the "very safe hands", in whose protection mother birds leave their day old chicks while flying off in search of food, would protect the pups till Jackie's return.

It was near the garden gate that I first encountered Jackie – growling, furious, menacing, - ready to attack! I had hardly slackened the chain on the garden gate that she forced herself in throwing me off-balance and within moments disappeared under the culvert shoving children aside. "So, this is Jackie!"

Heavily built – like German shepherd, eyes of a labrador, drooping ears, 4-5 wrinkles on either side of the nose a bit of doberman, a bit of what not; colour, a bit of each – a 'mongrel cocktail' – yet, a fiercely protective and dedicated mother. Since I wanted to ensure that Jackie faced no problems in accessing her pups I left the garden gate open for the night - unaware that unknowingly I was making the job of a thief easier. By sunset, everyone in the neighbourhood was talking about the pups. The beauty of the tiny creatures had enamoured everyone some others too, but for different reasons!

I returned home to face an anxious wife: " The pups should have been brought home? They are so pretty ... anyone would want to pinch them".

I thought of a second visit to the park for retrieving the pups. Yet Jackie's ferocity, the darkness of the night and the problems associated with accessing the pups hidden below a narrow culvert made me give up any rescue-by-night effort. And having decided to postpone rescue to first light next morning, I went to sleep.

It was past midnight. We were hardly asleep, when Jackie's crying and howling woke us up. We rushed out to ascertain as to what has gone wrong and saw Jackie rushing towards the 'Jhuggi' (slum) lane. This provided us an opportunity of being able to peep under the culvert. What we saw, with the help of a torchlight made us miss a heartbeat! The pups were gone – taken out of the "safest" hands of Providence! It should not have been five minutes when Jackie returned – whining and in total distress. She disappeared expectantly below the culvert only to re-emerge within seconds from the other side. Thereafter, she sat back howling piteously for a few seconds before resuming her run towards the jhuggi lane.

It was past one and that too on a night unusually dark and cold. Realising that any retrieval effort would need to pend till daybreak, we returned home. I had mentally resolved that come morning I would visit each house in the colony and solicit help in the restoration of the pups to their mother. Aware that people in my Colony respected me for my age, I was sure that my efforts would succeed. As the night grew darker, Jackie's howling and whining grew louder – the interval between one spell and another became shorter and her search area got extended to the entire Colony. God's gift of resilience to mothers – Jackie cried and ran non-stop throughout the night, no food, no water, no rest – and soon enough it was another day!

* * * * *

Day two – *Jan 18 2003*: Jackie's search, crying, howling and running entered the second day. Anyone would have been exhausted – would have given up but not Jackie – a mother who had lost her pups on the very day of their birth. Accompanied by 10-12 children, I did a 'padyatra' inside the Colony visiting each household. I pleaded that the pups were too young – that without their mother they would die. The mother would die too without her pups! Each household promised help. I returned home convinced that Jackie's problems were a matter of hours and that very soon the pups would get reunited with her.

My wife thought that Jackie might be starving – no end. She therefore prepared a broth of bread, eggs and meat in lukewarm milk and left it in front of the Park gate. During one of her rounds Jackie stopped near the bowl and bent low, sniffing at the food. We thought – now she would eat. However, soon enough she looked towards the culvert and walked away, leaving the food untouched. May be that she thought "my pups would be hungry? How can I?"

It was two in the afternoon and no news of the pups! Children came to tell me that it is being talked about in the Jhuggi lane that the pups had been sold in the night itself to a highway driver, for a paltry sum of rupees twenty. The pups, therefore, might never be retrieved! I immediately shifted my focus to saving Jackie. If she ran like this, without food, water or rest, for another night, she might die? I rang up my friend Dr. Saxena in the Veterinary Hospital. He held the view that since animals are endowed with innate resilience, Jackie too would get over her problems...of course after enduring a lot of suffering. However, according to him Jackie's case was slightly different since she had been separated from her pups within 24 hours of delivery, without getting a chance to breast-feed the pups. Now unless there was medical or surgical intervention, Jackie's mammary glands would continue to secrete – her udders would become heavier and painful with every passing hour – she might develop temperature and since she continued to run without food water or rest, she might even die! The doctor wanted Jackie to be brought to the hospital. And since we always had dogs in our house, I assured him that this would be no problem.

The loss of pups had however made Jackie furious, vengeful and unmanageable – even half-mad. With every passing hour she was becoming more and more panicky. Once extremely docile and gentle Jackie, who would allow even a 2-year old to twist her tail or pull her ears had started dreading the very sight of human beings. I tried to collar her by using all possible tricks enticing her with the choicest food, drinks, meat, bones, dog biscuits, chocolates, ropes and chains. Nothing worked! Increase in her bodily discomfort had made her extremely suspicious, fierce and threatening! Having failed – I called off my efforts!

My wife suggested implantation of a dart laced with strong sleep inducing drug. This she thought would give doctors an opportunity to empty her udders and to inject medicines preventing further lactation. I rang up Dr Saxena again and he found the idea workable. Since it was already dark, he promised a visit first thing next morning, accompanied by his 'catchers' and compounders and armed with an improvised dart. He saw no difficulty in being able to immobilize Jackie and thereby save her life!

* * * * *

Jackie's search for her pups – her crying and howling continued well into the second night. With every passing hour, the pitch of her wailing became louder and shriller. It should have been past midnight – just about the time when her wailing and howling had become unbearable, that it became – all quiet – abruptly. Five minutes – ten minutes – no howling – no sound!

My wife said, "Jackie is dead!"

I said, "No, she has got back her pups!"

And comforted by one make believe dream we went to sleep – undisturbed.

* * * * *

Day three – Jan. 19 2003. When children informed me of Jackie's death, I could not but curse myself. Had I requisitioned help from the Corporation or Veterinary Hospital a day earlier instead of wasting precious time in my own efforts, Jackie's life could have been saved?

Approaching the garbage dump I saw Jackie's lifeless body, tired, exhausted, paws drawn inwards, udders bloated, eyes open! Was it in the hope of being able to get a glimpse of her pups as life ebbed out of her? In a few minutes about a dozen children gathered around the lifeless body – grown ups did not come! Not even those residing in the houses next to the garbage dump? Two-year-old Aakash who a day earlier had removed the pups from under the culvert and then restored them back, arrived in tears – a marigold garland and a raw egg in his hand. No one spoke - everyone was sad! The revelation that animals who are generally taken forgranted, also suffer like humans, was lost but upon that small gathering of children!

Truth was never known-though it appears that it was a paltry sum of rupees twenty – also a general lack of concern towards the sufferings of animals that took Jackie's life!

* * * * *

God may not grant such destiny to any one! Let there be no other Jackie! I am sure you would be as sad as I am over Jackie's death! We therefore, leave the pups to face their Fate!

* * * * *

‘Bare Babu’ (Head Clerk)
(बड़े बाबू)

I prefer calling him ‘Bare Babu’ the only name by which he was known in the town.

Way back in 1960, Chhindwara town had just about a dozen offices with one ‘Bara Babu’ (Head Clerk) each. But, if one got down at Chhindwara bus stand and hired a cycle-rickshaw for being dropped at Bara Babu’s residence, it was a near certainty that he would be dropped at the residence of the one and only one Bara Babu of Chhindwara town – the Bara Babu of SP’s (Superintendent of Police) Office.

Bara Babu was a small man – at the most 5’-2” tall. He was thinly built but was very fair complexioned. He was a shaving addict. He shaved sometimes even twice a day and that too with blades blunted by torture of over dozen shaves. His face therefore bore visible imprints of prolonged encounters with blunt blades. He shaved daily since his British bosses did so! And in order to make his face appear like the surface of glass, he not only ran his blade up and down, and down and up but also left to right and right to left leaving tell-tale marks of this daily torture upon his face. To make matters worse, he sported – what those days was known as a ‘Makkhi’ (big fly) moustache – made famous by its mentor-Hitler – half inch wide at the widest – in Bare Babu’s case just noticeable enough. He was more than bald. Yet he successfully camouflaged his bald top by donning round the clock-except while going to sleep – a pith-hat, of the type worn by polo players – chin up with a shortened chin-strap.

Around the time when I met him, he should have been 57. He was due to retire in one year's time. He was always dressed in a pant – styled as a pyajama – heavily starched and ironed and creased as a pant, and a white khadi round-neck shirt. Whenever, outside his house, he sported a coat – also heavily starched. No one ever saw him without this famous coat, tailored 20 years earlier by a tailor in Jabalpur cantonment – famous for having tailored hundreds of suits for the Brown Sahibs. This famous coat, which should have been grey in good old days had turned totally off-white. Two leather patches adorned it's elbows. He always carried a walking stick made of cane – rounded on the hold. Come rain or sunshine it was impossible for Bara Babu to be on the road, except when spickly and fully dressed – as above!

Bara Babu's daily routine included reaching SP's office – where he worked, dot at 9 O'clock, inspect the cleanliness of the entire office, rearrange neatly, all files, papers, pens, pen stands etc. on the tables, get waste-paper baskets emptied and get all the drinking water containers in the office recharged. He used to clean, dust and neatly re-organise all the artefacts on the SP's table with his own hands. Bare Babu's punctuality was phenomenal – people used to set their watches to 9 O'clock seeing him pass on the road in front of their houses, day after day, morning after morning.

Attending office was a habit with him. He attended office Monday and Sunday – Holi and Diwali – pouring or stifling hot – SP being in town or on tour.

In 1960, when after completing one year's training as an IPS officer in Mt. Abu, I arrived in Chhindwara – for one years' practical training, Bara Babu was one of the two officers who received me at the bus stand and reached me to the Circuit House.

Bare Babu was recruited in the police set up way back in 1923, by the Britishers. It were they who saw in him qualities which they thought would endear him to any administrator. That year he had just passed his BA examination from Nagpur University – in first division. Thirteen years into independence he still reflected in his official and private life, the highest values imbibed by him from the British administrators.

Impeccable turn out, punctuality, rigid compliance with laws, rules and orders and absolute honesty – not only in action but also in thought and words – was his habit. His life was just another name for honesty and integrity, of thought and action as also of outstanding ethical values.

A clerk in SP's office once told me that a couple of years earlier Bara Babu almost died in a rage having discovered ten rupees kept neatly hidden in an envelope on his table. The money was supposedly sent by a supplier as his share in the supply of stationary to the SP's office. Bara Babu was mad with rage! 'How did anyone dare to bribe him? There perhaps, should have been something amiss in his own conduct that made some one bold enough to bribe him?' Bara Babu suffered from high blood pressure. Luckily, the fit of rage did not end up in a stroke. All the same he collapsed – firstly on to his chair, then on to the hard floor before becoming unconscious. In life, he nourished just this one regret – it should have been some unknown weakness in his own character that encouraged a rank outsider to think of bribing him!

He took a lot of pride in mentioning that an IGP of the stature of Mr. Rustamji did find him fit to be entrusted with the responsibility of training young I.P.S. officers – and of moulding their character. For him, this responsibility was an obsession. He therefore was not willing to allow the wastage of even half a day of the officer's training, and specifically for this reason, he never took leave. When he was unwell or sick, he on the quiet swallowed pills and came to the office pretending as if nothing was wrong. Any disruption in the training schedule of the IPS officers was unacceptable to him.

Bara Babu's family comprised just himself and one nearly bed-ridden wife. In lighter vein people used to say that Bara Babu's addiction to office work was so total – was so overwhelming that he never found time to think of having children.

Bare Babu was always the first one to reach office arriving there by 9 O'clock sharp. I used to arrive at 10 and the SP arrived at 1030 sharp.

This sequence of arrivals was fixed and never changed until one day arriving office in my usual time I found Bare Babu missing. Unbelievable! However, as I was trying to figure out the likely reasons, I saw him entering office – rather sheepishly. Questioning one's trainer was considered unethical those days. I therefore summoned one of the senior clerks to find out the reason for this very unusual event. The clerk informed me that Bare Babu's wife is very unwell and has to be shown to a senior doctor in the civil hospital every morning. He also told me that the consulting doctor was on a visit today and therefore Bare Babu had to wait which delayed his arrival in office.

I wanted Bara Babu to take 2-3 days casual leave for looking after his ailing wife. He however was unwilling. Any disruption in the IPS officer's training schedule was unacceptable to him – totally.

It should have been just three days when I bumped into him again at the office entrance. Enquiries revealed that his wife's condition remained unstable as before and that he has just returned after consultations with the doctor, leaving his wife behind at his residence with the required medicines stacked by her bedside. Bare Babu went on to add that he has already cooked both the meals for the two of them, and has left his wife's lunch by her bedside. Putting up a great show of confidence he told me that according to the doctor his wife was getting better and that there was no need for worry.

I once again offered him leave. He again refused. I then ordered him to ring up his wife thrice daily and to report to me, about the status of her health. And with that I thought I have settled the matter for a couple days. Bare Babu however, was faced with one great dilemma of his life. An office telephone had been installed at his residence some five years back. He was, however, yet to make an outgoing call from this number. He believed that the telephone had been installed at his residence, not for his convenience but for the convenience of senior officers – to enable them to reach him whenever required, not for his own use. Would anyone be ready to believe this today?

Having said 'yes' to my orders Bare babu had no choice. He was however finding it difficult to bring himself round to committing a breach of his self-imposed code of conduct which prohibited him from using official telephone for making private calls – in this case for ascertaining the welfare of his ailing wife.

After a wait of fifteen minutes when I sent a peon summoning him to my room, he was left with no choice.

It needs to be recalled that fifties and early sixties were the years in Indian telephony when every time you picked up your receiver a honey-dripping voice welcomed you asking 'Number – Sir!' Calls were unmetered and no account was kept of calls – official or personal. My Bare Babu, however belonged to an endangered species – one fast-disappearing Institution in which steadfast observance of principles was legendary. In fact my Bara Babu today can become an ideal subject for research by newer generations!

Left with no alternative and apprehending that any further delay might cause me annoyance, he summoned the telephone clerk with the telephone register. Then in his very emphatic handwriting he entered in the register one private call to his residence – handed over two annas to the clerk which was then the charge of one private call as per the GOP (Gazette Orders Police) and obtained from the clerk an official receipt. Then also he did not allow the clerk to leave his table. He insisted on his presence till the call was over.

When he did finally ring up his residence, his wife was stupefied! Five long years have gone by since the installation of telephone at their residence and she was yet to hear her husband's voice over the telephone instrument. And when she did finally hear him, she found it difficult to believe her ears and trust her fortune. 'Hope all is well with my husband' – she thought. 'Hope her continued ill-health has not made her husband loose his self-control'. She folded her two hands in a prayer to Almighty. She was certain of one thing – stress and strain notwithstanding, her husband would not have compromised with his principles – even in making that 'one' call to her.

The call was brief. 'How are you feeling? My A.S.P. Sahib wants to know'.

'Much better?,' she replied and the line went dead.

When the senior clerk passed on these details to me, my eyes filled up with respect for a person who that day incidentally happened to be my 'trainer'. In my life, whenever I rang my residence from an official telephone – and I did that so often – I found – Bare Babu standing next to me saying: "Sir, this I did not teach you – Did I"?

Now can there be any explanation for such rigid conduct? I have none!

Bara Babu – by making an example of your own life and by your words and deeds you tried to inculcate in me, the highest regard for integrity and high moral values. Yes, you did. You might not have succeeded in preventing me from making telephone calls to my residence, from official telephones. But every time I committed such a breach, I found you standing by my side reminding me that I was doing something which was ethically and procedurally wrong. The high examples set by you always reminded me of you. And today sixteen years into my retirement, I still remember you and what you taught me.

We believe in the multiplicity of Gods. We believe that every one who gives us something is God. Sun becomes a God since it gives us light and warmth! Moon is a God since it gives us cool light. Water and wind are Gods since they give us life. Earth is God too, since it provides us a place to live, gives us food and nourishment, gives us vegetables, flowers, medicines and fruits. Mother is a God since she brings us into this world. Father is a God since he brings us up. Guru or teacher is a God since he educates us. A guest is a God since he gives us an opportunity to serve people. What wrong therefore, if I see you Bara Babu amongst my many Gods?

I was told that when Bare Babu took leave of this mortal world he left behind just a one bedroom, thatch roof house – plastered with mud from inside and outside – and just about fifteen thousand rupees. More that 40 years of Government service and one bed room, thatch roofed house, mud plastered! Will anyone believe, today?

Ready to cross into the sunset of my own life, my very humble remembrances to you – Bara Babu. May God return you to our country times and over again – and may I get as many chances to train under you! I couldn't live up to the very high example set by you – perhaps couldn't have? People like you are born only once in a blue moon as a compensation, for multiple good deeds in several lives and as a consequence of special blessings from God Almighty – and father and mother. Of one thing I am certain: I never forgot you or the training you imparted through my about forty year long career – not even when I became a Governor – not even today when I am sitting comfortably in my own house, warming myself against one dying-out fire. My respectful remembrances to you – Bara Babu of Chhindwara SP's Office – Shri Prashadi Lal Srivastava.

The Life and Times of Dacoit Queen Putli Bai

Introduction

The infamous Chambal river, acknowledged over centuries as the safest hide-out for dacoits, flows through the districts of Bhind, Morena and Gwalior, all in Madhya Pradesh and parts of Etawah and Agra districts of Uttar Pradesh. In common parlance this area is referred to as 'Panchnada' or 'Chambal Ke Beehar' (ravines). The area is criss-crossed by five big rivers and many rivulets. The big rivers include famous names like Chambal, Kunwari, Sindh, Wesley and Pahuj, each leaving behind their own set of ravines. Resultantly this area is full of high ravines and low gullys –covered entirely with scrub forest, comprising low thorny bushes and medium height thorny trees.

Chambal ravines have for over centuries remained the safest and and therefore the most-preferred hideout for the 'Baghis' (rebels or outlaws) – now known as dacoits. Folklore recognises Bir Singh as the first 'Baghi'. He is believed to have lived and terrorised villages in the Chambal ravines, for over 50 years, in the second half of the fifteenth century. Villagers of this region believe that these ravines are cursed and therefore, they can never become totally free of dacoits. They have great faith in the cult of 'Rakta Beej Rakshasa'. They say that as and when one dacoit gets killed, many new ones arise from the drops of blood shed by the deceased. In the days gone by the 'Baghis' followed a very strict – self-evolved code of conduct, which gave them a Robinhood image. The current set of dacoits suffer no such infirmities.

Till 1955, Chambal ravines had just one big dacoit gang led by Man Singh, also known as 'Dau' (grand father). Dau was one clever and wily old man who ensured that no other gang except his own, survived. He was a great leader endowed with a very high sense of fair play and neutrality. He was also equally ruthless in curbing dissent or unacceptable conduct on the part of his gang members. He, therefore, remained the undisputed leader of a gang which contained members from many castes and communities. He treated each and every member of his gang equally – made no distinction between a Hindu and a Muslim, Rajput and a Brahmin, Gujjar and a Gadariya, Lodhi and a sweeper. He also made no distinction between people belonging to low and high castes. Every member of his gang received equal respect and was treated with equal dignity by their leader.

'Dau' ran out of luck in 1955 when following one excellent piece of information, Bhind police finally got him below a banyan tree, not far from Bhind-Gwalior road. The chase lasted three days and three nights. When adversity finally caught up with him, 'Dau' was well outside his favourite hideout in the ravines, not very far from Bhind town. The encounter was acclaimed by the press, both a success and a failure – success since police succeeded in killing Man Singh and failure since his entire gang managed to escape.

Senior police officers involved in anti-dacoity operations those days believed, that the remnants of the Dau's gang would remain intact and any second rung leader would assume the gang's leadership. Subsequent events however proved every-one wrong. The gang splintered, with Lakhan Singh assuming the leadership of the Rajputs and the Thakurs and Rupa assuming the command of the Brahmins. Gujjar dacoits walked away under the leadership of Kalla Gujjar.

Overnight liquidation of Man Singh signalled the end of single unified leadership. It also led to smaller castes raising their own gangs. Resultantly, Gadarias got together under Shripala, Lodhis under Jimipala and Muslims under Sikandara. Gujjars came up with a very powerful gang led successively by Bahadura, Gabbar and then Mohar Singh.

Putli Bai started her life of crime with dacoit Sultan Singh whom she adored and whom she subsequently married. When Sultan Singh met his end at the hands of Freddie Young – the then SP, Gwalior, Putli was left with no option but to join Dau Man Singh. Dau, however was uncomfortable with a woman in his gang. He, therefore, encouraged Putli to join Kalla who was then in the process of raising his own gang. Putli subsequently married Kalla and remained a part of his gang till Kalla's liquidation in yet another encounter. Kalla's death left Putli with no other option but to have her own gang, which she put together, soon enough.

* * * * *

Anuj

In 1958, Anuj, the then Assistant Superintendent of Police (ASP) was just 24 years old. He had appeared in the Central Civil Services Examination in 1956 and had made it to the Indian Police Service in his first attempt. Finishing one year's basic training in Mt Abu and another years' practical training in Chhindwara – Madhya Pradesh, he had joined Bhind district as ASP in December 1958. Enthusiastic and courageous, dutiful and compassionate, he knew no fears.

He sincerely believed that the dacoity problem was not going to get resolved by liquidation of a few dozen dacoits, annually. He believed in a 3-pronged approach for the solution of this problem which inter alia included – preventing ordinary criminals from finding refuge in big gangs; encouraging new recruits in the gangs to surrender – persuading senior dacoits to come overground and return to normal life after enduring the legal consequences of their past actions. Encounter to him was – if at all, only the last option, to be resorted to in cases where the first two options have been tried and have failed.

In pursuance of the above strategy Anuj used to tour continuously – the most inaccessible areas of his charge for remaining in touch with the family members and relatives of the active dacoits.

Segments of the society which had remained the beneficiaries of the dacoits and dacoities – and who had flourished because of them, started feeling threatened by Anujs' activities. They, therefore, started getting threatening letters sent to him – more or less on a daily basis, in an effort to cow him down. They wanted him to either retrace his steps or to seek a posting outside Bhind. Anuj, however, was made of sterner stuff and therefore continued undaunted. Gradually it became a daily habit with him to drive all alone to some village or other for interacting with either the family members or the near – distant relations of the dacoits. He believed that sooner than latter he would succeed in persuading them into making their relatives, who had taken to the ravines, to relent and surrender. He believed that this alone can eventually lead to their return to normal life after having endured due processes of law.

When threats failed, these very segments started approaching the SP and the DIG concerned, seeking placing of restraints on Anuj's activities. Soon enough Anuj started receiving instructions from his senior officers directing him not to move out unaccompanied into the ravines and to exercise caution while contacting family members of the dacoits.

In 1958, in pursuance of a well-thought plan of action, the then IGP of Madhya Pradesh, solely on an experimental basis, decided to replace ex-army officers with young IPS officers as Superintendents of Police (SPs) in dacoit infested districts. He also decided to personally interact and brief these young IPS officers prior to their posting in the dacoit-infested areas. His intention was to familiarise these officers personally, with the complexities of the situation in these areas, and also to make them aware of the Government's expectations from them. Anuj too got a chance to meet his IGP on a one-to-one basis and to hear his views on the dacoity problem. In this meeting – quite unhesitatingly, Anuj extended one assurance and made one request. By way of assurance he made a commitment that as long as he remained posted to Bhind he would not do anything which made the approach of an informer to him, difficult. He also assured that he would start off on a raid, within half-an-hour of the receipt of information – day or night, good or bad weather, darkness, blistering heat, storm or freezing cold, notwithstanding. He added that he would proceed on the raid even if no other officer was available or was willing to accompany him, or even if the force available for the raid was not sufficient enough. Anuj remained true to these assurances throughout his posting in Bhind.

By way of request, he sought an assurance from the IGP that should there be any complaint against him, or should his name be dragged into any controversy by gossip-managers, the IGP should be kind enough to hear him out first before forming an opinion. The IGP was not only kind-hearted but was also an experienced officer. He not only agreed to Anuj's request in as many words – but also extended an assurance that he would jealously guard Anuj's interests. He also wished Anuj a professionally productive stay in Bhind and as this story reaches its end, the readers would realise that the IGP too remained true to his words, all along.

In keeping with his decision to keep himself open to informers, Anuj refused to have a police guard at his residence. He believed that armed policeman at the gate questioning visitors would scare away informers who remained perennially worried about the protection of their identity.

This was a bold step – risky too. The upshot was, that within a month or two, everyone in the district came to know that Anuj's was the only house and Anuj was the only officer who could be approached without being questioned by policemen at the gate. Resultantly, informers started crowding Anuj's residence and stopped visiting the residences of the SP – and the Commandant of the 23rd Battalion of the Madhya Pradesh Special Armed Force (SAF), at whose residences they were not allowed entry without a gruelling cross-examination by the policemen manning the gate. The SP and the Commandant, who felt miffed by these developments, started putting obstacles in the execution of Anuj's operations against dacoits – even on 'grade one' information. Sometimes enough force was not made available and sometimes officers for leading various columns were not spared. (Since such developments are quite frequent in day-to-day police working, and since they have no bearing on Gudiya's story I leave them to rest, as they were).

* * * * *

Anuj joined Bhind district on December 18, 1958.

For several months things remained under control. Then in November, 1959 there was a string of offences that shook Anuj. To begin with one Kachi youth was murdered in broad day light in a Kachi village within Ater police station. Gudiya's gang claimed responsibility for the killing. Close on the heels of this murder, one late evening, Gudiya herself, accompanied by her gang, descended upon the same Kachi village and got all young Kachi youth rounded up. Thereafter she got their hands and feet tied firmly with ropes and on her instructions the gang members started beating them – mercilessly. Some women, who were shaken by the beating of their husbands or brothers or sons got together and prayed to Gudiya for putting a stop to the beating. Gudiya, however, remained unmoved. Leading the protest was one sixteen year old girl whose husband had been murdered by Gudiya's gang, a couple of days earlier – on suspicion of being a police informer.

Resistance put up by the women unnerved Gudiya. She threw her lathi amongst the protesting women and stayed frozen for a couple of minutes. The beating too remained suspended. Gudiya, however, recovered soon enough and signalled her gang to resume beating. She even called her gang members to beat the Kachi youth dead. The beating, therefore, resumed with greater vehemence. Some women from amongst the crowd who could not tolerate this intense thrashing of their husbands or of their near and dear ones, intervened physically, in an effort to shield the victims. They brought their own bodies between the youth and the assailants. Such open defiance enraged Gudiya no end. She lost control over herself and started shouting:

'These vermins – these 'haramis' (bastards) have become 'mukhbirs' (police informers) against me. These 'behen ch..s (sister fu....rs) – deserved to be taught a lesson. Gudiya will spare no one. Keep on beating the bastards, these mother f....ers till they become dead bodies. Break their bones. If 'chinals' (bitches) try to intervene, tear their clothes off. Make them naked! Kill everyone..."

During those moments Gudiya was demented – was possessed. She kept on mouthing filth. When one dacoit tore off the blouse or another one ripped off a petticoat or 'lehnga', she screamed with delight and let off an uncontrolled laughter. Gudiya's reactions encouraged the dacoits to harsher and unprintable barbarities. They crossed all parameters of decent behaviour.

Fifteen minutes later – which then appeared to be hours, this dance of indecency, destruction and killings came to an abrupt end. On Gudiya's command, the dacoits retreated into the ravines – as swiftly as they had come, leaving behind five dead, three Kachi youth and two Kachi women, both naked – both dead.

The place of occurrence and the Ater police station were under Anuj's charge. By eight in the evening he came to know of the incident and within an hour he was in the village accompanied by a small escort. He found the villagers in a state of shock. He consoled them. Over his wireless set he ordered the police doctor to reach the village forthwith, with an ambulance – some nursing staff and emergency medicines. He informed the doctor that many of the villagers, both men and women, have received grievous injuries and would need urgent medical attention. He got a police guard posted in the village. The station house officer (SHO) of Ater Police Station, who had arrived in the village an hour earlier was directed to register an offence under appropriate sections of law, against Gudiya and her gang, and to start vigorous investigation. No sooner enough police force became available on the spot, Anuj split them into two parties. He despatched one for laying an ambush on the likely escape route of the dacoits and the other for tracing and chasing Gudiya in her retreat. Placing these arrangements in position took time. It was getting 11 O'clock when Anuj thought that he can now return to Bhind.

The cries and tears particularly of the women folk, overwhelmed Anuj. He quietly took a vow to chase Gudiya no end till she got punished for her crimes and till she received exemplary punishment for her sins. Deputy Superintendent of Police (Dy. SP) Madho Singh who had accompanied Anuj to the village suggested:

"Sir, it may not be a bad idea to arm the aggrieved Kachis. They are mortified by this outrage and are itching for revenge. In their anger we have a golden opportunity for getting even with Gudiya".

Yet another officer suggested that it would not be a bad idea to send some policeman to Gudiya's village and to get her parents thrashed, red and blue. That would compel Gudiya to think one hundred times before repeating another such offence.

Anuj, however was an idealist in uniform. He believed firmly in the rule of law and in policemen functioning within the limits set by rules and regulations. Extra-legal methods had no place in his lexicon. Collecting himself, he ordered,

"We need good informers for tracking down Gudiya. We should be able to arrest her within a couple of months. We must maintain continuous pressure against her so that she remained on the run ... never got time to repeat such an offence".

* * * * *

Anuj arrived Bhind past midnight. Was dog-tired and therefore went to sleep. The morning dawned with many thoughts agitating his mind: "Gudiya's crime is unpardonable. She did not spare even women! She needs to be taught a lesson. She needs to be arrested forthwith and got punished for her crimes. Her sins are unpardonable. All this, however, would remain a pipe-dream as long as we did not stumble upon one good informer. There are other ways too. Surrender is one! If Gudiya agreed to surrender then we can get even with her – without bloodshed. But who would motivate her? And how? Her parents are alive. May be they can help. There is no harm in talking to them. May be they would succeed in persuading Gudiya to repent for her crimes by surrendering. If she remained adamant then encounter would remain the only option. But there too – good informers would be necessary. Raising of informers, therefore, remained priority one. All preparations notwithstanding Gudiya deserves to be offered one last chance to repent Who knows she might agree to surrender?'

Above soul-searching notwithstanding, Anuj knew fully well that it would be wrong to hold punitive action captive to an uncertain hope of surrender. Gudiya was obstinate – was head strong. It would therefore be right to prepare the police force for an encounter with Gudiya.

Anuj, therefore, decided to convene a meeting in Bhind, that very afternoon, of all concerned officers. By 3 O'clock all the thanedars (police stations in-charge) inspectors and Dy. SP's arrived for the meeting, which lasted just about an hour. The officers present were generally of the view that it would be futile to expect Gudiya to surrender. She never had any faith in the courts or in the processes of law. If she had, she would have approached the court for the redressal of her grievance, when as an innocent girl of thirteen on that fateful night, she was kidnapped and raped by the zamindar and his hangers on. On the contrary, driven by rage and a desire for revenge she took the shortest route to ravines and joined a dacoit gang. She neither hesitated for a moment, nor flinched. Yes, it is probable, that one of the important considerations in her rushing into the ravines could have been a feeling that a rape victim had no place in society. Yet that too is a fact that she found her desire for revenge so overwhelming that she became blind to reason. She has since kept on moving inside the ravines – has joined many gangs in one faint hope that one of these days she would be able to get even with the Zamindar by killing him and his cohorts – all her rapists.

Seven years have gone by. Gudiya is now twenty or twenty-one. She had since been in three gangs – one after the other. Two of these have already been liquidated by the police. But she has survived. She had got even with seven of the nine rapists. Two however are still alive. They have policemen protecting them and their residences – round the clock. Constant police presence around them has given them undue self-importance. They have become difficult targets for Gudiya. She, however, refuses to give up hope. She has boundless courage!

She felt lost just once when Kalla's gang, of which she was a member, got liquidated. Being the lone survivor she didn't know where to go? She therefore disappeared from the ravines and went into hiding. She remained in hiding for three years, spending time in Bombay, Agra and Delhi. She even got it circulated that she (Gudiya) had breast cancer and therefore had perhaps died – in a hospital in Agra. Many police officers in Bhind district bought these rumours more so since all these three years Gudiya was not sighted anywhere in the dacoit-infested areas, either by the villagers or by the informers.

Then suddenly one late evening, after an absence of over three years, Gudiya then 23-24 years old, reappeared in Badagaon, Police Station Ater, leading a gang of her own. After usual drama of firing and beating up youth, she left the village taking with her three children, 2 to 3 years old, belonging to business families. The children were released unharmed by her within a month after she had extorted a sum of rupees four lakhs as ransom. Then started the inexorable routine of kidnappings, dacoities and murders. The Kachis and the Rajputs were her special targets. Soon enough, people in about fifty villages, situated in the ravines between Chambal and Kunwari, in Bhind and Morena districts, started trembling under her fear.

It was around such time that Anuj assumed special responsibility of the area, terrorised by Gudiya. In the meeting with the police officers of his zone one thing became vary clear – no one was willing to believe that Gudiya would ever agree to surrender! How wrong human calculations can be!

Anuj was keen upon putting an immediate end to Gudiya's reign of terror. He, therefore, directed all the officers to go out for raising dependable 'mukhbirs' (informers). The meeting also decided to keep Gudiya on the run through combing operations and forays in her beat, so that she got no opportunity to plan another heinous crime. All officers present agreed with the decisions taken.

* * * * *

Half-an-year went by uneventfully. None of the police officers present succeeded in raising a dependable informer. None of Gudiya's close relatives were found willing to broach the subject of surrender with her.

One wintery afternoon as Anuj was passing close enough to Gudiya's village a thought crossed his mind – why not meet Gudiya's parents? Acting on an impulse he turned his jeep towards Gudiya's village and in about five minutes, he was in front of Gudiya house – one tiny, rickety shack of thatch and mud, ready to come down any moment. He found the distressed parents worse off – old bodies weakened by catastrophe – clothes nearly in tatters, a few worn out utensils – father and mother both nearly blind. No sooner the jeep came to a halt in front of their house and Anuj dressed in uniform alighted from the vehicle, the two came out with folded hands. A cot was quickly summoned from the nearest neighbour and Anuj was requested to take his seat. Gudiya's sister Puniya, around eighteen or twenty hurriedly went outside for borrowing some milk and sugar from the neighbour and started preparing tea. Anuj accepted the sizzling hot tea with gratitude.

He stayed in Gudiya's house for about half-an-hour, and utilised this opportunity to broach the subject of Gudiya's surrender with parents. He explained to the old man that once Gudiya had surrendered and has undergone the punishment awarded to her by the courts, she would be able to get out of the ravines and return to normal life. The two parents kept on listening, attentively. Both confirmed that Gudiya had not visited them for over five years. When Anuj reiterated his request the old man started speaking haltingly.

"Maharaj, we too want that infamous girl to surrender. Because of her, we have not been able to get our second daughter married so far. No one wants to marry her. People say – marriage in Gudiya's family means having police on one's back all the time. As it is Maharaj, whenever policemen visit our house, they do so to shower us with insults and abuses. Their visits invariably end up in lathi blows, sometimes a few, sometimes many. We have endured all these indignities and lathi blows – what for? For whom? For that wicked girl who has not shown us her face in the last five years. Policemen think that she visits our house every night and that we do not inform them".

Anuj smiled, "That is alright Kakku. You send her a letter asking her to surrender. Once she has done so, all her's and your problems would be over".

"Arre, Maharaj does Gudiya listen to anyone? She would not listen even to God. If she was visiting us or listening to anyone of us, we would have certainly asked her to surrender – many times. Our bodies are tired receiving the beatings both of the police and the thakurs – also of the police at the instigation of thakurs. So many of our teeth have got knocked out. We have become almost blind. Doesn't she know all this? She does. But she does not care! About six years earlier when we had almost been beaten to death by the police she sent a message through a gadariya (shepherd)".

"Kakku, whatever is happening to you has torn my heart apart. Just bless me enough so that I can kill the remaining two rapists .... Let me have my revenge... I had vowed revenge in front of Kali Ma. I shall surrender no sooner I succeeded in killing the remaining two. Forgive me till then .... Kakku. Excuse me till then Amma".

"Now tell us Maharaj, what do we do? We ourselves are sick of getting hammered every now and then. Please get into our house and see for yourself ... no doors, no rooms, no locks. Would any Baghi want to come and rake refuge in such a house?"

Anuj saw reason in Kakku's argument. Therefore in an effort to assuage Kakku's hurt feelings, he replied: — "Absolutely, not Kakku. This house can prove to be a death trap for any baghi. However, don't you see what your daughter has now started doing? She has started attacking women! She is getting women's clothes ripped off! She is making them naked in public! That is why the police is so desperately after her. The moment she surrendered both of you will be able to live and breath in peace".

"Maharaj, we ourselves are dead with shame. Everyone now hates us for Gudiya's shameful conduct with women. The day we heard of her unpardonable crime, we both decided to commit suicide by jumping into the mouth of a 'gharial' (crocodile) in Chambal. But Maharaj we still have to get our other daughter married. A boy in Agra has since agreed to marry her. The marriage is fixed for Basant Panchmi. We would certainly commit suicide by jumping into Chambal, after her marriage. We are so sick with this life of ours! We can tell her to surrender if we met her. But she does not meet us anymore".

Anuj realised that the parents were speaking plain and simple truth, and that persuading Gudiya to surrender was at present beyond them.

"Kakku! Won't you invite me to your daughter's wedding?" Asked Anuj.

"Arre, Maharaj! How can we poor people dare to invite you? The villagers are so scared of the police that even our neighbours have stopped visiting us. The village pandit has agreed to conduct the 'pheras' – and other ceremonies. Puniya's marriage would be a weight off our chests. We are tired of this life of ours – Maharaj – very-very tired!".

"What about wedding expenses, Kakku? Have you made some arrangement? Will Gudiya be willing to help you out?"

"What expenses, Maharaj? The village pandit has agreed to get the entire ceremony performed in just twenty rupees. Our neighbours have promised a gift of rupees five hundred to our daughter. Pandit will be paid off out of this amount. The boy is a working and earning hand. He just wants Puniya's hand ... nothing else. No one in the village dares visit us. Therefore what other expenses can be there? None whatsoever, Maharaj".

The evening has started turning grey. Anuj had no escort. He therefore decided to leave the village forthwith.

"So Kakku, I leave now. My congratulations to both of you – for the wedding of your daughter. May God bless you and may your younger daughter shower upon you the care and affection which the elder didn't!"

Waving his hand in a gesture of farewell Anuj soon got out of Gudiya's house. In one motion he was into the driver's seat and in the same motion he had switched on the ignition bringing the engine to life. Soon enough the jeep left Gudiya's village with a sputtering sound, leaving the two parents – the onlookers and the lengthening evening shadows behind.

* * * * *

Gudiya

Basant Panchmi was still a month away. Everyone in the police department had come to know of Gudiya's sister's wedding having been fixed for Basant Panchmi. Everyone was confident that Gudiya would certainly attend the marriage since she loved her sister so dearly. No special information or an informer was needed to confirm her visit. All that was needed was one well-calculated, well-planned, down-to-earth operation.

Police officers in Bhind, got busy planning encirclement and raid on Gudiya's village on the wedding night. Everyone believed that if the raid was carefully planned – leaving no escape routes, and if the operation was meticulously executed there was no chance of Gudiya getting away – at least this time. D.I.G. Gwalior and S.P. Bhind started pressurising Anuj into submission of an operational plan, well in advance of the wedding day. They also started emphasising the need for a well-rehearsed raid in which everyone knew his role and the 'how' of it.

Anuj gave in to the aforesaid pressures with just one modification. He wanted the raiding party to be compact, comprising just about thirty young and fit policemen, all dressed in civilian clothes and disguised as villagers. He wanted the raiding party to be armed with revolvers, pistols and about half a dozen carbines or stens.

A week before Basant Panchmi, Anuj under the guidance of his DIGP and SP completed the tasks of selecting policemen for the raiding party – earmarking and test firing of weapons; recce of routes and earmarking of guides for various columns. It was agreed that each column comprising five policemen would approach the village adopting a route different from the others. Looking into the intensity of preparations, policemen earmarked for the raid started believing that Gudiya was as good as dead. Consequently they started dreaming of promotions and cash rewards.

Closer to the wedding day, Anuj made some further modifications to the operational plan. He decided to allow Gudiya to arrive at the venue-without any let or hindrance. The encirclement was to be put in place only after her arrival in the village. Anuj also decided to send one of his informers into the village, at least 24 hours prior to the marriage. The informer was supposed to stay put in the village and was to signal Gudiya's arrival to Anuj. The encirclement plan was supposed to be put in operation half-an-hour after the receipt of confirmation of Gudiya's arrival in the village. The raiding parties were to move half-an-hour after the completion of encirclement. For facilitating quick movement of the raiding parties a 3-ton truck was placed at Anuj's disposal at the Kali-Ahroli road junction on Ater-Porsa road. The raiding parties were to stay put there – awaiting orders from Anuj.

Gudiya however was no ordinary woman. She had survived in the ravines and had remained on the run for over ten years and had acquired a good knowledge not only of the police practices, but also of the complicated moves of the world of crime. She also perhaps had an informer within the police force who regularly alerted her – in advance, of the plans being made by the police for her liquidation. It is also likely that she had a very strong commonsense which enabled her to assess in advance police moves. She should have simply concluded, that the police would be on the look out for her on the wedding night, and would try to encircle her.

She therefore landed in the village, in broad day light, three days prior to the date of marriage. The two sisters – Puniya and Gudiya came face to face and their eyes became Ganga-

Yamuna. Gudiya blessed Puniya and prayed for her long life – a very happy married life. "May Ma Durga keep you Suhagin, till eternity", prayed Gudiya. She spent half-an-hour with Puniya. Her parents came to know of her arrival in the house. But they refused to come to her. Bad omen! Unlucky girl! Brings disaster wherever she goes! Why has she come on this very auspicious occasion? The police would definitely come to know of her visit and would turn everything upside down. And if they failed to find her they would rain lathi-blows upon the two parents – in an effort to find out where she was. Their honour and prestige would be mud in front of the entire village and that too on an auspicious occasion. It would be a catastrophe for Puniya and her would-be husband.

Bidding goodbye to sister Puniya, Gudiya walked over to her parents. She was wearing a plain white borderless Sari made of coarse Khadi. Her hair were tied tightly in a bun at her back. She wore very dark sunglasses and carried a Khadi bag, slung loosely over her shoulder. The bag contained books and literature, mainly writings of Mahatma Gandhi. She also carried in her bag a letter of identification issued by an important newspaper from Agra. Gudiya noticed that her mother had difficulty in recognising her – perhaps due to her failing vision. She therefore, rushed towards her and hugged her. A fraction of a second and the mother recognised her blood. Tears started streaming down her eyes. Gudiya too started crying resting in the comfort of her mother's bosom.

How sun-tanned has Gudiya become? How thin? Is she ill? What if some-one informed the police? In that case it would be the parents who would become instrumental in sending their own blood to the gallows. Weighed down heavily by these fears, the mother dragged Gudiya into the darkest corner of the house. She was sobbing and saying: "Gudiya why don't you say goodbye to the ravines? Why don't you come back to us?"

At that very point of time Kakku entered the room shouting at the top of his voice.

"We have suffered so much because of you – we have been suffering for such a long time! How many more lathi-blows we would need to endure because of you? You have kept yourself away from us for so many years. Why you have to come on this very day? Parents getting beaten by the police on the wedding day of their innocent daughter. Don't you care? Do you want your parents to continue to suffer at policemen's hands – perennially?"

Kakku would have gone on for any length of time. But the entry of a boy shouting 'A police jeep – a police jeep – coming this way' stunned everyone. Gudiya alone remained unmoved. With tears streaming down her eyes, she dropped at Kakku's feet. The old man was touched. "Why am I scolding my child – poor innocent daughter of mine! She has to be on the run constantly. No rest – night or day – running constantly from ravine to ravine, avoiding police – avoiding other predators. After all she is the one who was sinned against – was gang raped! What fault of hers if she now cries revenge?"

"Gudiya beti, surrender some day – before the Chotey Kaptan (ASP). He appears to be a good man. My heart says that he would be considerate and compassionate towards all of us".

"Yes Kakku – yes! Who can be a bigger well-wisher of mine than my own father? Your words are my command. They will ever remain etched upon my heart – will always remain at the back of my mind. I accept them Kakku most respectfully." All this while, Gudiya was shedding tears at her father's feet.

The horn of the police jeep sounded close enough and Gudiya for the first time became panicky. 'She has to run out of the house forthwith or else everything would be over for her.' Hurriedly she took out a bundle of ten thousand rupees from her bag, and leaving it on Kakku's feet – in just one motion she ran towards the back door – which opened into the ravines. At the sight of money Kakku's blood started boiling – money tainted with the blood of innocents. If such money was spent on Puniya's wedding, her future too would get cursed. He therefore picked up the bundle and in one motion hurled it towards escaping Gudiya. The bundle hit Gudiya on her back. She turned to see what had happened and since there was no time to loose, she ran back, picked up the bundle, touched Kakku's feet again and ran towards and out of the back door.

Just at that very moment, the police jeep came to a halt in front of Gudiya's house with Anuj making a swift entry into the room. He saw tears rolling down Puniya's cheeks and those of her parents and guessed what had been happening there.

"Kakku, did Gudiya come to meet you all?"

"Yes, Maharaj! She has just jumped into the ravines through the back door. If you run fast enough you would be able to catch her. Go quickly. Hurry, Maharaj, hurry". Kakku was sobbing and words were coming out of his mouth haltingly.

"Kakku, today I have not come here to arrest anyone. I have come to see the arrangements for my sister's wedding".

Anuj's words calmed everyone. He continued: "I had known fully well that Gudiya would come to bless her sister. Which sister won't? And since police would be maintaining vigil on the day of marriage, she would find it safe to come a few days earlier ... if she was intelligent – which she obviously is! But I am not here today to spoil the atmosphere. If I ever wanted to have an encounter with Gudiya, I will have it any other day – but certainly not today. Why should I be shedding blood on my sister's wedding day. If I did so, Ma Durga will never forgive me!"

A brief pause ensued. He then started speaking again.

"As in my life, so also in police work I have followed certain principles – rigidly. I would never allow anyone to fire upon someone who had raised his hands and has taken the first step towards surrender. Similarly, I would postpone an encounter with anyone who had realised the futility of a life of crime; shown an inclination for return to normal life – of course, after undergoing the legal processes. The duration of the process or punishment can be short or long – can even be 20 to 25 years. But it offered a hope that ultimately the offender will be able to return to the society as a reformed citizen".

About 20-25 villagers had gathered around Anuj and were listening to him attentively. They were ready to trust Anuj and were willing to give him a chance. Anuj's words therefore were acting as a balm to them. Jointly they blessed Anuj and prayed to God that he sent officers like him to the crime-ravaged ravines – again and again. Gudiya's sister was so overwhelmed that she rushed to where Anuj was standing and bent low to touch his feet. Anuj stopped her half-way and held her close to his heart.

"No Puniya, for God's sake, no! Don't be unfair to your brother. It is I who should be touching your feet. Come on – smile. Let us both laugh. Let us share a smile. After all today is the day when everyone is happy preparing for your marriage."

Puniya was grateful. She went into a fit of laughter – for the first time after Gudiya's escape into the ravines and kept on laughing hysterically, for a long time.

It was one of those usual winter evenings. Anuj looked at his watch and noticed that it was getting to be 4 O'clock. "It would be dark very soon" – mumbled Anuj. He had left Bhind for a meeting with an informer at a pre-fixed R.V. (rendezvous). The informer was to give information about the whereabouts of D-7 (Rampala). The 'R.V.' with the informer was just outside Gudiya's village. The prefixed time was 5 O'clock – plus minus ten minutes. Anuj therefore had to rush. Bidding goodbye to everyone assembled outside Gudiya's house, Anuj jumped into his jeep. As he was about to take off, he remembered that he has missed out on something – important. He therefore got out of his jeep in a flash and re-entered Gudiya's house. He took out one thousand rupees from his pocket and deposited them at Kakku's feet, adding meekly, "A humble gift for my sister".

Kakku was overwhelmed. Tears filled up his eyes. He respectfully picked up the money and in a gesture of gratitude and respect touched it to his forehead. Then in a voice choked with emotion, he started speaking:

"Chotey Kaptan, I would want to address you as my son. But my tongue gets frozen. I am poor, rough and crude, so crude that it becomes difficult for me to even pronounce your name. Today itself Gudiya wanted to leave ten thousand rupees for Puniya's wedding and I refused. I was not ready to get Puniya's married life poisoned by use of tainted money in her wedding...tainted with blood and tears of innocents. I threw Puniya's money back at her. Now you give me a much smaller amount. I know it is hard-earned money. May God give every sister a brother like you and every father – a son like you!"

Kakku was so overwhelmed that he would have gone on and on. Anuj, however, was in a hurry. It was already getting 5 O'clock and he was nowhere near his R.V. He however, had the advantage of plus ten minutes. He, therefore, knelt a little to enable his hands to touch Kakku's knees. Then taking old man's permission he jumped into his jeep and drove off. Gudiya's sister wanted to add something to what Kakku has already said but Anuj's jeep was well past the village.

* * * * *

To begin with no one from the village or even neighbourhood was willing to risk attending Puniya's wedding. However, in the context of Anuj's expressed views, everyone decided to participate. They came forward not only with small amounts of money, but also agreed to help in running errands for the family. There was total unanimity in everyone wanting to cooperate with Anuj. Villagers started propagating that any hope of seeing an end to bloodshed and mayhem in the ravines, lay in cooperating with the Chotey Kaptan.

It should not have been a week and Anuj's views on resolution of the dacoity problem, as also the news of his compassionate relationship with Gudiya's family got circulated into the neighbouring 30-40 villages. Everyone agreed to support Anuj – spontaneously. They saw in Anuj a spark, not seen by them earlier in the police officers.

Gudiya too was able to hear first hand, the entire conversation between Anuj and her parents. As she ran out of Kakku's house, she realised in good time the futility of running in the ravines all dressed up in a sari. She, therefore feigned an escape by first crossing the father's back door and then disappearing into the ravines for a few minutes. However, no sooner, she was convinced that no one was watching her and that everyone would believe in her escape to safety, she retraced her steps taking the first gentle slope leading into the neighbour's backdoor. For the neighbour, Gudiya's entry into their house was an unwelcome sight. But they had no choice.

They therefore agreed to help Gudiya by allowing her to hide behind some bags of wheat lying stacked in one corner and by locking up the house from outside. No sooner Anuj's jeep was out of the village, they returned to their house and told Gudiya all that had transpired. They conveyed verbatim, the entire conversation between Anuj and the villagers as also everything that Anuj has done for the family – also his suggestion of surrender being an option for Gudiya.

Gudiya remained quiet for sometime. Then almost in a whisper, she started speaking:

"How can you trust police? I may surrender and they may shoot me down in the ravines, staging a false encounter? After all they earn their rewards and get promotions by killing dacoits".

The neighbour butted in and said, "Gudiya, this officer appears different – seems to be trustworthy. Kakku informed him that Gudiya had just jumped into the ravines and would not have gone far – that if he so desired he could chase her and capture her. You know what was Anuj's reply? He said that he has not come today to spoil the atmosphere of his sister's wedding. Listen Gudiya, would any other police officer behave in this manner? Anuj is compassionate. He is wedded to certain ideals. He would not resort to illegalities even if it was going to get him awards, fame and promotion. Understand Gudiya ?"

"Haan, yes!"

"Chotey Kaptan mentioned that if someone raised his hands in a gesture of surrender, he would not shoot at him. Not only that, even if someone exhibited the slightest interest in surrender, he would put-off an encounter – perennially, till the person concerned has made up his mind – either way".

Gudiya sat engrossed – quiet – eyes glued to the ground.

"So Gudiya why don't you surrender – before Chotey

Kaptan? Your parents have become old and infirm. They may not live long. If you are willing, we can all go to Chotey Kaptan".

Then after a brief pause- "Say something, Gudiya! Shouldn't we be talking to Chotey Kaptan?"

Gudiya however sat unprovoked – totally quiet.

Puniya came to know of her Jijji's (elder sister) presence next door. In excitement she leaped across to the neighbour's house – shouting "Jijji, Jijji, how long you have been here? Are you not scared? Chotey Kaptan has just left –a few minutes ago. He is a very good man. He has given thousand rupees for my marriage. He even touched Kakku's feet. He touched my feet too and blessed me! He said that he would not allow any untoward incident during my wedding. He has announced that he would be attending my wedding and would be participating in 'Per Pujan' – (Worship of bride's feet who on her wedding day is considered to be equivalent to Durga)".

"Is that so?" Gudiya's answered.

"Jijji, why don't you surrender? To begin with we may not get much time together. But even if we got a couple of years towards the end of our life, that too would be worth living for. Kakku-Amma both are now really old. Don't know how long they would last? Once you have returned to the ravines we do not know when and if at all we would meet. God alone knows who amongst the four of us is going to survive – whom? And Jijji, the police is after us today since you are in the ravines. Once you have surrendered, our troubles with the police would be over!" Then after a pause – "Say something Jijji – why don't you speak?"

Gudiya once again returned a blank face to Puniya's pleadings. However, it should have been just two or three minutes when she instantly got up and putting her right arm firmly around Puniya's shoulders – started dragging her towards the back door – and into the ravines. Neighbours tried to follow the duo but were signalled by Gudiya to stay put. Gudiya's gesture frightened every one.

Slowly the two walked down the nearest gentle slope and in seconds disappeared into the ravines. Having walked about 200 metres Gudiya found a lonely spot and signalled Puniya to sit down and relax. Then pulling her bag from the shoulder she took out her loaded revolver. The sight of the revolver frightened Puniya, 'What is Jijji up to? Why has she taken out her revolver? For whom?'

Puniya, however was not required to wait long. Gudiya very soon came uncomfortably close to Puniya...loaded revolver in hand! Puniya's heart sank! The suspense however came to an end as abruptly as it had started, with Gudiya taking her seat next to Puniya and putting her revolver back into her shoulder bag. It took good 4-5 minutes for Puniya's breathing to become normal. In the meanwhile no one spoke. Then gradually summoning strength, Puniya resumed conversation.

"Jijji, why have you brought me here? Amma and Kakku would be tense thinking that Gudiya has abducted Puniya for forcible enlistment in her gang".

Gudiya offered no answer and stayed quiet. Then after good about five-ten minutes she started speaking – to begin with in a really faint voice – so low that even Puniya had difficulty in following her.

"Listen, Puniya, I am a dacoit and all dacoits are reprehensible criminals – one more reprehensible than the other. Even within themselves they don't trust each other. People are bumped off on slightest suspicion. For women like me, keeping one's skin safe – is in itself a tight rope walk. I have endured such inhuman existence for ten years – surviving amongst terrible criminals. I have picked up – involuntarily though – one habit – not to trust anyone! I now suspect each and everyone. Just tell me Puniya if I started discussing subjects like surrender, in public, I would be inviting certain death. I therefore remain quiet when people ask me such questions. I have no choice. Can I trust policemen? If Kakku says Anuj is trustworthy – I have to agree. After all Kakku is our father. He has seen more of the world! He has endured greater sufferings, than either of us. But no one knows, who in our village is in touch with the police or giving them information. We also do not know who is in touch with whom – with which dacoit gang – with which criminal. In such a situation talking surrender openly means taking grave risks. Anuj moves around in the villages, alone. Any informer can get him killed. Any gang would be happy to kill him. If I start speaking in front of so many, nothing would remain a secret and every word of what I say – even what I don't say would get conveyed to my enemies. That would be dangerous, not only for me, but also for Anuj".

"There is another angle to surrender. All dacoits take surrender to be a blot on the 'glorious' traditions – set by the 'baghis' of yore. For them becoming a baghi is as good or as bad, as becoming a sanyasi – wandering mendicant. Once a sanyasi always a sanyasi! Once a dacoit, always a dacoit! They believe that the only respectful end for a dacoit can be receiving police bullet on his chest. That alone is considered to be a glorious end for people like us".

Gudiya paused for a few minutes trying to regain her composure. When she started talking again she was back to a whisper.

"You know very well Puniya, why I took to ravines – at that very tender age. Every minute detail of what happened that evening is etched upon my memory. I can describe even today each turn of event that evening, in all its gory details. It was at the tender age of thirteen that I was gang raped – not by one person, but by eight beasts. So many times in the past I have tried to forget everything that happened that night – but I have failed. I have succeeded in killing six out of the eight rapists. But the fire of revenge still burns inside me. I used to think that killing Zamindar would be tough. But Ma Durga made things easy for me. On the day I killed the Zamindar, I was passing in front of his haveli dressed in low-on-waist pants, a flower bedecked, colourful, navel-exposing shirt, and short hair. Lecherous beast that the zamindar was, he thought that some new 'maal' (woman of loose character) has come into his village and that as per tradition he had the first right to enjoy her. He therefore came out of his haveli twirling his moustache and announcing, "Hai Jaani" (Hi darling)". Within seconds he was close enough to me trying to catch my breasts and molest me. I looked around and noticed no one close enough. Instinctively my hand went into my bag and came out with the loaded revolver. He had by then stretched out his hands in an effort to fondle my breasts. Within twinkling of an eye I attached the revolver to his chest and fired – twice! My eyes refused to believe when I saw him collapse, instantaneously – his hand upon his injured chest. Hearing gunfire, people started running from all directions. But then their priority was to save the Zamindar. They, therefore, ran towards him with no one thinking of giving me a chase. Ma Durga – facilitated my escape!"

"I got a few seconds only. But they were enough to allow me to vanish into the safety of the ravines. Two-three policemen from Zamindar's guard tried to give me a chase. They fired a few rounds too in the air. No harm done! This happened when I was not even a member of any gang. Dacoit leader Kalla Gujjar used to laud my courage. He had therefore given me a revolver for my security. No sooner the news of my having bumped off the Zamindar – in broad day-light – spread into the ravines, dacoit gangs started queuing up asking me to join them. I had however decided to throw my lot with Kalla. He had been sensitive to the sufferings endured by me. He was appreciative of my courage. He had given me his personal revolver – even when I was nobody".

"My joining Kalla gang was not only an occasion for Kalla to celebrate. It also boosted my self-confidence – sky high. Kalla arranged a 'Mark – V para-trooper rifle' for me, through his contacts in Agra. The rifle had a telescopic sight. I killed three of the rapists using that rifle! I killed the first one when he, accompanied by his bodyguards was watering his field. He should have been still for just half a minute. But that was enough for me to take a long shot from a distance of about 4 – 500 metres. Taking the help of the telescope I fired two rounds and saw him collapse on the spot. It was only then that I moved away. I killed the second one with the same rifle when he was returning to his village driving his tractor. I finished him in between the words of a 'rasiya' (amorous song), that he was singing".

"I killed the third one when I found him standing all alone on the Porsa-Ater road, waiting for a bus. Bahadura Gujjar killed one more when he approached him appealing for peace and seeking forgiveness. The last one was killed by some goondas (bad characters) who used to act as go-between collecting 'panihai' (ransom) from the families of the kidnapped children".

"Puniya, all this has taken me ten years! Yet the overpowering thirst for revenge, that drove me into the ravines that night, is not yet fully quenched. Two of the rapists – Jaswanta and Ram Bharose are still alive! Killing them is the raison de'etre of my existence. To fulfil that vow, I have to put those two also to sleep. I cannot surrender unless I have killed

Jaswanta and Ram Bharose. If I left the security that the ravines offer, these two would not take even a month to get me killed. They are people with long arms. They have access to very important politicians – ministers. They also enjoy the support of some senior police officers. They have several cases of murders and rapes pending against them. Yet they still walk freely and fearlessly. Policemen accompany them whenever they move out. It is therefore not easy to kill them. But I am willing to wait and I am sure Ma Durga will smile on me one day – sooner than later".

Having said all this and having bared her heart to Puniya, Gudiya became quiet. No one spoke. Puniya too didn't find words to console Gudiya. She just sat there, shedding tears.

After sometime Gudiya got up and replaced the loaded revolver into her shoulder bag. Then she turned towards Puniya and putting her arms around her she lifted her off her feet in a very tight embrace. Puniya looked bewildered. The suspense however remained short-lived. Placing her right hand on Puniya's head, Gudiya broke into a prayer.

"May you live long, Puniya! May God grant you a very long and very happy married life. May you remain for ever, a pillar of support to Amma and Kakku".

Tears rolled down Gudiya's cheeks as she pronounced the aforesaid blessing. Soon enough a moment arrived when she could no longer speak. She therefore became quiet. It should have been a few minutes when she started speaking again.

"I wanted to remain present in your wedding and to share the joy of your becoming a Suhagin (married woman). I wanted to lead you into the mandap. But now I will not come. I don't want to become a source of trouble to anyone of you on your wedding day. Therefore Puniya, please excuse my absence and accept my blessings today itself. Accept my congratulations. Tell Kakku that his desire that I should surrender is a command.

But since I am presently tied to a vow, I would need some more time". As she was getting ready to leave she once again caught hold of Puniya and said, "I leave now, Puniya! Don't know when we would meet again. Therefore, even if it is going to be one last laugh, let us laugh together, that very innocent laughter, which we shared when we were children – same laughter which was exclusively ours till that evening when the catastrophe struck!"

The two struggled hard to put up some semblance of a laughter, but it all ended in a short-lived smile. The tragedies of life and times had taken away from them their very precious full-throated laughter of childhood. Gudiya looked towards Puniya again – tapped her on her tear-drenched cheeks – and wiped away her tears with her palms. Then she turned away from her and towards the ravines. She would have gone just a few steps when she remembered something and turned back to Puniya, saying:

"Don't tell anyone what I have just now told you. Don't tell whether I would be attending your wedding, or not. Don't tell Amma and Kakku that I won't be coming. Also don't mention it to them whether I am thinking of surrender".

By the time the full impact of these words could sink into Puniya's head – Gudiya was gone – swallowed by the ravines!

* * * * *

Puniya's wedding day arrived in a wink. Pandit from Puniya's neighbourhood got the marriage solemnised by going through the rituals of havan, seven pheras and exchange of solemn vows. And with the conclusion of these rituals, Puniya was a married woman. Pandit had demanded twenty five rupees as his 'dakshina'. He collected that money in advance and offered the entire amount to Puniya during her 'Per Pujan' (the ritual of worshipping the feet of a virgin, as a Goddess on her wedding day). Villagers were earlier hesitant to join the marriage celebrations. However, Anuj's assurances emboldened them and everyone joined and blessed Puniya. They also prayed for a very long and happy married life for her.

Gudiya heard the happy news in a far-off ravine and quickly went down on her knees in a gesture of thanks-giving to Ma Durga – little realising that the Commander of Destinies had up his sleeve – some other plans.

* * * * *

Someone had complained to the DIG and the SP that there would be laxity in the execution of ambush by Anuj, enabling Gudiya to attend the marriage ceremonies. They, therefore, landed in the village a day ahead of the marriage for an on the spot inspection of the police arrangements. They also decided to spend the wedding night in the nearby Kali-Ahroli Armed Police post, forcing Anuj to spend the wedding night in Gudiya's village.

Anuj was overjoyed receiving these orders. It enabled him to attend Puniya's wedding without let or hindrance. When time came for the 'Per Pujan' or of worshipping the feet of the virgin, he quickly changed into Kurta/Pyjama and performed the ceremony.

Readers would remember that Gudiya had decided three days earlier – not to attend Puniya's wedding. She didn't.

After the barat left the village in the morning and after it had been confirmed that Gudiya did not attend the marriage, the ambush was lifted.

Puniya left for her husband's home – bidding goodbye to her aging parents and leaving everything that was part of her existence so far – behind, as a matter of fact leaving every thing that she had known and was a part of her existence since birth, behind.

Kakku and Amma were left alone, broken–hearted. They would have probably ended their life by jumping into the river. But a faint hope that Gudiya might some day agree to surrender enlivening their grey days – made them revert to normal life.

The DIG and the SP, sitting in Kali-Akroli camp were congratulating each other for the very strong 'bandobast' (arrangement) made by them which prevented Gudiya from attending the marriage. Just then a wireless message landed into the DIG's hands informing him of the murder of Jaswanta – another rapist, outside Gormi town. The message, which confirmed Gudiya's presence in Gormi at the time of Jaswanta's murder went on to add that the lone police man accompanying Jaswanta was also killed on the spot. According to the message, Gudiya murdered Jaswanta just about time when he was boarding his jeep in preparation for leaving Gormi en route to his village.

News of Jaswanta's murder by Gudiya brought to an abrupt end the festivities in Kali-Ahroli police camp where the DIG and SP were camping.

Police officers, posted in Gudiya's village on the marriage day heaved a sigh of relief – their report that Gudiya did not attend Puniya's wedding got authenticated!

The last of the eight rapists, Ram Bharose, started living on Ram-ke-bharose – depending on Divine intervention for his protection!

* * * * *

Talks of Surrender

Bureaucracies all over the world thrive on back-stabbing, back-biting, malice and slander. In India, mainly due to long spells of rule by the Rajas – Maharajas and Nawabs as also due to the imperialistic style of functioning of the British, this was perfected into a fine art and fine-tuned to an extent that it came to be recognised as professionalism per se. Most bureaucrats perfect this art at the very beginning of their service and do nothing else thereafter, only run down their colleagues and fellow officers by carrying tales and circulating slander about each other – rarely factual – mostly imaginary. Such officers thrive better – in comparison to those who make professionalism the mainstay of their career.

It was under the pressure of such deviant – but generally accepted behaviour – that some vicious police officers got it secretly conveyed to the IGP in Bhopal that there were reasons to suspect the role of the police parties during the wedding of Gudiya's sister in the village. They also got it conveyed that the police parties would not have behaved as such without Anuj's connivance, since it was he who was in-charge of the arrangements in the village on the wedding day.

Consequently, no sooner Anuj returned to Bhind, he found a wireless message from the Police Headquarters, waiting for him in his office. The message conveyed that the IGP was visiting Gwalior the next morning and expected Anuj to meet him in the 2nd Battalion Police Mess.

Anuj had no inkling of what had gone on behind his back. He took the IGP's visit to be routine and the summon for a meeting to be the IGP's interest in the welfare of the young

IPS officers. He even felt that the IGP might be wanting to congratulate him for his hard work in the anti-dacoity operations. Unaware of the intrigues, he spent the day merrily.

He reached Gwalior Police Mess the next morning at about 10 O'clock. The DIGP was sitting in the lounge surrounded by senior police officers. The IGP had arrived in the morning by train and after some preliminary discussions with the officers at the railway station had retreated into his room for receiving a telephone call from the Chief Minister. While waiting for the IGP in the lounge Anuj noticed some oddity, in the behaviour of his colleagues. He felt as if everyone was trying to avoid him.

It should have been good fifteen minutes when the IGP emerged from his room with everyone standing up and coming to attention. All other officers except Anuj had met the IGP at the railway station. Therefore only Anuj saluted. The IGP was moving towards the DIGP when he noticed Anuj. He immediately checked his steps and walked towards him, shook hands with him and asked, "How are you, Anuj? When did you arrive".

"I am fine, Sir – with your blessings. I arrived about 10-15 minutes earlier."

The IGP put his hand over Anuj's shoulders and motioned him to move towards his room. He also asked the mess orderly Phool Singh to serve two cups of coffee in his room. The DIGP initially wanted to accompany the two into the IGP's room. But on second thoughts he retraced his steps.

The officers seated in the lounge were certain that Anuj was going to receive a severe dressing down today – might even be thrown out of Bhind district.

No sooner Anuj had taken his seat, the IGP in brief conveyed to him the suspicions of the senior police officers, particularly with regard to his dealings with the Gudiya gang. The IGP went on to add that some senior police officers had complained that the ASP was not taking them into confidence in planning operations and that he was soft towards D-7 (Rampala Lodha) gang. In between mess orderly Phool Singh entered the room with two cups of coffee of which the IGP took one and passed on the other to Anuj. The IGP finished bulk of his coffee in one go while Anuj's coffee remained untouched – lying on the table.

Anuj took a little time in organising his thoughts. Then in very carefully selected words he started telling the IGP that he had received information about Gudiya gang wanting to bid farewell to arms and to surrender. It is essentially for this reason that he has been going soft on Gudiya. He mentioned that in his scheme of things he wanted the police to earn an image of honesty, fair-play and of being wedded to law. He did not want the police to earn the reputation of being blood thirsty, cruel, deceptive and partial towards the rich and the powerful. He asserted that Gudiya has committed several unpardonable crimes and she deserved the severest punishment. But police should not be the one taking over the responsibility of punishing her. She needs to be punished by the courts and that too strictly within the framework of law. Encounter should only be the last resort – to be attempted if all other methods have been tried and have failed. D-7 Rampala's gang is a fit case for encounter and he has deployed many dependable informers against him. He is sure that as and when D-7 entered any of the villages accessible to his informers, encounter will ensue."

Anuj went on to add that "he wanted to take each and every officer along. But many of them are unnecessarily suspicions of each and every informer and of every bit of information that such informers cater. I have given you an assurance that I would launch my myself into a raid within half-an-hour of receiving information. If I have to stay back trying to convince my colleagues as to why the information is trustworthy, the convincing process can go on for hours and the value of information would get lost. That is why whenever I feel that it would be impossible to satisfy my colleagues, I launch myself alone into the operation which might have become the reason for their's feeling unhappy. Sir, I do admit that I am inexperienced, especially in dealing with the dacoits. But I loathe being required to waste any chance or any information. Sir, you are highly experienced in anti-dacoity operations. I would follow-hundred percent and with all sincerity – any advice that you might choose to give me".

The IGP had nearly finished his coffee. Putting down his cup on the table he got up and putting his hand on Anuj's shoulders, patted him. Then said: "you are doing well Anuj – keep it up. I am pleased with your work, with whatever you believe in – also with your methodology. I also believe that in areas specially like Bhind, Police should try to earn the confidence of people. They should earn the reputation of being harsh – only on criminals. Their image should not be of a government mafia, fond of shedding blood – fond of encounters. If the police started behaving like goons, people would have hardly anything to choose between them and the dacoits. I sincerely believe that the police needs to involve itself more seriously in enforcing the law through efficient and effective police working and by tackling crime as first priority. Go ahead Anuj – my best wishes to you!"

The IGP slowly moved out of his room with Anuj following a few steps behind. As the two appeared in the lounge, the officers present did a summary scrutiny of Anuj's face. They mumbled to themselves: "The IGP has surely rebuked him – given him serious tongue-lashing. Might have even threatened him that he is going to be thrown out of Bhind disrict". All officers who only half-an-hour earlier were avoiding him, quickly made a bee-line towards him and surrounded him – wanting to know 'what all did happen?'

"Boss, how was the meeting? What did the IGP tell you? Hope all is well?"

Anuj did not reply. He knew that these officers believe that he had been castigated and subjected to serious tongue-lashing by the IGP! Let them continue to believe so.

Soon enough he put on his peak-cap and saluted the IGP. And then in one swift right-about-turn he was out of the Police Mess. Once out in the porch he jumped into the driver's seat of his vehicle, shoved in the ignition key in the keyhole and turned it on. The engine fired and soon enough he was on his way to Bhind.

Rumours started flying fast and thick that Anuj has been put on notice by the IGP and that his days in Bhind were numbered.

* * *

Facts that three days prior to the date of Puniya's marriage; Gudiya had visited her village and met her infirm parents – that she did succeed in escaping into the ravines in the nick of time due to Anuj's unexpected arrival in the village; that Anuj was informed of Gudiya's escape into the ravines by Gudiya's father but he refused to give her a chase; that Gudiya had not gone far into the ravines and had returned soon enough into the neighbour's house through the backdoor and remained present there as long as Anuj was present in Gudiya's house, and that a proposal to surrender was made to Gudiya, firstly by her neighbour and then by Puniya herself – became the talk of about 30 to 40 villages – in no time. Rumours started flying thick and fast, reaching the community leaders first and then the dacoits. Gudiya could have put a stop to these rumours by pronouncing a categorical 'yes' or 'no' to the surrender proposal. But she decided not to react. Gudiya's silence therefore was given many mischievous twists by gossip-mongers. They started circulating that Gudiya's silence should be interpreted as half-assent. They asserted that Gudiya had an opportunity to counter the proposal vociferously which she did not which means that she was keeping her options open. They also started circulating that no sooner Gudiya succeeded in eliminating Ram Bharose – her last rapist and had fulfilled her vow of avenging rape, she would surrender.

Likelihood of Gudiya's surrender became a topic of hot discussions and street-corner gossips, in Bhind and Morena districts. Dacoit gangs started speculating over the likelihood of Gudiya's surrender. Gudiya's gang members were the first to suspect their leader's moves. She however convinced them by laying bare the facts – as they were. She addressed them firstly in a group and then individually and told them in very clear terms that the proposals for surrender had been made so far more or less publicly by the neighbours in their houses, where it was not possible for her to react either way due to fear of misinterpretation. The gang members saw reason in Gudiya's clarification and reiterated their absolute loyalty in her leadership – which had for ages been the most important mantra for survival in the ravines. This also explained Gudiyas presence with her gang at the time of Jaswanta's murder.

Allaying the suspicions of other dacoit gangs was however not easy. Gudiya started receiving threatening messages from various gangs. She was told that if she considered surrender as an option then her entire family – even her distant relations would be wiped out – she herself will be murdered even if she preferred to walk into the security of police or jail. Gudiya met several gang leaders personally and sent trusted lieutenants to talk to others. But no one was willing to trust her fully. Jaswanta's murder did convince some that she perhaps has not given up the path of crime. But mischief-mongers started propagating afresh that Gudiya was all ready to surrender and would do so no sooner Ram Bharose, the last rapist – was killed.

Influential people from Gudiya's own community were the first to feel threatened and insecure. If Gudiya's gang surrendered who will be left in the ravines to protect them. Therefore, in an attempt to dissuade Gudiya from surrendering, they got it conveyed to her that if she surrendered, Anuj's life too would be in jeopardy since her surrender would easily get linked to Anuj.

The severest threat – also the first formal one, came from D-7 Rampala. That night Gudiya was camping in the ravines of Tehengur Police station. She had arrived there to dissuade the hench man of a local politician from contesting for the Sarpanch's post, by administering a direct threat to him. The politician (a local MLA) opposed to this person had promised Gudiya rupees twenty thousand for running this errand.

It was 11 O'clock in the night when one messenger arrived announcing that D-7 Rampala was arriving in a short while, accompanied by his gang, for meeting Gudiya. Gudiya had no difficulty in guessing the reason for this nocturnal visit.

It wouldn't have been long – about half-an-hour, when Rampala arrived. Tall and strong – muscular, long arms, blood-shot dark eyes, black open beard reaching down to his navel and a long blood-red vermilion 'tilak' in the centre of the forehead reaching right down to the nose bridge. Having come face-to-face, he caught hold of Gudiya in his very strong arms and embraced her. Then after a brief pause he explained to her – in great details, the purpose of his visit. He mentioned that the Baghis (dacoits) were unhappy knowing that Gudiya planned to surrender after she had killed Ram Bharose and avenged the inhuman crimes against her. 'Listen Gudiya for the Baghis of

Chambal, surrender either in victory or defeat is equally infamous. I have been entrusted with the responsibility of reiterating to you the long established tradition of the Baghis. Gudiya – we only go down fighting. We embrace death – with a smile on our lips. So Gudiya don't ever think of surrender. We believe that you are intelligent. You have spent ten years in the ravines fighting alongside other Baghis. We follow only one law – that of the gun. Smallest lapse gets punished by it – by the gun. You chose to be a Baghi. You must abide by the glorious traditions set by the Baghis. A Baghi never surrenders – never! He dies receiving police bullet on his chest. So Gudiya, don't ignore those glorious traditions! Don't think of becoming a blot on the revered traditions set by the Baghis. And don't forget this is going to be the last – also the final advise from us. No one else will ever approach you again – on this subject.'

The conversation ended as abruptly as it had begun. D-7 did not revert to the topic of surrender again. He asked Gudiya the reasons for her visit to Tehengur. He also shared some news about his own (D-7's) area. It was well post midnight. He stood up as abruptly as he had arrived and in one gesture took leave of Gudiya. All other members of his gang – about a dozen of them, got on to their feet. Gudiya's gang members got up too. Together they shouted "Jai Durga", "Jai Kali". And in a few seconds D-7 along with his gang had disappeared into the arduous terrain.

An hour went by with Gudiya sitting motionless – going over and over again into the contents of her conversation with D-7. One thing was clear; the threat to her life was definite and imminent. She could ignore it only at her peril – at grave risk to her own life and to the lives of her gang members.

* * * * *

Dacoits follow one thumb rule – call it superstition. Whenever someone visits them in the ravines, they vacate that hide out forthwith and shift to another one – soon after the visitor's departure. The older generation of dacoits even used to leave that area – altogether. Gudiya however sat transfixed, for over an hour. Then she got out of her trance and ordered her followers to get ready for leaving the hide-out – at once. And in five minutes or so, Gudiya's gang too was lapped-up by the ravines.

In the morning when those very villagers who had conducted D-7 to Gudiya's hideout the previous night – arrived on the spot, they found the area cleaned up with no tell-tale signs left behind, by either of the gangs. On getting information about the presence of both Gudiya and D-7 gangs in their area, the Tehengur Police got active trying to find out where the two gangs would have gone? But by day-break both the gangs were well out of Tehengur area – D-7 being located two days later near Ron Police Station in South Bhind and D-3 Gudiya in Gormi Police Station, in the North-west.

* * * * *

It should have been three days past the meeting between D-3 and D-7 in the Tehengur area when on a hot and sultry evening Anuj was accosted by a shopkeeper-cum-money lender in Gormi town, just outside his shop. It was getting 8.30 in the evening and Anuj was driving his jeep past Gormi town, unaccompanied. This unusual gesture startled Anuj. He however gathered his wits soon enough and brought his jeep to a complete halt.

"What do you want? Who are you?"

"Maharaj I own this shop. And please visit my home. It is important", replied the shopkeeper.

"If what you wanted to tell me was so important why don't you tell me here itself" questioned Anuj.

"No Maharaj, my sister is sitting at home. It is she who wanted to speak to you urgently".

"But why don't you bring her here?" queried Anuj.

"Maharaj, she is very unwell. She can't come here. You would have to take the trouble of visiting my house".

"Why don't you go home and ask your sister as to what she wants to convey. I am willing to wait here. You can come here and pass on her message to me", suggested Anuj.

"No, Maharaj no! Please visit my house – just for two-three minutes. I swear by my only son that no harm will come to you and that there is no ulterior motive in my request. There is something very-very urgent that she wanted to tell you. She is not willing to tell me what it is. But it is important," replied the shopkeeper.

Anuj on the basis of the police station records knew the shopkeeper. It was on record that he was a receiver of stolen property. He bought not only jewellery and other looted items from the dacoits and thieves, but also handled their cash. The police station, however, had no information that he also passed on information about the movements of the police to the dacoits, or gave them refuge in his house. It was also on record that he had at times acted as a go-between in ransom deals between dacoits and the families of those kidnapped.

Anuj was all this time wondering as to whether the shopkeeper can be trusted?"

"Which one is your house"? Asked Anuj.

"There – Maharaj – you can see – in the shadow of that lamp post" said the shopkeeper – pointing to a house about 30 meters away.

Anuj noticed that the house stood bang on the main road. Being late for people to venture out in dacoit-infested areas, the street was deserted. Not a soul anywhere. Anuj thought for a while and then decided in favour of taking a chance.

"Come on – let's go", said Anuj as he started walking towards the designated house. The shopkeeper followed him. The house being just 40-50 steps away, they reached there instantly. The door to the main entrance was lightly shut. The shopkeeper gave it a gentle push and it opened ... without making any noise.

Anuj entered the room and found it well lit. In one corner sat a woman, on a chair, covered from top to toe with a sari. As Anuj entered, he heard the woman mumbling: "Vyapari (trader) bhaiya – please wait outside and give me a signal only if you smell any danger. 'theek' (OK)".

The shopkeeper walked out past the main entrance without making any noise and in no time the woman on the chair uncovered her face. Anuj just got enough time to have one good look at her as she started speaking.

"Chotey Kaptan...I am Gudiya...You are absolutely safe here...I have given my word to Puniya – my sister, therefore don't feel scared. Sit down comfortably and let me have my say. I am alone here – just like you. You can arrest me right now and here, if you so desire. I will not protest. Choice is yours".

Gudiya waited for a couple of minutes to give Anuj time to take his seat and to react. Anuj, however, was dumb struck.

"I promised Kakku and Puniya that I would make one sincere effort to meet you and that is why I am here. My sister wants me to surrender – to undergo court awarded sentence and then return to society and family for living life like an ordinary women, after having endured the sentence awarded by the Courts".

Gudiya broke her dialogue for a few seconds in the hope that Anuj might have something to say. Anuj however sat speechless.

"Chotey kaptan, I am sick of my life in the ravines. I do not want to stay there a minute longer than absolutely necessary. You know that it was one seething desire for revenge that drove me into the ravines. One rapist still survives. He not only is wily but has secured police protection or else I would have killed him long back! My vow for revenge would get fulfilled only in the death of Ram Bharose. Ten years have gone by. Only Ma Durga knows what is in store for me. I definitely want to surrender but that had to await the death of Ram Bharose. My father too wants me to surrender to you – forthwith, leaving Ram Bharose's fate in your hands. Can you get him hanged, Chotey Kaptan?"

Having exhausted herself, Gudiya pressed pause and silence ensued.

There was enough light in the room but not enough to allow Anuj to see Gudiya's face clearly or to allow him to watch reactions on her face. Puniya's faith in him that he can get Ram Bharose hanged, made Anuj feel uneasy.

Silence was becoming unbearable. Therefore, in order to keep the conversation going, Anuj started speaking.

"Gudiya why do you link your surrender to that of Ram Bharose's killing. If you have come to believe that surrender was the way out for you, then do it straightaway. Leave Ram Bharose to his own fate. Leave Ram Bharose into the hands of administration, courts and God. Somewhere, he will be made to pay for his sins".

Gudiya sat quiet!

Anuj resumed after a brief pause: "I do not say all this since I don't want to help you. Far from it! The fact is that in order to convict criminals, the courts need conclusive evidence and in your case we don't have it. Rape per se is a heinous crime. Gang rape is an unpardonable sin. However, in order to have a strong case against Ram Bharose, the court would need FIR (First Information Report), medical examination report and your contemporary statement. None of these are on our records. You ran away into the ravines from the scene of crime itself. That has made the case against the rapists, extremely weak, particularly since we have no F.I.R. from the victim and no medical examination report to prove rape. I may extend to you an assurance that I would get Ram Bharose sentenced. But that may not happen due to the case being very weak. I do not want to give you an assurance which I might not be able to fulfil. I do not want to be proven untrustworthy before you or your sister Puniya – more importantly before God!

"Chotey Kaptan, I appreciate your views. I am aware that in cases of rape one can never get enough evidence and therefore one can never feel certain that a rapist will get punished. That specifically was the reason for my taking to the ravines. Now you appreciate that. Don't you? It is perhaps Ma Kali's wish that I remained in the ravines a little longer – at least till Ram Bharose's death. I would honour Her wish! It is also possible that in this process I may get killed – felled by a bullet. In that case Ram Bharose will live and I would die. But today Chotey Kaptan, I just wanted to express my inner feelings to you and I have done that".

The twist in the conversation was not to Anuj's liking. Gudiya's arguments non-plussed him a bit – but for a few seconds only. Organising his thoughts he started speaking again:

"Gudiya, you don't seem to follow what I have said. Please, try to understand me. I told you not to link your surrender to Ram Bharose's death. If you thought surrender was an option, then surrender. Leave Ram Bharose's fate into the hands of administration, courts and God Almighty".

"Chotey Kaptan, you don't know Ram Bharose. Once I have given up the security of the ravines and of my 'MK-V', he will get me eliminated in less then a week of my surrender, irrespective of where I was kept. If I somehow managed to save myself from him, then the leaders of my own community or even an odd Baghi would get me finished. They have sent me a very stern warning .... Gudiya, if you surrender then anyone of us will kill you. Yes, anyone! Even inside the jail. Pay heed to this warning! Don't take us lightly! In their lexicon a dacoit dies just one way .... felled by a bullet to his chest. He never ever surrenders".

"Gudiya, I appreciate your fears. You firstly, appear worried about your own security and secondly about Ram Bharose. Administration will ensure your security – hundred percent. Whether you were kept in a jail or in an open air jail or in a women's prison, or in your own house, or in anyone else's house or on parole, it would be the responsibility of the administration to ensure your security. However, I do not want to give you such an assurance, off hand. I need ten days time so that I could visit Bhopal and discuss your fears, in details, with the IGP. I will certainly get back to you, thereafter.

Gudiya did not react at all to Anuj's assurance. She was personally very worried and remained so till the very end. Then getting in control of her emotions she started speaking again:

"So then Chotey Kaptan – I would go now. We would meet again after 10 days...March 10".

"But where?" asked Anuj.

"Please come to Agra on that day and visit Puniya. She will inform you of the time and place of our meeting". Then hesitating a bit, she added, "I leave now, Chotey Kaptan. I will go out first and you will leave after me. I shall be hoping to see you again – on March 10. Rescue me from the ravines, Chotey Kaptan!"

Halfway through her sentence Gudiya was out of the back door and as she receded into the shadows, Anuj got a chance to see her – fully. Tiny like a Gudiya (doll) – hardly 5 feet tall – extremely fragile – shouldn't be weighing even 40 kilos! How has she survived the rigours of the ravines? Anuj felt really sorry for her.

* * * * *

Next morning itself, Anuj applied for three days casual leave on ground that he had hurt himself during one of the raids in the ravines – that his knee was troubling him greatly and therefore, it has become necessary for him to visit Bhopal to get himself checked up in the Police Hospital. By the evening he received the leave sanction-order and by early next morning he was in Bhopal, having arrived there by an overnight train. The IGP used to give appointments to officers coming from anti-dacoity areas and Nagaland, preferentially. Anuj too got his appointment the same evening at 7 O'clock..

When he met the IGP in his office, he found him cheerful – notwithstanding an entire days work in office. In exact and just few words Anuj conveyed to the IGP Gudiya's proposals – also her fears. The IGP took some time to assess the full implication of the proposal. Then he started speaking in a voice, hardly audible.

"Anuj when you meet Gudiya next please tell her that we

want her to surrender – as soon as possible and to refrain from committing crimes till then. Tell her that once she had surrendered, her security will be our responsibility. She needs entertain no fears".

"Sir, I will explain all the three points to her in our next meeting scheduled for March 10. I envisage no difficulty in being able to do that. Problems may arise, if the court decided to send Gudiya to judicial custody. In that case the responsibility for her security will get transferred to the jail authorities and the police will find it impossible to keep its promise – to Gudiya".

"Yes that can pose a problem", said the IGP. "However, I am sure the Police would be able to take the court into confidence before hand, and would be able to impress upon them the grave threat to Gudiya's life emanating from diverse elements. I am sure the court would agree to send Gudiya to a 'Special Jail' and to her's being kept under police protection. This is permissible under the existing laws". Then after a few moments the IGP added:

"Incidentally – will Gudiya agree to confess to her crimes before the court or will she contest?"

"Sir, I do not know. I'll ask her in the next meeting. May be she would agree to confess".

"OK, all the best, Anuj. Take care".

* * * * *

March 10 was there in a blink. Nothing untoward happened in between to distract Anuj. He left Bhind in plain clothes early in the morning and reached Phup Police Station. Then on the pretext of visiting Kosad Police station, he crossed river Chambal and reached Agra via Etawah reaching there before 12 O'clock. Leaving his police jeep in the parking lot of Agra hotel, he arrived in Puniya's house riding a cycle rickshaw. Puniya was overjoyed seeing Anuj. She mentioned that she has not heard any thing in the recent past from Gudiya and is not in a position to say – if she would be coming. Anuj was hungry. He gratefully accepted Puniya's offer of lunch. The lunch got over at about two in the afternoon. Anuj was wondering as to what needs to be done now, when all of sudden the back door opened and a woman covered in a black burqa, entered the room, shutting the door carefully behind her. In a fraction of a second the burqa came off and lo and behold it was Gudiya – standing in front of Anuj and Puniya.

Puniya welcomed her sister and laid out the left overs of the food for her and when Gudiya wanted to be left alone with Anuj she quietly walked out of her house.

After a brief interregnum, Anuj started speaking and conveyed to Gudiya the gist of his conversation with the IGP. He also told her that the Chief Minister has been taken into confidence and he is in agreement with the IGP's views – that they both want to convey that Gudiya should surrender soon and that the administration would take care of her security – post surrender.

Gudiya kept on listening carefully. She did not utter a single word and when her lunch was over she pushed the 'thali' (plate) aside and started speaking:

"Chotey Kaptan, I am eternally grateful to you for whatever you have done for me. On my part, I have decided to surrender. That is my own decision with no pressures or persuasion from any one. However, I would delay my surrender till the start of rains and in between I would try to get even with Ram Bharose – would try to finish that 'harami' (bastard) and feed his bones to the dogs. I am aware...I can fail and Ram Bharose can survive. In that eventuality I would leave that 'harami's' – that f......'s fate in the hands of God – and would surrender accepting defeat. However, I would not surrender unless I have made one more attempt to kill that 'kutta' (dog). Committing crime gives me no pleasure. But I am leading a gang of dacoits. I can't keep the gang intact unless I kept them involved in dacoities, murders and kidnappings. They start feeling restless if they have to sit idle for even half a month. They start suspecting that Gudiya has got friendly with the police and may get all of them killed. As long as I am in the ravines, I have to pay the price for being there – by committing crimes. Maharaj, no dacoit has ever survived in the ravines by doing pujas or preaching Hari-katha – please understand this harsh reality".

She stopped speaking as abruptly as she had started. Anuj found her agitated and worked up. It took her about a minute to calm down. Then in a very low voice – almost in whisper, she started speaking again.

"Chotey Kaptan – may be I would be ready to surrender by July first week – earliest by middle of June. Nothing is certain yet. I would need to deliberate my decision with my gang members. So Maharaj, have some patience".

Anuj thought that Gudiya has not grasped the spirit behind the IGP's instructions. Therefore, in an effort to elucidate, he said,

"No, Gudiya – no! We are only keen that you surrender at the earliest. It does not mean that we want you to surrender right now. Any date in April-May is O.K. However, if you want it to be a date in June or July – we'll agree to that too".

"Maharaj, I have followed you exactly! Incidentally where would I be kept after my surrender – in Mahila Jail? There I would get murdered in ten days. You don't know what goes on in your jails – and how?"

"The IGP plans to keep you in a special jail under the security of very trusted policemen. Have no worries Gudiya?"

Gudiya got up from her chair abruptly and started putting on her burqa. She also simultaneously summoned Puniya from outside.

"Chotey Kaptan, I shall leave now. As on the earlier occasion this time too I would go out first. You would need to wait here with Puniya for say about five more minutes".

Puniya had in the meanwhile entered the room. The sisters embraced each other and exchanged words of farewell. Both had tears in their eyes.

As she was exiting through the backdoor a fear crossed her mind and she stopped to ask:

"Chotey Kaptan, can you save me – your sister – from being murdered, till my surrender?"

"Of course, Gudiya, my word of honour for that!" replied Anuj – emphatically.

It is, however, unlikely that Gudiya heard those words, since she was gone before Anuj could complete his sentence.

Words – prophetic per se – her's or his?

Anuj stayed on for another half-an-hour with Puniya – then left for his hotel and from there for Bhind.

* * * * *

The IGP was keen to know all that had transpired in the meeting? He therefore rang up Anuj early next morning. He himself was on the line.

"What happened in Agra – Anuj?"

"The meeting went off well. But sir, I have difficulty in conveying details over telephone".

"OK, remain ready. I shall be summoning you to Bhopal, today itself". And the line went dead.

When he arrived in office, he found the IGP's wireless message on his table.

The message read: "GOI (Government of India) is worried over the existence of four vacancies in the SP's rank in Nagaland and is seeking volunteers from amongst IPS officers – on a rather lucrative 150% deputation allowance plus Rs.800/- North-East special pay. Should you be willing to be considered for this deputation please make it convenient to meet the IGP in Police Headquarters in Bhopal – tomorrow at 1030 Hrs.".

Anuj left Bhind forthwith for Bhopal and en-route called on the DIGP in Gwalior to put him in picture with the contents of the IGP's message. The DIGP wanted to know from Anuj whether he was willing to be considered for this deputation. Anuj said, "yes" adding that the job appeared challenging.

Anuj arrived in Bhopal by train early next morning, and after a bath and breakfast in the police mess, he reached the police headquarters. The IGP was already in office and no sooner he sent in his card, he was ushered in.

He found the IGP relaxed. A small pocket radio placed on another table played – "come September". Without loosing any time, Anuj gave a verbatim account of his conversation with Gudiya – in Agra. He found the IGP listening to him in rapt attention and as he came to the end of his reporting – silence ensued.

After about a minute the IGP started speaking – measuring his words:

"She has agreed to surrender – is good news! Will not surrender immediately – is not good news! She might even commit a few crimes prior to surrender, is positively bad news". A minute's pause ensued.

"We don't seem to have any choice – Anuj. If our intention as policemen is to bring criminals back into the society – without bloodshed, we'll need to be patient. Go and tell her – first of July is OK with us. But that is the final date We may not be able to wait any longer.

"Right Sir. ... Understood. ... Will comply. Can I leave now, Sir?"

"OK, Anuj...all the best. Incidentally, is your DIG aware of your contact with Gudiya?"

"No, sir... not yet".

"OK. Keep it that way. I will take him on board as and when it became necessary".

"Right, sir". Anuj saluted the IGP – did a right about turn and within the blinking of an eye was out of his room".

Once outside – Anuj was a worried man. Agra meeting was fixed at Gudiya's request and in the Agra meeting he had committed the blunder of not fixing the 'where' and 'how' of the next meeting with her.

No future RV (rendezvous) existed. No arrangements were in place for any further exchange of messages. No d.l.b's – (dead-letter boxes) were either discussed or agreed for exchange of information with Gudiya. The IGP now wanted some proposals to be passed on to Gudiya. How does he do that? How does he go about fixing a meeting with her?

Lost totally in such worries he arrived Bhopal railway station and having boarded a first-class compartment on a train to Gwalior he straightaway went off to sleep. He was woken up by the train attendant early next morning – shortly before the train pulled into Gwalior railway station. He had left his jeep the previous evening in the parking lot of the GRP Police Station. Out of the train – out of the railway station, he went straight to his jeep and drove off for Bhind.

While crossing Mehgaon village, the Shopkeeper or the 'Sahukar' (money lender) from Gormi came to his mind. He instinctively turned his jeep towards Gormi – arriving there and in front of the sahukar's house in less than an hour. It was getting to be eight in the morning and a very pleasant surprise awaited him. He found the 'sahukar' squatting on the stone slab outside his house – busy brushing his teeth. The 'sahukar' invited Anuj for a cup of tea which Anuj accepted, gratefully. Sipping boiling hot tea – Anuj informed the 'sahukar' of the need for yet another meeting with Gudiya. To Anuj's bewilderment he found the 'sahukar' to be a straight talker. Without 'ifs' or 'buts' he 'promised' – doing his best. He requested Anuj to visit Gormi again, unaccompanied, on the morning of March 20th, assuring that he would have some information ready by then. Anuj made a mental note of the date and time.

By 10 O'clock Anuj was back in Bhind. The news of his having accepted a posting to Nagaland was all over the place. It had also been circulated that he would be leaving Bhind shortly.

* * * * *

<u>**20th March, 1959 – 7.00 A.M.:**</u> 'Sahukar's' promise was the first thing that came to his mind as he got up in the morning after an undisturbed eight hours sleep. He got up instinctively and left for Gormi in his jeep - unaccompanied – arriving

there shortly before nine. As good luck would have it, he found the 'sahukar' once again outside his house – squatting on the same stone slab, brushing his teeth. The 'sahukar' once again offered Anuj a cup of tea, which offer he once again gratefully accepted. While sipping hot tea, 'Sahukar' revealed that he had been able to contact Gudiya and that she was ready to meet Anuj in Jayandraganj Gwalior on·25th March at 7.00 PM, outside the Agarwal Sweet House – and that Anuj should reach there dressed in 'civvies' (civilian clothes). He went on to add that all other details about the actual RV and the 'how' and 'where' of it would be worked out by Gudiya.

Nothing was left for discussion. Anuj therefore, hurriedly finished his tea and thanking the 'Sahukar' profusely he left for Bhind – where he reached well before 11 O'clock.

<u>March 25, 1959 – 7.00 P.M.:</u> Anuj, dressed in jeans and a white loose cotton shirt, arrived at the RV (rendezvous) slightly before time, leaving his jeep in one of the many side lanes. As he was getting out of his jeep, a small girl, 7 – 8 year old approached him and directed him to follow her, saying 'Didi waits for you'.

Maintaining ten yards distance, Anuj started following the little girl. He experienced no difficulty in following her since the girl had two shocking pink ribbons tied to her two pleats and since she was putting on a shining 'taveez' (talisman) in a black thread around her neck. The two should have zig-zagged for about ten minutes through narrow/stinking lanes when the little girl came to an abrupt halt in front of an old and dilapidated house. Directing Anuj to keep following her, the girl climbed on to the narrow platform in front of the house and gave a gentle push to one of the two doors. The door opened straightaway revealing the sitting room inside. The girl signalled Anuj to get in and take his seat and having done so, she quietly walked out of the room through the same door the two had come in – bolting the door, rather noisily from outside. The girls' last act frightened Anuj. He could see in the rather dim light, that the room had two other doors. But one had an ancient looking Aligarhi lock upon it and the other opening on to the back side, was bolted – from outside. His heart started beating faster. His blood pressure started rising.

Has he been cheated? Has he been double-crossed? Has he been trapped by some dacoit gang? He started examining the other artifacts present inside the house, but could find nothing that could help in identifying the owner. In one corner he found a rolled up 'jai-namaz' (carpet used by the Muslims for offering namaz), in another corner a utensil for doing 'wuzu' (washing hands) and on the wall a picture of 'Kaaba'. One thing was certain: the owner of the house was a Muslim. This however was no help! If he has been trapped he would need all his wits intact to get out of the ordeal. It would however be unwise to let go an opportunity, howsoever slim it might be of meeting Gudiya – in nervousness or hurry.

Fifteen minutes went by and nothing happened. Anuj was literally getting bathed in sweat. As he was at his wit's end he heard the bolt upon the rear door being pulled apart – from outside, and a figure dressed in a black burqa – covered from tip to toe, entered the room with a revolver in hand – held menacingly. This suspense too didn't last long. In one single motion the incumbent transferred the revolver into her shoulder bag that hung loosely from one of the shoulders. With that Anuj's breathing, normalised. It would have been another minute when Gudiya uncovered her face.

"Hope you had no problems reaching here? Did I make you wait long, Chotey Kaptan?".

"Oh no, not at all. But that revolver in your hand knocked the hell out of me" – replied Anuj.

"Chotey Kaptan, this house belongs to Rafiq Chacha. He was once a dacoit in my gang. One evening he decided to indulge himself by visiting the house of a 'bedni' (local prostitute). It was then that his luck ran out. Either the 'bedni' herself or someone from the neighbourhood, leaked the information of his presence to the police. He got killed in the ensuing encounter. Presently Rafiqa's uncle is very ill and is hospitalised. No one therefore, lives here. I can still offer you some tea. The girl who brought you here has left some tea-leaves, some milk and sugar in the kitchen".

Anuj had sweated a lot. A cup of tea therefore was welcome. In about five minutes Gudiya returned to the room with two cups of steaming hot tea and some biscuits. Setting the tea cups on the table she collapsed on to the chair nearby and started talking.

"Seeing you again bhaiya is such a big relief. I am grateful to Ma Kali for that. Now, tell me what happened that made it necessary for you to summon me?"

Anuj started explaining – in carefully selected words, the purpose of his visit:

"The Government is very happy with your decision. It wants to assure you that your security – post surrender, would entirely be its responsibility. My IGP wants you to surrender latest by July one. He also wants that you refrain from committing any crime in the intervening period. The Chief Minister has been informed by my IGP of your proposed surrender".

"Will I be surrendering before the Chief Minister", asked Gudiya.

"That can be arranged, if you so desire", replied Anuj.

"Please do that. I should presume that in that case my post surrender existence would become more secure".

A long spell of silence ensued. Neither of them said anything. Putting her thoughts together, Gudiya started speaking again:

"Your IGP seems to believe that I enjoy bloodshed. It is emphatically not so. As a child I could not even kill a fly or a mosquito. My heart revolted at the sight of blood. Yes – I loved singing. Even when five or six years old, I used to get invited to singing sessions in front of small audiences. My singing skills were self-acquired. No one taught me. I learnt singing by listening to the radio programmes and the gramophone records. I enjoyed listening to songs since I loved singing. I hated dacoits and detested the crimes committed by them. In due course, I started singing film songs, songs of love – also ghazals, which ended up in my being invited to marriages – and other social get-togethers, including birthday parties and parties thrown by the rich and neo-rich. On 26th January, I sang 'sare jahan se accha' at The Republic Day Parade in our district headquarter. The Collector gifted me three hundred rupees. I still fondly cherish the memory of that day. Singing gradually started bringing enough money, and my parents started believing that their days of penury were over. That proved to be our undoing – mine and of my parents".

"From singing in families, I graduated to singing bhajans in temples – and then to singing in wedding parties – moving up the ladder from singing bhajans to singing 'dadras', 'birha', 'kajri', 'thumri' – ending up with singing amorous films songs.

"Chotey Kaptan, the wheel of time had not stopped churning – was constantly on the grind. Imperceptibly it might have been, but I was moving towards becoming a teenager. My body was getting filled up. I was in the process of transformation from childhood to youth. Road romeos and youngsters from our locality had started whistling and flinging indecent remarks at me. My outings however were still restricted to marriage parties, where in addition to singing bhajans I had started singing film songs – also songs of love".

"It should have been just a short hop, when I started receiving invitations to private parties and since the payments at such functions were lucrative, my parents saw no difficulty in my accepting these invitations. On that fateful day too – it was an invitation to a birthday party and as a matter of abundant precaution my mother had accompanied me. The party got over by about 8.00 p.m. and we were out of the host's house soon enough. We would have taken just a few steps towards our house when the Zamindar's men stopped us and ordered us to visit the Zamindar's house for singing a few songs. I did not want to go but they started pulling and pushing me. My mother wanted to accompany me but she was threatened into returning home – directly from the spot of obstruction.

"And Bhaiya – this is how I landed into the Zamindar's house".

"The Zamindar was half-sitting, half-lying down on a wooden bed surrounded by 6-8 goons – all dead drunk. The Zamindar asked me to sit next to him and forced a glass of country liquor down my throat. It all started soon after – a long chain of incidents of which I had no inkling fifteen minutes earlier. There was only one lamp in the room which too was quickly extinguished. My clothes were forcibly removed – those that didn't came out were torn and in just a few moments I was stark naked. I struggled to save myself for as long as I could and then collapsed. The barbarities and the rapes continued even when I had become unconscious".

"No one came forward to save me! Not even Lord Krishna whose Bhajans I had been singing from age five. I should have endured their atrocities the entire night. I, however, was not aware of what was happening to me since I was unconscious.

When I regained consciousness it was already day-break. I was lying stuck in the barbed wire fencing of a field – about one hundred yards away from the Zamindar's house. A woman going for her ablutions just around that time, took pity on me and draped my body in her shawl. The women also passed information to my parents who came to the spot soon enough".

"Kakku wanted me to come to the Zamindar's house seeking a settlement. He wanted me to report to the police only in case the Zamindar was found uncooperative and unhelpful. I was crying all the while. I was also pitying myself. Gradually the state of helplessness inside me got transformed into deep anger – bordering upon madness. Curious crowds had gathered around me, trying to ogle my semi-nakedness. To save myself from those lecherous gazes, I ran into the ravines. My first thought was to kill myself by jumping into Chambal. However, once in the safety of the ravines, I changed my mind. I remembered Ma Kali and vowed revenge. In the ravines I found a few children grazing sheep. They had known me and therefore they decided to help me out by sharing their clothings – a shirt, a turban and a dhoti – with me. I quickly converted the dhoti into a sari, shirt into a blouse and safa into a loose dupatta. I spent two days and two nights hiding in the ravines – no food – no water. Then I chanced into a gang of 'baghis', led by Sultan Singh and Kalla – both Gujjars. They appeared God-sent! They had heard of the rape and atrocities perpetrated upon me, by the Zamindar and his cohorts. Kalla promised me all assistance in the execution of my vow of revenge. Sultan Singh helped me by providing me a place in his gang".

"So commenced the journey of one tender-aged girl, into the ravines – a journey from which no one returns. It has been ten years since and I have remained separated from my family – from my Kakku and from my Amma. I am wandering from one ravine into another. Rifle and bullets have replaced the tanpura and harmonium in my hands. Having endured all this and for so long Chotey Kaptan, how can I think of surrendering, as long as Ram Bharose is alive? How can I surrender and yet be at peace with myself with that 'harami' in one piece. Tell me Chotey Kaptan – Can I?"

Anuj was dumb-founded. He wanted Gudiya to spend herself out fully – to hear from her in her own words, the long story of the misfortunes of a tiny girl – the story of the transformation of a bhajan singer into a dreaded dacoit. He, therefore, maintained discreet silence. And after a brief pause Gudiya started speaking again:

"Bhaiya! I don't like bloodshed – at all! I hate spilling blood. Yet as long as Ram Bharose is alive, I would need a gang – which is active. And this will require me to keep on committing – at least minimum crimes. I respect your IGP's wish and since he wants me not to commit any crime, I will try not to. I will try to ensure that my gang stayed away from committing any major crime".

"And Chotey Kaptan, I will try to stick to July 1 given by you – would try to surrender by that date – along with my entire gang – of course subject to my remaining alive till then. Life of a 'baghi' offers no certainties – living one moment – dead another moment! I however want to live. I do dream of a settled family life like that of Puniya. I have, therefore, decided to confess to all my crimes in the first hearing itself. I cannot think of wasting another 10-12 years fighting cases in courts. I am around 25 now. Even if I got 20-25 years in jail, I would be 55-60 by the time I got out. At that age too I can acquire a life partner – have a house, bring up a family. But Bhaiya, there is a chance that court may award me death sentence. In that case what can I say – Jai Shri Ram! On the day of my execution I would pray that I was not re-born into a village which has Zamindars – rapist Zamindars – other rapists like Jaswanta and Ram Bharose!"

Anuj, for the first time, found Gudiya emotionally charged – tense. She was noticeably running out of breath and had therefore put a pause to speaking. Two-three minutes went by – in total silence. Anuj too sat quiet. He was not wanting to break Gudiya's chain of thoughts. Regaining her breath, Gudiya started speaking again:

"Chotey Kaptan, please arrange my surrender in front of the Chief Minister. Also please keep everything secret till the actual date of surrender. If the information got leaked out – prematurely, anyone from my community, or any of the 'baghis' or even Ram Bharose would get me murdered. Understand?"

Silence ensued. Gudiya had said all that she wanted to say. She suddenly got up from her chair with a jerk, pulled up her burqa sleeve to have a look at her watch. It was past ten p.m. She was worried.

"Bhaiya, I am terribly delayed. Do not know what got me so involved with my past – so useless now – so irretrievable. May be that for the first time in my life I found a brother before whom I could unburden myself. Bhaiya, skipping meals does not hurt me. In ravines, we are used to not getting meals at all – or getting meals at irregular intervals. But not getting dinner on time would be making you miserable. I can't serve you anything. This house has no arrangements – not even sugar or milk. So I would go now. If I remained alive, I'll meet you again. I will surely surrender – will bid good bye to this life of crime – will laugh with friends and well-wishers. I'll pray to God that he gave me a brother like you, in my next birth – to guide and protect me from the evil ways of the world".

"And please Chotey Kaptan, keep the news of my surrender secret, or else you might be required to see your sister's dead body".

Anuj noticed that Gudiya has already got up – had while talking collected herself inside her burqa and pulled the burqa cape over her face. She was ready to leave. As she passed in front of Anuj, she stopped for a few seconds, bent her head low in front of Anuj in a gesture of submission, and without looking back she walked away. The back door opened slightly as she pulled one shutter towards her while pressing on to the other. And within seconds Gudiya had vanished into the darkness of the night.

April 15, 1959: Twenty days went by – eventlessly. Police started receiving information about Gudiya's movements in Chambal ravines along the borders of Bhind and Morena district. Gudiya had kept her promise and had not committed any violent incident. April 15 was Anuj's birthday and he had invited some friends and colleagues from Bhind and neighbouring districts for a simple dinner at his home. In pursuance of this invitation, two senior police officers from Morena district had also arrived in the morning for joining the dinner. These officers informed Anuj, that they had seen a news item in the local press, quoting a reliable source saying that Gudiya gang was going to surrender in front of the Chief Minister by July 1. In confirmation, they produced a copy of the newspaper 'Agnibaan' – a cheap, local, yellow press hand out – not bigger than the size of a leaflet, published from Morena. The news item was brief. It stated that according to a very reliable source, the Gudiya gang has decided to surrender before the Chief Minister in Bhopal on July 1 and that the Chief Minister has agreed to accept the surrender.

Such a brief news item, that too in a flimsy news paper with circulation of not more than 50 copies was enough to rattle Anuj and shatter his peace of mind. For him the fun of the party was over. He started praying that may this news item never reach Gudiya – also Gudiya's enemies hands. After all, that was the only request that Gudiya had made – "Chotey Kaptan, please keep the news of my surrender absolutely secret or else my life will be in serious jeopardy". What can Anuj do now? Who leaked the information and why? This information was known only to the Chief Minister and his office. But politicians are generally self-seekers, insensitive to other's troubles. By no stretch of imagination, the Chief Minister would have leaked it out. Some minion in his office could have done it? But why? The information was only known to the Chief Minister and perhaps one of his personal staff.

Who would have played this mischief – or what? Why? Anuj remained rattled, restless and worried.

The dinner got over in due time and Anuj decided to go to bed. His mind, however, remained engrossed and agitated with the 'why' and 'how' of this 'leak' – as also the threat that it now posed to Gudiya's life.

April turned into May. Nothing happened. No state newspaper or even local newspaper picked up the information about Gudiya's impending surrender. Anuj was lulled into believing that the 'leak' is as good as dead, a forgotten episode with no one having read it – neither Gudiya, nor her enemies.

The wheels of destiny however were churning – slowly, unnoticeably, mercilessly, ruthlessly – squashing dreams and fond hopes!

May 5, 1959: It was past eight in the evening. Anuj was planning to sit down for an early dinner when he heard a desperate knock at his door. On loosening the door slightly he found the 'Sahukar' from Gormi standing outside, shivering unusually, on a very hot summer day.

"Maharaj, Gudiya has sent this letter. I am ill – down with very high fever. I can't wait. I'll leave straightaway".

Sahukar left as quickly as he had come. Anuj got no opportunity to either stop him, or to make him wait, or to help him with some medicine.

Closing the door behind him, Anuj entered his room, switched on the tube light and started reading the letter.

"Chotey Kaptan – something really terrible has happened. News of my surrender has got published in a local newspaper. You might have read it too? My life now is in real danger! Whom should I blame – my fate. How will I surrender now? I could have surrendered only if I remained alive till July 1? Now I have grave doubts! Your unlucky sister – Gudiya".

Anuj folded the letter and pushed it inside his daily diary lying on a table nearby. Apparently, the Government has goofed up on its promise of total secrecy. Gudiya however exhibits no rancour, either against the Government or him. She complains against no one – only against her fate. Such a small women – such a vicious casualty of evil that men do – of sports that Gods play!

Tears started rolling down Anuj's cheeks!

* * * * *

The Tragic Encounter

<u>*May 9, 1959 – 6 A.M.*</u>

Anuj was sleeping when the noise of a motor bike outside his door woke him up. It was the police despatch rider who had come to deliver a wireless message. Anuj opened the envelope hurriedly and went through its contents.

"Previous night, Gudiya gang entered a small village in Khipona area and beat up several boys and girls belonging to the Lodhi community. The gang not only looted money from the households but also abducted two Lodhi children aged 3 and 7. A ransom of 3 lakhs per child has been demanded for their release. The gang was in the village for about an hour and is reported to have moved towards Ater police station after the commission of crime. Eight Lodhi youth who received minor injuries and two who received grievous injuries have since been moved to Ater Civil Hospital. An inspector from police station Ater has arrived on the spot and has taken over investigation. EOM (End of the message)."

The contents of the message were enough to rattle Anuj. "So Gudiya didn't keep her promise too...like the State Government" muttered Anuj to himself.

In 10 minutes Anuj was off for the place of occurrence and it was ten in the morning when he arrived there. The police inspector on the spot has already done a lot of spade work including registration of an offence, seizure of incriminating evidence from the spot and examination of the eye witnesses. He informed Anuj that at the time of offence the gang was not led by Gudiya but by her number two – dacoit Sikandara. The villagers confirmed that the gang was that of Gudiya, but she was not present at the time of commission of offence. The villagers went on to add that Sikandara's parents were murdered some years back by a Lodhi gang led by D-7 Rampala and that the offence was then instigated by the local Lodhi villagers, who wanted to grab 30 acres of land owned by Sikandara's parents. The inspector went on to add that Sikandara had jumped into the ravines a year earlier, only to avenge the death of his parents and that he was pressurising Gudiya into helping him settle scores with the Lodhis. The inspector had also been informed by the villagers that the two children were not going to be released – were going to be murdered – payment or non-payment of ransom notwithstanding. Villagers were also of the opinion that Sikandara did commit this crime in a hurry – in Gudiya's absence – since rumours were afloat that Gudiya was planning to surrender and since if that happened, Sikandara might be required to wait – God knows for how long, for revenge.

It was clear from the statements of eyewitnesses that Gudiya was not a party to this crime and that this crime was committed by just three dacoits from her gang. Was it perpetrated without her approval – or did she approve it? If so, then there is one larger question – is her gang splitting? What happens to the surrender then?

Having supervised the investigation and having made arrangements for the protection of the village, Anuj left for Bhind.

May 13, 1959: Anuj received one more wireless message from police station Ater informing him of the recovery of two dead bodies – of the children kidnapped by Gudiya gang from

Khipona village a few days ago – worst fears coming true. The bodies were recovered from a field just outside the village. The message went on to add that according to the medical report the two children were strangulated to death.

Anuj left once again for Khipona and found the inspector already at the P.O. (place of occurrence). Right from the day of crime the villagers believed that the children were not going to be released – that they were going to be murdered to avenge the death of Sikandara's parents. All the same many villagers did try to negotiate their release – on payment of ransom – hoping against hope that the lives of the children would be spared. Rumours were afloat that the Lodhis of Khipona have already requisitioned D-7 Rampala Lodha's help – in negotiating ransom and in getting the kidnapped children, released. Villagers believed that the intervention of a gang of the stature of D-7, might result in saving the lives of the two innocent children. Outcome, however, belied expectations.

Having given appropriate directions relating to on the spot investigation, raids on suspected hideouts and ambushes on escape routes, Anuj returned to police station Ater and convened a quick meting of the concerned officers.

Anuj was angry with Gudiya for having gone back on her assurance. Officers present in the meeting felt that D-7 Rampala was going to visit Khipona area soon seeking revenge against Sikandara – the two Lodhi children having been murdered in contemptuous disregard of D-7's warnings. It was generally believed that D-7 might not succeed in laying his hands upon Sikandara. Therefore, he would go about murdering as many of Sikandara's close relatives as he could lay his hands upon. As an instant measure therefore, Anuj created two special task forces from out of the existing P. Stn strength – one for keeping an eye on the movements of D-7 within Kali Ahroli-Chomoh area and another for keeping a watch on the activities of the harbourers in the ravines on Ater-Khipona-Pabai axis. The task forces were to keep strict watch upon the movements of D-7 and send daily situation reports (DSR's) to the headquarters.

"We have to finish this game of killings – early", ordered Anuj. Meeting dispersed and Anuj returned to Bhind via Porsa and Gormi.

May 27, 1959: One of the DSR's received by Anuj in the morning made a mention of D-7 (Rampala) having been seen in the ravines of Pabai on May 25. Next day, the DSR from Ater Police Station mentioned of both D-3 and D-7 having been seen within Ater Police Station area. The DSR went on to add that D-7 is reported to have met D-3 (Gudiya) in the ravines of Ater and has threatened her, in the presence of several villagers, to produce within 24 hours – Sikandara and all other dacoits involved in the kidnapping and murder of the two innocent Lodhi children of Khipona. He has also threatened Gudiya that if she failed in producing Sikandara and all his accomplices within 24 hours – he (D-7) would be compelled to trace, chase and kill Sikandara and his colleagues first – Gudiya thereafter – and all her remaining gang members latter.

"Take this as last warning from us," thundered D-7. "We are not bluffing you. That is why we have brought these villagers here to remain a witness to the fact that we warned you in good time".

The DSR went on to add that Gudiya did try hard to explain the situation to D-7 – also her difficulties. She was however summarily overruled by D-7. On intervention by villagers, D-7 hesitatingly agreed to allow Gudiya to have her say. Gudiya added that Sikandara accompanied by three other dacoits had been missing from her gang for over a fortnight and therefore she was in no position to present him before

D-7, as ordered, and that D-7 was at liberty to locate the three of them and cut them into pieces, if he so liked.

Gudiya's explanation enraged D-7 further. Boiling with rage, he showered Gudiya with the filthiest of abuses and then said, "Don't act innocent – like Sati Savitri....you bitch! You 'chinal'. If you have been in the ravines for 10 years, we also have been here for 20 years. Dacoits don't desert gangs just like that – just like you describe. Such 'haramis' – (bastards) get killed within 24 hours. Whom are you trying to fool? You are the one who connived with Sikandara in Khipona incident – got Lodhi children murderd. Now you are giving shelter to Sikandara and his 'badmashs' (scoundrels) – trying to save their skin by telling lies. Pay heed to what I say....or else you too would not survive beyond a week. I am a very old 'papi' (sinner). I am a very old harami! I can see through you. Now go you bitch – go sing and dance... and f..k off".

Contents of the DSR alarmed Anuj. Apparently, the person who had passed on such detailed information to the police should have been a trusted man of D-7 and should have given this information only on his directions. Such exchanges between dacoits are common. But they invariably remain secret. No one, not even the most trusted gang member remains privy to such exchanges. Why such secret information is therefore being leaked out to the police? What can be the motive?

Anuj had no answers to these questions. He therefore decided to visit Ater for ascertaining the goings on, personally. In the meanwhile, another wireless message arrived from Ater announcing that while D-7 (Rampala) and D-3 (Gudiya) were busy in the above discussions one dacoit from D-7's gang, forced his entry into the house of a teacher in one of the nearby villages and tried to rape the teacher's wife. The teacher who himself is a Lodhi, had earlier been a very trusted harbourer of D-7. The message went on to add that the teacher's return to his house was unexpected and hearing his wife's cries he tried to grapple with the dacoit, who finally managed to escape. The DSR added that the above incident has however not been corroborated by any independent sources – even by the teacher himself. Anuj paid no attention to the second part of information and that is how destiny moved one more notch towards denouement.

If the information about the attempted rape upon the wife of the teacher had been properly evaluated – and in good time, the entire chain of events that followed could perhaps have been reversed. But in dacoity area officers generally remain overwhelmed with information and events – round the clock and such insignificant looking yet vital signals do sometimes get ignored. That is what happened to the most vital content of the DSR and the destiny took one further turn towards tragedy!

Anuj spent just half a day in Ater. The local officers confirmed to him the presence of both D-3 and D-7 in Ater area. They also confirmed the contents of the meeting between the two gangs. It was also confirmed that Sikandara has not been seen with Gudiya recently – that he was hiding somewhere on his own, but in Ater area only. What baffled everyone was that a one time trusted harbourer – the teacher – a Lodhi and a confident of D-7, did visit Ater police station of his own accord and did convey the details of the D-7 + D-3 meeting. He also tried to convince that he knew the hiding place of D-7 (Rampala) very well, and if the police promised a sumptuous reward, he was ready to guide the raiding parties to the hideout and get Rampala's gang liquidated, in its entirety, as a means of avenging the molestation and attempted rape of his wife, by one of D-7's gang members. In a society badly riven on caste lines such information is generally not forthcoming. No one ever volunteers information about the movements etc. of gang members belonging to ones own caste. Anuj struggled hard trying to understand the 'why' of the information catered by the teacher', but failed. He therefore gave up. Nothing else remained to be done. He therefore returned to Bhind.

The night between May 28-29, 1959

Anuj was fast asleep in his house when someone started banging his door – loudly. With loaded revolver in hand he relaxed one of the two shutters and found a rather small man, 35-40 years, standing outside his door.

"Maharaj, I am the teacher from Akon. It was my wife who was molested by one dacoit from Rampala's gang! I have come to give you some information".

"Come in", directed Anuj, opening the door fully.

"Maharaj, you would have known by now that day before, a member of Rampala's gang molested and attempted to rape my wife. The place where Rampala is hiding these days is very well known to me. If you so desire, I can lead the police party to his hideout – and Maharaj you can finish the entire gang". The teacher appeared to be in a hurry.

"Why should I trust you" queried Anuj.

"Why not Maharaj? Would I not be wanting to avenge the molestation of my wife? My blood had been boiling ever since. I cannot take revenge except with the help of the police. I swear by my son that I would take the police parties to the exact spot".

Information about the presence of D-7 in Ater area was already at the back of Anuj's mind. He thought for a while before pulling out from amongst his papers, the topo-sheet of Ater area. Then with the help of the informer he drew an approximate circle around the area where D-7, according to the informer, was hiding. Then he drew another – yet bigger circle around the first circle covering roughly an area 3 km in radius. The operational plan of the raid had already started taking shape in his mind.

"Master ji, taking advantage of the darkness, you can now return to your village. I'll speak to the DIGP before launching a raid. If there is going to be a raid, you would come to know sitting in your own village. In that case you should meet me again – tomorrow might – around 11 p.m. Don't wake me up later than eleven. Arrive punctually. Understand"?

"Sir, I can't return to my village right now. The night is so dark. I'll spend the night in Bhind itself in the house of one blacksmith from my village. Maharaj, can I leave now"?

'OK', replied Anuj and as the teacher was out some distance he closed his doors.

Anuj wanted to have another 2-3 hours sleep. But he was too agitated. He decided to prepare some black coffee and as he sat sipping it, the entire chain of events, including the information furnished by the teacher rolled past his mind. It was good information alright – but it came from a person whose credentials remained unverified. All the same no harm in taking a chance – thought Anuj.

It was getting to be four in the morning. Anuj, decided to give up the idea of going back to sleep. He entered the bathroom and took a leisurely shower. As he came out he finished his puja and then entered the kitchen for cooking some breakfast – two toasts, one poached egg, a fistful of cornflakes with milk and another cup of black coffee. Finishing his breakfast, he put on his uniform. By 5 a.m. he was out of Bhind.

May 29, 1959: Anuj reached Gwalior around 7 a.m. and went straight to the 2nd Battalion Police Mess, from there he rang up the DIGP seeking his permission for an urgent meeting. The DIGP asked him to join him over breakfast – in half an hour's time. The mess orderly had in between, brought a cup of tea. Anuj found it God-sent. He drank it – unmindfully revolving the operational plan in his mind.

Half an hour and he was ready to leave for the DIG's residence which was located close by. In the bungalow, he found the DIGP already in his uniform – ready for the day. The two made a bee-line for the dining table where the breakfast had already been served. Over the breakfast table Anuj, in few selected words, conveyed the gist of the information catered by the teacher. The DIGP appeared satisfied. He however asked Anuj whether he was willing to trust the teacher.

"Sir, it depends on – if we are ready to believe the story of his wife's molestation by a dacoit from Rampala's gang – then yes. If that story is considered untrustworthy than the rest of the information too should become doubtful", answered Anuj.

The DIGP mulled the information in his mind. Then started speaking:

"From the radio messages that I have been receiving from Police Station Ater, it appears that both D-7 and D-3 are present in Ater area. A police raid, therefore, appears called for. 'Agar D-7 ko maar bhee nahin sake to bhee insdad-e-jurm to ho jayegee.' (Even if we did not get D-7, the police movement in that area will result in preventing commission of any serious crime by either of the gangs..)

"Right sir, police raid seems to be in order".

"Anuj, do you need any assistance from me", asked the DIGP.

"Sir, we need to encircle a large area. We would, therefore, need extra force – some officers for leading columns and also sir, your personal guidance in the encirclement plan. Your advise based on your long experience in dealing with the dacoit gangs and your blessings both are essential".

Anuj's words pleased the DIG – 'young officer, so what? Doesn't want to proceed without my guidance. Education in itself is not everything. Experience too is one great asset'. Lost in such thoughts the DIGP twirled his moustache twice and then spreading the topo-sheet on the table and covering the area between Chambal and Ater with his right palm, he proudly announced, 'rok-party one' (stop-party or ambush party one). Then covering the area between Kali-Ahroli and Chambal river with his left palm he ordered, 'rok-party two' (stop-party or ambush party two). Then he picked up a ruler from his table and putting it across between Kali-Ahroli and Ater he announced 'rok-party three' – also 'thonk party (attack parties) one and two'. Having made these suggestions, he became quiet – rather abruptly.

The D.I.G. was an ex-army officer and therefore preparing operational plans came to him as naturally as organising a 'beat' for a wild animal.

Anuj was noting down DIG's instructions – obediently.

'Sir, your operational plan would require at least 350 O.R's (other ranks), 20 JCO's and six senior officers'.

'Don't worry. I am getting in touch straightaway with the SPs of Bhind and Morena as also the SAF (Special Armed Force) Commandants. I would get you the required numbers. Operation Launch – 1330 hrs. – okay. Any doubts – any questions?...No! Then, good luck'.

Anuj said, 'thank you, sir' and straightaway got busy in sending wireless messages conveying DIG's instructions.

The DIGP spent another half-an-hour telephoning. By the time he finished, the total force requirement for the raid has been marshalled. When SPs Bhind and Morena came to know that the D.I.G.P. was organising this raid, they felt involved and therefore threw their strength and heart into it. Both promised to the DIGP that they would be reaching Kali-Ahroli, accompanied by the required force, by 1300 hrs. DSP Radio Ram Singh, promised to equip the 'rok' (stop) and 'thonk' (attack) parties with one wireless set each – for on the spot communication. DIGP sent radio messages confirming that he will be in Kali-Ahroli by 1315 hrs. and would be in-charge of the 'command post'.

In a nutshell, the arrangements were elaborate and grand and given the hype – as also the DIGPs personal involvement in the raid, everyone started believing that D-7 Rampala was as good as dead. Everyone became desirous of joining the raid. No one wanted to be left behind in police stations/SAF posts even for essential security duties. Everyone started looking forward to sumptuous rewards and promotions.

It had rained heavily for over half an hour in the operational area, the previous night. The weather therefore had become quite 'bearable'.

Anuj left for Ater straightaway from Gwalior arriving there by about twelve in the afternoon. The DIGP arrived in Kali-Ahroli exactly at 1315 hrs. and SP, Morena reached Udotgarh slightly before 1300 hrs All wireless sets came to life simultaneously at 1330 hrs.

After preliminary exchange of information about presence of senior officers with the parties the operational plan got going.

1331 hrs. — all parties started moving towards their target areas – in operational formation.

1400 hrs. — all 'rok' and 'thonk' parties got in position – ready to attack.

The DIGP was pleased with the precision of his planning. He twirled his moustache twice in a gesture of satisfaction.

1401 hrs. — DIGP manning the 'command post' came on air – on his wireless set – and ordered all 'rok' parties to watch front and fire to kill if the enemy got in sight. 'Thonk' parties commenced search of the ravines for destruction of the enemy.

SP, Morena and Anuj were in-charge of the two 'rok' (stop) parties. Sitting in ambush, they started monitoring closely, the movement of the two 'thonk' (attack) parties – towards the killing area.

It was getting to be 16:30 hrs. The two 'thonk' parties had searched every nook and corner of the ravines without getting in sight of a single dacoit. High hope had turned into high disappointment.

The DIGP, having felt that the raid was proving infructuous left for Gwalior, handing over the charge of his command post to the SAF Commandant Kali-Ahroli. At 5 p.m. the command post relayed the final order directing the two 'thonk' parties to recheck the target area and then close the raid. All officers and other ranks were terribly disappointed with the outcome. Various columns soon received orders to close force at pre-determined locations and to return to camps. The entire force was back in their barracks by 7 p.m.

Anuj had not slept properly the night before. Tired and exhausted with almost 24 hours of non-stop work, he started boiling with rage at the informer.

It was pitch dark when his jeep came to a stop outside his house in Bhind. In the glow of the headlights he caught the glimpse of a figure crouching in front of his door. He was ready to fire when he heard the figure screaming!

'Chotey kaptan – Chotey kaptan! please don't fire. I am the 'Sahukar' from Gormi. I have a letter for you from Gudiya'.

Anuj snatched the letter from the Sahukars' hand and started reading it standing in front of the jeep headlights.

"Chotey Kaptan forgive me! I could not keep my words. On the day the news of my impending surrender appeared in the newspaper, my number two in the gang deserted with two others, and their weapons. I did try very hard to prevent their desertion but failed. I have now decided to surrender on June 5th itself along with the leftover of my gang comprising seven baghis. Please arrange my surrender at Ater Police Station itself – moving outside appears to have become so hazardous.

Rampala has sent word, threatening that he is arriving in Ater Police Station area shortly – to liquidate me.

Where do I hide – till June 5th – Chotey Kaptan? Your sister – Gudiya."

The Sahukar added that Gudiya has asked him to bring a reply to her letter.

Anuj pulled out a pen from his pocket and without wasting another second, started scribbling on a piece of paper.

"Please enter Ater area which is under our total control. I shall be arranging your surrender in Bhind – not Ater – on June 5. I'll let you know more after discussing your request with the DIGP — Anuj'."

–With the letter safe in his pocket – the Sahukar left immediately for Gormi.

* * * * *

__*Night between May 29-30:*__ Anuj was fast asleep when the teacher from Akon knocked angrily at his door. Anuj checked his watch and found that it was well past midnight. He woke up, alarmed.

'He thought to himself – should be that damned teacher. I am going to settle accounts with him – today itself. Damned liar!'

Loaded revolver in hand, he slackened the door slightly and peeping outside he saw the teacher. Without wasting a minute he thundered:

'So you are here again – you bastard'.

The .38 Webly and Scot in Anuj's hand was enough to knock the hell out of the teacher. His anger evaporated instantly. He was down on his knees pleading.

"Sir, listen to me please – Chotey Kaptan! If I was cheating then why would I come back to you – again?"

The awestruck, flushed face of the teacher filled Anuj's heart with compassion. Would he have walked thirty miles to Bhind – in the night – if he was guilty?

"Well, come on now. What explanation do you have for your information going wrong?"

"Maharaj...you are unnecessarily getting angry with me".

"Arre, you bastard...you now come quick with what you have to say. Is it something worth listening to? The DIGP is so angry with you that he will shoot you at sight. You made 400 policemen sweat out one entire day – in a wild goose chase!"

"Maharaj, at least listen to me? You can then get a canon fired at me if you were not convinced", pleaded the teacher.

Anuj nodded and gave him the go ahead signal. The teacher started going into great details explaining why the raid failed. He added that D-7 is still in Dau Bharak and if the encirclement was slightly enlarged, the raid would be succeeful.

He started pleading once again: "Sir my wife was molested – nearly raped. Place her in your sister's position. Won't your blood be boiling with rage? – Maharaj, Rampala is a Lodhi, like me. Yet my desire for revenge is so consuming that I have stopped taking him to be a Lodhi. I consider him to be a vermin – a guttersnipe – a harami – a behen c...d, a criminal – a rapist. If the police refused to help me then where would I go? Rampala is a dacoit and his gang is armed to the teeth. What am I against him? He knows that! Now you are my only saviour. You are known in the ravines as one who has always helped people in distress. Please help me too! Please – Chotey Kaptan!!

Anuj was feeling terribly sleepy. He therefore wanted to cut the conversation short.

"You mean you want the police to raid Dau-Bharak again?"

The teacher nodded in affirmation.

"Ok. you go now. I would be talking to the DIGP in the morning and if he agreed, I'll organise a second raid. If the second raid too failed, then in your own interest don't show your face again. If you did, I would get the hell knocked out of your skull. Understand?"

"Yes Maharaj – and very well too!"

The teacher walked out of Anuj's house mumbling a few words. Anuj, however, was not interested in knowing, what he said. He checked up with his watch. It was well past midnight. 'Getting up tomorrow morning I will reassess the information.' And so mumbling he went to sleep.

* * * * *

May 30, 1959: The nocturnal visit of the teacher notwithstanding, Anuj slept well and peacefully too. As he got up in the morning he was calm and in control of himself. He mentally recalled his conversation with the teacher and mulled it over. It might have taken him ten minutes or so, but he came to the conclusion that the teacher was not fabricating. However, since the information catered by him had gone wrong once there was need for extra caution before committing the force to a second raid.

As he was moving towards the breakfast table he heard the despatch rider (DR) at his door. The DR delivered an entire bunch of radio messages received by the control room during the night. He decided to go through them prior to sitting down for his breakfast. Bulk of the messages were routine. There was however one from police station Ater catering information identical to the one catered to by the teacher. Gist of the message was:

'The police encirclement fell slightly short. Gang was about 100 metres outside the encirclement. It stayed put there itself – all the time watching the activities of the police. No sooner the police force withdrew, it returned to Dau-Bharak and is reported to be still there. Gudiya gang too has been noticed in the Dau-Bharak area. D-7 Rampala has ordered Gudiya to 'present' herself before him – with her entire gang and answer the killings of two innocent Lodhi children in Khipona, by Sikandara.'

As a postscript, the inspector in-charge of Ater P. Stn. added, that since the dacoits believed that the police never raided the same ravine twice – within 24 hours – they might be taking Dau-Bharak to be the safest place, for the next 2-3 days. He also informed of having received another report suggesting that D-7 has already left Ater police station area and Gudiya gang has arrived in Dau-Bharak the previous night – though no other source was ready to confirm this information.

Finishing his breakfast, Anuj rang up the DIGP and updated him with the contents of his meeting with the teacher. The DIGP was obviously unhappy.

"Anuj, you seem to trust just each and everyone. Be cautious in choosing your informers", warned the DIGP.

Anuj however went ahead seeking DIGP's permission for launching another raid on D-7 in Dau-Bharak area – that very afternoon – on the strength of the information catered by the teacher.

The DIGP expressed no disagreement. On the contrary, he conveyed his good wishes to Anuj.

Anuj had hardly any time at hand. The raid therefore needed to be organised in a hurry. Anuj rang up personally all units which could help him with force. With great difficulty, he managed to collect about 90 men. No officer was willing to join the raid. Their argument was that Dau-Bharak had been extensively searched only yesterday – by over 400 men. If such a big operation could yield nothing, what will 90 men produce – rats or cats?

Anuj however was not disheartened. His heart was riveted on to a low-level operation with very small columns. He thought that may be this would ensure greater secrecy and greater element of surprise – greater chances of success. He therefore decided to introduce 90 men in Dau-Bharak – secretly, quietly – under cover of low gullys.

It was getting 12 in the afternoon and Anuj had no time to loose. He therefore put the entire force in two 3-ton police trucks and left for Ater police station – unaccompanied by any other senior officer and without even one pair of wireless sets for inter-communication between columns.

Arriving in Ater police station, he divided the entire strength into 3 parties – 40 men forming the 'search' or 'raid' party – to be launched from Udotgarh (Morena district) flank. For the purpose of setting up 'stops' and laying ambushes he decided to use the remaining 50 brought from Bhind and another 30 provided by Ater police station. These 80 were to be used as 'stops', all the way from river Chambal to Kali-Ahroli with each stop being manned by one policeman each instead of the normal two. The decision was fraught with risks, but Anuj had no choice. He has decided to head straight for Dau-Bharak at 2 p.m., leading a party of 10 – all armed with stens and grenades. All 'stops' were therefore ordered to be in position before 2 p.m.

At exactly 2 p.m. Anuj stretched his 10 men in a straight line and started leap-frogging towards Dau-Bharak – arriving there in one hour. No dacoits were there and therefore there was no opposition. However, in Dau-Bharak the raiding parties found cooked food for 30-40 persons. Obviously, the dacoits were somewhere close by but had slipped out getting information of the police movement.

Food for 40 persons? Was there going to be a big dacoit's get-together in Dau-Bharak?

Leaving a party of 30 policemen for guarding the spot, Anuj kept an pressing till he established physical contact with the nearest 'rok' or ambush party. At this juncture the raid was ordered 'closed'. Police vehicles were summoned inside the ravines for picking up police parties. Ater police station was directed to confiscate the cooked food and other material left behind by the dacoits on the spot. Police station staff returned to Ater and Anuj to Bhind.

On return journey Anuj handed over the wheel to his driver. He sat in his seat –eyes closed – all the way to Bhind. No one could make out what was going on in his mind. It was almost pitch dark when he reached Bhind.

He ordered his driver to take him straight to the 4th SAF Bn. headquarters located near his bungalow. He went straight into the Commandants' residence and when he returned to the jeep he had two Gorkha jawans accompanying him, both armed with stens. Arriving home, he directed the jawans to hide themselves in one of his two rooms. He thereafter sat down to a light dinner and then went to sleep.

* * * * *

Night between May 30-31: It was getting to be three in the morning. The wind outside had become really chilly. Anuj was woken up once again by a knock at his door. He knew that it had to be the teacher. Positioning the two Gorkhas behind the main door, he slackened the shutters a bit – just enough to allow the teacher to get in. Then in one motion he threw the teacher on the ground, face down, and pulling his two arms backwards – applied the handcuffs. This unprecedented welcome startled the teacher but didn't quite rattle him. It should have been 5-10 seconds when he started speaking:

"Maharaj, what is this? The police fails to capture the dacoits and the 'mukhbir' (informer) gets punished. Rampala with his entire gang was in Dau-Bharak – all along. The villagers had prepared a feast for his gang. Rampala was certain that the police will not return to the same ravine twice – on two successive days. Gudiya was also to reach there the same evening – trying to work out a settlement with Rampala. Now some villagers would have come to know of the police movement in the vicinity, and informed the gang. I don't understand Maharaj as to how you set your ambushes. The entire gang managed to slip through your cordon.'

Anuj allowed the teacher to continue talking. He was aware that the scarcity of manpower had forced him to put stops too far apart which might have made it possible for the gang to slip through – unnoticed.

"Maharaj I was present in a village – just half a mile from Dau-Bharak. Immediately after your raid, the gangs returned to Dau-Bharak again. Both the gangs are there now – Rampala and Gudiya.

The villagers have convinced the gangs that the police has searched these ravines twice on two successive days and they would not return again. Maharaj, that is why I am here. Last night while coming to Bhind, I passed quite close to Dau-Bharak and heard lot of noises coming from there – even sounds of gun-shots and screams. Yes, I heard sound of gunfire too – about 8-10 rounds having been fired in Dao-Bharak. God alone knows, what was happening."

Anuj scolded the teacher and asked him, 'So, daddu (big brother) – now tell me clearly – as to what do you actually want?'

'Arre, Maharaj. I just want that you organise a raid again and kill Rampala. Let me have my revenge and reward.

Anuj feigned a tantrum. "Ok. I will organise a raid, but only on one condition that you accompany me and lead the raiding parties to Dau-Bharak – dressed as a dacoit. You would be required to take us to our destination i.e. Dau-Bharak by using the secret footpaths – used by the dacoits. And if I get no dacoits there, I'll kill you instead – dressed in dacoits costume. Do you agree? Do you? Speak."

"Maharaj – this is very unfair – a sure recipe for my murder". Then after a long pause.

"Ok, I agree. But I have three pre-conditions. Firstly, instead of the dacoits uniform, I would put on police uniform. Secondly, I insist on keeping my face covered all the while so that my identity is not revealed – not even to your policemen.

And thirdly, no sooner the encounter is over you would get me dropped at a lonely spot – in your police vehicle, where I could change into my normal clothing and disappear. I promise to come back to you after a month – may be two months – after I started feeling safe".

"Deal daddu (elder brother) deal! In totality!" announced Anuj.

* * * * *

<u>*May 31, 1959:*</u> It was not yet first light and the force was getting ready for a third raid on Dau-Bharak – in as many days. Anuj rang up SP Morena who agreed to contribute 120 policemen – two Dy. Superintendents of Police included. Anuj collected another 90 policemen from within his own units and another 90 from SP's task force. Three Dy. SPs from within Bhind district also agreed to join the raid. Police station Ater agreed to spare 20 policemen from its strength. Anuj requested his close friend Dy. SP, Madho Singh to head one of the 'thonk' (attack) parties. Madho Singh agreed. Dy. SP (Radio) – Ram Singh agreed to despatch five wireless sets alongwith operators – for maintaining inter-party communication and synchronising the movements of various parties. Informer wanted impregnable encirclement of the 'target area'. Anuj agreed. Informer, as a part of attack tactics also wanted the encirclement to press inwards so that after sometime the 'thonk' parties could launch an attack on the target area from Kali-Ahroli side. Anuj suggested continuous assessment of the raid by him – importantly prior to the launch of the "thonk party" into attack on the target area. This was mutually agreed. Anuj had decided to keep the informer under his control and within talking distance from him – throughout the raid.

It was getting to be 11.30 AM. Anuj rang up his DIGP in Gwalior informing him of the raid and seeking his participation – for on the spot guidance. The DIGP thanked Anuj for keeping him informed but politely declined his request. He saw no wisdom in raiding the same target area successively, on three days. He however, was not willing to curb the enthusiasm of a young officer – so didn't say 'no' to the raid.

"Best of luck to you, Anuj. I do not think much of your informer. He seems to be drawing circles around you. All the same – all the best to you Anuj". And the telephone line went dead.

The D-time (departure time) for the raid was 12 noon. Anuj was about to get into his vehicle when his office phone started ringing. It was the IGP from Bhopal.

"What is going on in your charge, Anuj?" The IGP appeared visibly irritated. Apparently, the DIGP had rung him up some minutes back and apprised him of the 'madness' that seems to have overtaken Anuj.

"Sir, today the informer himself is leading us to the 'quarry'. I have decided to try him, for one last time."

"But Anuj, you have already wasted two days of the force, raiding the same area – on information of the same person? Are you not aware that none from amongst the senior police officers are ready to support your action?"

"Yes, Sir ... but one last chance, Sir – please."

"Okay. Take care Anuj. Best of Luck".

* * * * *

All reservations and doubts notwithstanding, Anuj left for the designated area slightly after, 1200 hrs accompanied by the assembled force, the communication equipment and the informer dressed as a police constable. Short of 1300 hrs, when Kali-Ahroli was about a kilometre away, the force was ordered to de-bus. Then hiding the vehicles behind trees and bushes and under camouflage nets, the force was asked to 'form up' and proceed to their designated areas on foot – in tactical formation. All wireless sets were ordered to observe 'listening watch' and 'radio silence'.

One column from Udotgarh and another from Ater, started the march at about the same time. The first radio contact was scheduled at 1430 hrs – earlier only if the sound of firing was heard in the designated area. Just one jawan whose uniform had been given to the informer had stayed behind at Anuj's residence in Bhind.

* * * * *

May 31, 1959 – afternoon: The network of intimidating ravines hewn by river Chambal is spread in the designated area (DA), between police stations, Ater of Bhind and Udotgarh of Morena districts. Kali-Ahroli is situated nearly in the centre of these two extremes. One, specially threatening stretch of this network, lies between Kali-Ahroli and Akon-ki-Madiyan to Pilua Danda to Baraiya Khar – a favourite dacoit trail. Ravines in this stretch are daunting, going up and down – 100 to 150 feet. In the North flows river Chambal – placid and peaceful – water span about 200 metres – not fordable. If one was lucky one could see several alligators floating like upturned boats in the river. Their movement agitates the water for a little while, but the river regains its composure soon after. The river, by and large, is peaceful at this time of the year. Across the river lies Uttar Pradesh and the famous Khera village of Agra district, also known as Khera Mansingh – Dau's birth place. Right opposite is situated village Chomoh of Bhind district. The river bank on the UP side is sandy and on any given day one can see 10 to 15 alligators lazing there.

It was getting to be 2 PM. Scorching sun had made the ravines stifling and oppressive. It was a clear day – not a patch of cloud in the sky – with flaming hot winds (loo) blowing at about 40 to 50 miles an hour. All around it was sizzling hot with temperatures in the open hovering around 47°-49°. The day was so scorching that if any bird dared to come out of its perch it would instantaneously die. The entire network of barren, uneven ravines was experiencing blistering heat.

However, in this blistering searing heat and in the midst of such intimidating landscape one could hear – sometimes vaguely – sometimes precisely – strains of music, floating in the air. What could be the source – thought Anuj! A transistor radio – he surmised, broadcasting 'Aap Ki Farmaish' from Vividh Bharati – AIR New Delhi – perhaps?

'Tu Ganga Ki Mauj Main Jamuna Ka Dhara, Rahega Milan.....'

('You' a wave of river Ganga, 'I' a current from river Jamuna – we are bound to meet)

The strains of music were generally low – scarcely audible. But whenever there was a sudden gust of wind and the sound waves drifted this side, the music became audible-loud and clear. Has some music-loving ghost taken over these ravines and is trying to entertain itself with music? Impossible. These ravines are haunted by dacoits and one can run into them on any turn. One can only find dacoits in these ravines – not musicians. And if one chanced into them unexpectedly, the face-to-face would be enough to drive the devil out of anyone. Is someone playing a gramophone record. Or is it a transistor radio receiving some radio programme. But transistors have so far remained a luxury of the rich, in places like Delhi and

Bombay. No one has heard of them yet in Madhya Pradesh. Has someone brought a transistor from one of these big cities and is now listening to music – in this scorching heat? But who would be wanting to listen to music in these ravines and in this heat? Is he mad? Or is he just music-crazy? Is he someone who loves music – more than his life?

'Chale Aoji – Chale Ao – Maujon Ka Lekar Sahara...'

(Come, come, riding on the waves)

Suddenly, Anuj heard some disturbance in the western flank. Someone had disturbed the birds in their shelter sending them up in the skies – screaming. The sky which was barren a few minutes earlier was now full of birds. Their twittering could be heard, sometimes clearly, sometimes not so clearly, depending upon the wind speed and direction. A few moments later similar commotion was heard from the eastern flank too – from the direction of Chomho and Ater. And a little later from the direction of Kali-Ahroli. The commotion created by the birds has now become audible enough – strong enough – to wake up a Sadhu from his trance, during meditation.

But who could be playing a transistor in the ravines – thought Anuj? Have they not become aware of the commotion on the two flanks?

The Vividh Bharati channel of the AIR continued playing as usual. Now on someone's farmaish it was playing:

'*O duniya ke rakhwale ... sun dard bhare mere nale*'.

(O protector of the world... listen to my songs of sorrows.)

Who is playing these very sad songs? Whom are they being addressed to?

It should have been just a few minutes when Anuj noticed columns of men clad in Khaki (dacoits or police) advancing in his direction from the two flanks. First column was noticed, about 200 metres away advancing from Udotgarh side and the second one from Ater-Chomho side. All men in Khaki. Can't be dacoits? So many of them. All dacoits in Bhind district – put together, would not make that many. Soon it became clear that they were policemen – in blue berets, rifles in hand. When the intervening distance between the two columns remained just about 250 metres, they came to a sudden halt – took lying positions and froze themselves. Some just took kneeling positions. Some went down on their stomachs and took aim. Whom were they planning to kill?

The transistor continued playing the 'farmaishi' programme:

"Ae mere dil-e-nadan tu gam se na ghabrana

Ek din to samajh legi duniya tera afsana"

(Oh my simple – sorrowful heart, don't let tragedies of life upset you. A day will come when the world will come to realise the tragic story of your life.)

It should have been a couple of minutes when Anuj with the assistance of on-the-spot directions given by the informer, decided to attack the 'target area'. Accompanied by 18 policemen, all armed with stens – primed grenades in hand – two jawans with G.F. (grenade firing) rifles – advanced quietly, totally unnoticed, through one of the several gullies and arrived at a spot about 20-25 metres away from the general area from where the sound of transistor appeared to be emanating. At this point everyone came to a sudden halt and formed up for assault. Anuj went to the informer once again and asked him 'who' and 'where' of the dacoit gang. The informer pointed to yet another gully close by and spoke just one word 'Rampala'! Anuj from behind his men ordered 'fire' and about 15-20 hand grenades plus another 10 rifle grenades landed into the target area. Another hundred rifles, light machineguns and stens, belonging to the two 'stop' parties also started firing – apparently for no reason. Everything appeared like the doom's day – all so noisy that even policemen, in well entrenched positions were unable to hear each other. Senior officers wanted to order cease-fire in a bid to control the situation in the field area. But they were unable to even raise their heads due to fear of getting shot.

Anuj started wondering as to what next? The enemy was no where in sight. Then why all this firing – shooting birds in the sky – or the sky itself?

This 'free for all' should have gone on for about five minutes when Anuj quietly appeared from behind his column and switched on his wireless set. Then in a voice authoritative and firm – he commanded:

'Panther here (Anuj's – code name for the day) – all forces – ceasefire ... forthwith and report .... No more firing unless enemy appeared in sight. Understand – over'.

A few seconds and one of the four wireless sets came alive and reported:

'Hallo Panther – column Alpha reporting – firing stopped – over'.

A few seconds later, another wireless set came alive:

'Sir, column Bravo reporting – firing stopped –570 rounds fired – over'.

Again – 'Column Charlie reporting – firing stopped – 100 rounds fired – over'.

And with that message the police radio network went into listening mode again. The strains of music continued as before – the transistor relaying songs from New Delhi station of the All India Radio.

'Jiski kismet mein gam ke bichone the,
Aansoo bhi salone the
Dukh bhari ankhiyan thee,
Dard hi sakhiyan theen,
Ghar bhi na tha koi, aur dar bhi na tha koi'

(Fate has granted her
Beds of misery
Tears of pain
Pain filled eyes
Pain as companion
No home, no hearth to call her own)

Anuj stared for quite some time at the vista unfolding before him – in slow motion. How could it be...such heavy firing and the transistor still continues to play?

It took him a couple of minutes to get in control of himself – also the situation. Then slowly but in carefully selected words, he came over his wireless set again and announced.

'All columns – stand by ... can anyone of you hear songs .... can you locate its source .... can anyone see D7 or any member of his gang .... O.kay – watch front and report ... over'.

Within a few seconds the wireless sets started responding.

'Column Alpha reporting Sir ... no trace of D-7 in my observation area ... Can't locate the source of music either ... over'.

'Column Bravo reporting sir... D-7 not seen in my area .... Source of music seems to be 12 O'clock (in front) of column Charlie .... 150 mts. upfront .... Over'.

Anuj intervened and announced:

'All columns attention .... column Charlie to despatch a recee (reconnaissance) party for search of area 12 O'clock of them ... objective to locate the source of music and the enemy... All columns to observe strict ceasefire .... No firing at all .... even on dacoits.... All forces will hold fire till my further orders .... Understand ... Comply .... over'.

Strains of music continue as before:

'Dil mein ye armaan the ek chota sa bangla ho;

Chand ki dharti pe, ek sone ka jangla ho,

khel hon jeevan ke jahan mel hon jeevan ke

ho mel hon jeevan ke,

Gaya bachpan to aansoo bhari aayi jawani,

Suno choti si guidya ki kahani'.

(In her heart she nurtured dreams

of a small house ... somewhere,

on the moon – a barricade done in gold,

living in which one could play the games of life and love

and make everlasting friends –

Giving way to the innocence of childhood arrived

Youth ... full of tears

Listen to long tearful story of the tiny doll – Gudiya)

* * * * *

The recce – party taken out by column charlie had just 12

policemen plus the informer. Anuj led the party himself. All twelve were armed with automatic and small firearms.

The party set off for Dau-Bharak in arrow-head formation and kept on leap-frogging towards its destination. In less than 10 minutes they were in Dau-Bharak. What they saw there on arrival – left then dumb-founded – stunned. The scene inside Dau-Bharak was heart-rending! Hand grenades had played havoc – everywhere. They had blown off to bits each and every article. The only thing that had survived destruction was the rather tiny National transistor radio, sitting atop a rectangular boulder, in one corner. It continued to relay the Vividh Bharati programme, broadcast by the Delhi station of the All India Radio.

Mutilated bodies of as many as eight dacoits lay sprawled over the ground – some staring vacantly into the skies. Some had received one full grenade blast. Others had received just a few splinters – but in vital organs. The head of one lay sliced into two with blood oozing profusely from the wound. Another grenade splinter had pierced the eye of one dacoit. One had received as many as four splinters in his heart region. In one corner of the 'Bharak' lay stacked, mattresses and quilts. They had all caught fire. Another corpse dressed in old, torn, khaki bush-shirt and pants lay face down – blood soaked, long, black grey peppered hair and thin small body. Plastic slippers have come out from the feet revealing a heel full of cracks. The corpse bore no obvious signs of injury. Could be that a really small splinter had entered the heart region – unnoticed.

Whose gang is this? Who are these dacoits? Is it D-7 Rampala's gang for whom this raid was organised? None of them looks like Rampala. Rampala is more than 6 feet tall – is heavily built, has a long flowing beard and long hair – tied on top of the skull in a massive bun.

Dance of death in the ravines notwithstanding the transistor continued to relay songs.

"*Pyar ke raste hon, aur phool baraste hon,*

Banna chahti thi ek din woh taron ki rani,

(She yearned for – alleys of love with showers of flowers

Aspired to become – one day, the queen of stars)."

Not able to fix up the identity of the gang, Anuj started getting worked up. In a fit of rage he summoned the informer, shouting:

"Get that bastard of an informer here. Let him speak out who all has he got killed today?"

The informer was close by. One of the constables caught hold of him by his collar and threw him on the ground in front of Anuj.

Anuj thundered, 'who are all these men whom you have got murdered? Look at the dead bodies closely and tell us'.

Informer took a quick look at the dead bodies. Then he turned towards Anuj and said:

'Maharaj, I can't see him among the dead bodies'.

'Which him?' thundered Anuj.

'Arre, Maharaj, ... Rampala, who else?'

'What rubbish are you talking .... you bastard?'

'Yes sir, none of these dead bodies is that of Rampala'.

Anuj's face turned pale. He queried:

'Then, who are they? They all look like dacoits. Have weapons upon them. Are dressed like dacoits. And that one body lying face down – whose it could be? Rampala's?'

"Can't be that of Rampala' Maharaj. Rampala is so tall that if he raised his hands he would touch the ceiling of your house."

Anuj lost his temper. In exasperation, he caught hold of the informer by his collar, shook him violently, then gave him a mighty right-handed slap which sent the informer reeling. As the informer was trying to get up, Anuj kicked him... saying:

'You bastard – you swine – you son of a bastard – you black guard – Saale – harami! If you have got innocent villagers killed, then you will be made to pay for it – right here. I assure you. I will turn you into the ninth dead body – here itself. Now quickly go and turn over that corpse lying face down and tell me whose is it?'

The informer tip toed to the dead body – Anuj following closely behind. The informer fearfully turned the corpse over and said:

'Maharaj, this is not Rampala... this is... this ...'.

Anuj was standing close by. It didn't take him more than a glance to identify the dead body. He took off his beret cap – came to attention and saluted the dead body. Tears started trickling down his cheeks, wetting his uniform. The dead woman's buttons on the bush shirt had come off revealing her stomach and bra. Anuj took off the towel that he was wearing around his neck as protection against the scorching sun and 'loo' (hot winds), and gently spread it over the exposed parts of the dead body, covering them fully.

In death, the woman's eyes were open – seeing dreams of a settled life after surrender. Anuj bent low over the dead body and with his hand, covered the eyes for a few seconds. As he withdrew his hand the eyes were closed. The grenade blasts had dishevelled her hair. They were spread all over her face. He moved closer to the head and using his fingertips shifted the dishevelled hair to over her temples – exposing her face fully.

It was getting 3 O'clock. The farmaish or request programme was getting over:

"Toote pal bhar me, sapnon ke moti bhi,

gayee aankhon ki jyoti bhi

Rah gaye andhere, ujre hue savere...".

(Vanished in a fraction were all the pearly dreams.

Gone was the light of the eyes.

What remained was enveloping darkness

A dawn of trampled dreams)

The Vividh Bharti Programme came to end – also came to an end the story of the little doll

'Chhoti Si Gudiya Ki Kahani'.

Anuj walked over to the place where the transistor radio was kept – picked it up carefully, switched it off – dusted it and lifting the woman dacoit's head slightly, with care and respect, slipped the radio under the dead woman's head. He, thereafter put on his beret cap, handed over his sten to the nearest constable and pulling the mike of his manpack set in front of him, in a hushed tone, he started speaking – slowly and carefully:

'All stations attention – Panther calling – raid is over – officers and men to close at Ater-Porsa road crossing... Dy. SP, Madho Singh with one section to take charge of the dead bodies and the encounter venue ... D-7 remains safe ... D-3 Gudiya with her entire gang liquidated... Gudiya is no more.... understand ... All Stations ... over and out'.

* * * * *

Noor Mohd. Sector Commander Noorabad had come to know, of the raid in the ravines surrounding Ater and Udotgarh Police Stations. He was keenly monitoring over his wireless set – the progress of the raid – listening to the chatter between various wireless stations. He was therefore the first one outside the ravines to hear of the liquidation of D-3 (Gudiya) gang. The other one to hear Anuj's last announcement over his wireless set was SP, Morena. Noor Mohd. lost no time in informing the IGP in Bhopal through a wireless message of D-3's death in an encounter. S.P., Morena went one step further and conveyed the news over telephone to the IGP – also to the news room of the All India Radio, in Bhopal.

Teleprinters in various News Agency offices started ticking. They had a sensational news story at hand. All of them started searching for Gudiya's photograph – which no one had.

Anuj had given a word to the informer that after the raid he would be carried in a police vehicle, and dropped at a place of his choice. Anuj however, got busy in completion of the legal formalities associated with the encounter. Dead bodies needed to be identified – sent for post mortem prior to their delivery to the next of the kin. Arrangements for sending bodies to their respective villages and for funerals required to be made. Cases required to be registered at police station Ater. All possessions found in Dau-Bharak, belonging to the D-3 gang were to be seized and Panchnamas (seizure memos) were to be prepared. All this was going to take time. Therefore, there was no question of Anuj returning to Bhind and informing all concerned.

* * * * *

No sooner the raiding parties – with the exception of skeletal staff required by Dy. SP, Madho Singh – left for Ater-Porsa road junction, Anuj remembered the informer and therefore summoned him. The informer had been hiding in a depression nearby. He had covered himself fully, from head to toe with a rug picked up by one constable from the site of encounter. Unless one came really close, it was impossible to know whether he was dead or alive. Anuj accompanied by Madho Singh went as close to him as possible and no sooner they were certain that they were not being watched he put the informer up on his feet. They found the informer shivering .... with fear. Madho Singh advanced one step ahead and slapped him hard, asking him the reason for this unusual behaviour. It took the informer a little time to recover from the shock. But once he did, he started speaking:

'Maharaj, I have definitely been cheated. There surely has been some foul play. How is it possible that when the information was about the presence of Rampala – Gudiya would get killed – on the same spot? Has such a thing ever happened – before?'

Madho Singh was on the verge of loosing his patience with the informer. He caught hold of the teacher by the scruff of his neck and asked: 'Now tell us Kàkku, what exactly were you plans and at whose behest you were acting? Else I am not going to leave you alive ... Bastard, you son of a bitch ... You have got a dacoit killed who was going to surrender – alongwith her entire gang, within a few days. He let go some more adjectives before quieting down.

'Maharaj, you are unnecessarily getting angry. I am not at all at fault. Chotey Kaptan, you know Sobarna – the dacoit from Rampala's gang who had entered my house in my absence and molested my wife? He came and told me that on the molestation issue he has fallen out with Rampala and that he now wants to get Rampala killed – by way of revenge. He went to the extent of telling me that he was ready to share – half and half - the entire reward money that they would get –

by getting Rampala killed. He was the one who was informing me regularly, about Rampala's whereabouts. He used to give the same information to the Police Station too. The two informations i.e. the one given to the Police Station and the other given to me tallied. I therefore, started trusting Sobarana. He visited me last night saying that Rampala is hiding in Dao-Bharak with his entire gang – though information in the village at that time was that Lodhi gang of Rampala has moved into Phup Police Station area, after handing over a very stern warning to Gudiya – even threatening her with her life. Villagers believed that only Gudiya gang was now in Dau-Bharak. So Maharaj, I believe that some one has short changed me – has used me to get Gudiya killed. And if this is true, then I now face the gravest threat to my life.'

Having said all this the informer relapsed into a long spell of silence.

Gudiya's death has already left Anuj shattered. She trusted him as she would, her real elder brother. She had accepted him as her real elder brother. She had entered Ater Police Station area only on an assurance of safety from him. He has failed a trusting woman! He has got his own 'sister' killed. He has betrayed not just a dacoit but a sister who trusted him, in totality – had even fixed a date for her surrender and had demanded security from him – for just those few ... intervening days. This is nothing short of murder – a deceitful and dastardly killing. It is the murder of a person who having decided to give up the path of violence was looking forward to return to a peaceful life!

Anuj got over such depressing thoughts with great effort and having done so started speaking –haltingly and then normally.

"Masterji (teacher) – please don't worry about your security. Police will look after you. On your part, you should also be careful. Should you at any time, want to join the police force – I will help you out – of course after taking permission from my IGP. Presently, according to my assurance to you, I will get you dropped at any place of your choice. It is going to get dark soon and once it was dark no one will recognise you. So get along'.

Then after some hesitation:

'Madho Singh – is this okay with you? You have to drop him ... wherever he wants.'

'No problem Sir – give me just a few minutes', said Madho Singh with alacrity and after coming to attention.

It should have been a couple of minutes when Madho Singh turned towards the informer and catching hold of him by his elbow he started walking him towards his jeep, which had since arrived in Dau-Bharak. The two should have taken just a couple of steps when the informer shook himself free from Madho Singh and having pulled out a white scarf form his pocket covered his face – minus the eyes – tightly with it. Then turning towards Anuj he said:

'Ram, Ram – Chotey Kaptan – shall meet again, if I survived!' Then turning towards Madho Singh he said, 'Let's go, Maharaj. I am ready – and no sooner it gets dark enough you can drop me anywhere – any place of your choice'.

And then without waiting for Madho Singh's response he started marching towards the jeep parked nearby – should have just gone a few steps, when from behind his tightly muffled face he started chanting – loudly and clearly ... the Hindu funeral chant.

'Shri Ram Nam Satya Hai ... Arre Ram Nam Satya Hai ... Ji Ram Nam Satya Hai...'

He continued singing the above chant rhythmatically and without break all through. Notes were loud and clear when the intervening distance was short. They started fading as the distance increased. They became inaudible no sooner the informer accompanied by Madho Singh turned a corner in the ravines.

Madho Singh's departure left Anuj alone ... in the wilderness of Dao-Bharak. He started feeling apprehensive. He realised that someone has made him a pawn in his game of deceit and murder. But who can he be? Why is the teacher so terrified? Whom did he fear – what were his fears? Such negative thoughts started making Anuj feel uncomfortable. He, therefore decided to shake such fears off, and to get on with the job at hand.

He decided to walk back to the scene of encounter in Dau Bharak. Which was just about 20 metres away. He should have normally walked this distance in a few seconds. But the uneven terrain and the gathering shadows of the evening made him loose his way. In a bid to recapture his bearings he climbed on to the nearest highest point and arriving there he re-set his bearings towards the scene of encounter. While descending, he landed into three fully prepared funeral pyres (*chitas*) minus the dead bodies – ready to be lit. Discovery of the funeral pyres surprised Anuj. For whom were they readied? When? Fear started crawling all over him. In a bid to confirm that they were actually funeral pyres, he walked close enough to them! Indeed they were *chitas* – but for whom?

It had become fairly dark by then. He therefore decided to retrieve his steps and walk back to the place of encounter. It should have been a minute and he was at the exact spot where Gudiya's body lay a couple of hours earlier. He bent down respectfully over the spot and touched that patch of ground where Gudiya's blood was spilled – with his hand – and then he touched the same hand to his eyes. He then came to attention and raised his hand in salute.

Officers from Ater Police Station were busy completing the legal formalities. About two dozens villagers from nearby villages had arrived on the spot. They all came to attention as Anuj arrived and started congratulating him for a successful encounter. Anuj ignored them. He saw the local inspector standing to attention and therefore asked him:

'Have you seen those funeral pyres, nearby. For whom were they readied?'

'Yes, sir! The villagers say they were readied only this morning – on Gudiya's orders. She had mentioned that she had to cremate three dead bodies by this evening ... before departure'.

'Whose bodies were to be cremated' asked Anuj.

One villager came forward and started speaking:

'Sir, Gudiya didn't tell us whose bodies were to be cremated. She just wanted us to ready the pyres. She had told us not to enter Dau-Bharak. Therefore, we know, no more.'

The local Inspector who was listening to all this quietly, lost his temper and cut-through the villager's dialogue by shouting: 'Why don't you 'haramis' tell the truth... you bastards? My Sir is wanting to know the truth – which all of you know. Do I need to kick your asses – for you to tell the truth ... you haramis (bastards).'

Inspector's outburst stunned the villagers. They knew that the Inspector meant business. One villager therefore came forward and on strict oath of secrecy started speaking.

'Maharaj, while we were busy collecting wood, dry grass, cow-dung cakes and bamboo for readying the pyre, we came to know that Rampala had visited Gudiya the previous evening seeking a settlement, but had ended up shooting down three of her colleagues. While we were busy preparing the pyres, Gudiya visited us twice or thrice – for checking the progress. She appeared tired and emaciated ... invariably on verge of tears.'

Anuj listened – in rapt attention. He was willing to believe what the villager has just said. He wanted to fix up the sequence of events and therefore he started going over mentally into the incidents of yesterday and today. Dead bodies should have been the reason for Gudiya sticking on to Dau-Bharak, police raids during the past two days notwithstanding. She would have been wanting to give a decent funeral in presence of a priest and all – to her three dead colleagues. It could also be that she had implicit faith in 'my' assurance of safety extended to her, that 'within Ater Police Station area she need have no fears.' However of what use is it now going over all those things. – he mumbled?

Anuj directed the local Inspector to seize the pyres since they would become useful pieces of evidence in case D-7 was ever brought to trial for those three murders. He was lost in thoughts when Madho Singh returned completing his errand. He confirmed having dropped the informer at a place of his choice, on Ater-Porsa road. He also mentioned that since it had become totally dark by then, no one would have seen the informer alighting from the police vehicle. Madho Singh added that the informer did keep on chanting 'Ram Naam Satya Hai' all along – even after he had got down from the police jeep.

It was nine in the night when the procedural formalities got completed. The dead bodies were sent to 'Porsa Civil Hospital' for post-mortem. The doctor in Porsa had earlier sent a radio message informing that rules prohibited post-mortems after sunset and therefore the police parties would be required to wait till day break of June 1. Arrangements were put in place for handing over dead bodies, after the post-mortem examination to the next of the kin of the deceased.

Anuj suddenly remembered Gudiya's sister Puniya. She needs to be told officially, of her sister's death. Anuj asked the driver of one of the police jeeps to leave for Agra straightaway – accompanied by one police officer – for informing Puniya of her sister's death in an encounter, and for bringing her to her village in the same jeep – if she so desired.

In the meanwhile, detailed lists were ready of the items seized from the place of encounter. Seizure memos had been prepared. A case under appropriate sections of law had been registered and investigation set in motion. Establishing the identity of the slain dacoits was no problem – many villagers were ready to identify the dead bodies. Sikandara and his two accomplices, responsible for the Khipona incident were among those killed. However, the three had just one bullet mark each on their temples and one bullet each in the heart region. Anuj wondered, how a grenade explosion could have caused identical injuries in as many as three persons. He, however, put off the solution of this mystery to some later date.

Finding on-the-spot proceedings satisfactorily completed Anuj thought of returning to Bhind. He therefore got into his jeep. In the last minute he remembered something. He therefore got out of his jeep again! Then he, resolutely walked over to the corner where the seized items were kept and picked up Gudiya's transistor from amongst them. Thereafter, with transistor in his hand he walked back to his jeep, got into the driver's seat and left for Bhind, reaching there in an hour's time.

* * * * *

***<u>1st June 1959</u>*:** Anuj was dead tired and therefore went to sleep no sooner he hit the bed – in uniform, sans jungle boots. When he got up in the morning he found himself in a state of shock, disgust and remorse. His head was still unclear when his telephone rang and he found the IGP on line.

'Anuj, how did you kill Gudiya? Was she not surrendering – in a week's time?'

'Sir! I'll get back to you in a couple of day's time. At the moment, I am myself unaware as to how Gudiya got killed when the information and raid were both for D-7. Sir! please give me a couple of day's time.'

'Okay Anuj. All the best – was it not your duty to protect her till her surrender?'

'Certainly sir,' replied Anuj.

'Okay'. And the telephone line went dead – abruptly.

* * * * *

Puniya arrived in Bhind from Agra, at about 1030 a.m. Anuj has already placed in position arrangements for her journey to Porsa where her sister's body lay in the hospital – also for her onward journey to her village, along with Gudiya's dead body.

Puniya was in tears all the time. Anuj too was finding it difficult to control his tears. Prior to her departure she collapsed on to Anuj's feet and amidst tears asked:

'How did this happen, Bhaiyya? A sister done to death – by her own brother? She trusted you, Bhaiyya – so completely?'

Anuj remained dumb-struck. He gave no answer. In fact, he had no answer! How can one answer for the games the Destiny plays?

On his signal the jeep started moving forward carrying

one sister in tears, for being with another sister who was alive and full of life 24 hours earlier – gone now!

Anuj received the post-mortem report from Porsa over wireless. The report confirmed the cause of death of Gudiya and of her five associates to be injuries caused by grenade splinters, penetrating vital organs. The report went on to add that Sikandara and two of his colleagues did not die in encounter, but died as a result of small-arms injury, inflicted upon their temples from close range – about 15-20 hours before Gudiya's death.

Anuj clenched his teeth and muttered to himself, 'Rampala – I will get even with you soon – you bastard?'

By evening all the bodies had been despatched to their respective villages – under police escort. Gudiya's parents decided to cremate their daughter – in the ravines only, on the bank of river Chambal – close enough to her own village.

Anuj decided to attend Gudiya's cremation. He was restless, remorseful and unable to concentrate on anything when one constable walked into his room. He was the very same constable who had been left behind in Anuj's residence, since his uniform had been loaned to the informer for concealing his identity. The constable saluted Anuj and informed him that less than half an hour after his departure on raid – the 'Sahukar' from Gormi arrived with a letter, which he received on his behalf and left it on Anuj's table. Anuj directed the constable to return to the police lines forthwith and that he would find out the letter himself.

No sooner the constable was out of his gate, Anuj started searching for the letter. More than hundred messages – mostly congratulatory – lay piled upon his desk. He, however, couldn't find the letter. He wanted to have a second-round search. But his orderly entered the room informing him of the dinner having been served. Anuj was not hungry at all. He, however, went through the motion. He then took the receiver off the hook and went to sleep.

* * * * *

__2nd June, 1959__: Nothing, that could be important for this story happened, till the early afternoon. Anuj attended office as usual and disposed routine work. He thereafter, returned home and sat down to a light lunch. Then, he left for Gudiya's village – escorted by a jeep and four armed policemen. In an hour's time he was in Gudiya's village.

There, he found Gudiya's body lying under the shade of a big neem tree – just outside her father's house. All items required for the cremation have already been procured. Women from the neighbourhood sat around the dead body. No one cried – except Puniya. Many from amongst the gathering felt that it would be wrong to mourn Gudiya's death since only in death has she found real 'moksha' (salvation) – real peace – freedom from her tragic and beleaguered existence.

Gudiya – in her death, appeared tranquil and relaxed – totally at peace with herself.

* * * * *

Bamboos, rope, white cloth, grass, cow-dung cakes, sacred thread 'Nara', Ganga Jal, fire from the hearth etc. – everything needed for cremation was ready. On Anuj's instructions policemen from his escort party started readying the *arthi* (pyre). In life all arrivals are so slow – so full of wait – all departures are so swift. It would have been just 10 minutes and the *arthi* (pyre) for carrying Gudiya's dead body to the river bank, was ready.

Anuj helped Puniya's husband in placing Gudiya's dead body over the '*arthi*'. Puniya used her fingers to rearrange Gudiya's clothes and her dishevelled hair...also by moving Gudiya's hands and feet she brought the body into a more relaxed position. Anuj covered Gudiya's body with white cloth – leaving her face uncovered. The body was then tied on to '*arthi*' with the multi-coloured sacred thread drawn over and over again. Puniya sprinkled Ganga Jal (water from sacred river Ganga) over Gudiya's dead body.

The two parents were the last to be brought for having a last look at their daughter. Mother started crying uncontrollably and the father collapsed upon the *arthi*. As he regained consciousness, he said his final farewell.

"My dear daughter .... what a life? What a death? Why did God ever sent you to this earth – full of wicked people? To suffer .... to suffer! Go bitiya (dear daughter)... Go! Find peace in the arms of Bhagwan Ram!"

The neighbours dragged the two parents inside and left Puniya behind – for looking after them.

And so started Gudiya on her final journey – on mother earth – earth which gave her life but nothing else ... except tears and struggle.

Still one should be thankful to Providence for smaller mercies – Ma Durga gave her strength to fight injustice – made her die at the hands of a very good soul – her own brother!

* * * * *

Anuj and Puniya's husband lifted the '*arthi*' on to their shoulders – almost the entire neighbourhood joined in. Everyone started chanting "Ram Naam Satya Hai...".

It should have been ten minutes, and the funeral party was on the banks of river Chambal. Gudiya's body was taken straight from the '*arthi*' on to the 'chita' (pyre). Anuj asked one of his jawans to fetch Gudiya's transistor from his jeep. He wanted to play some music for her. After the transistor had been brought, he switched it on and tried several stations of the All India Radio. Unfortunately, none was playing songs at that time. At Anuj's request it was agreed to delay the cremation by about ten minutes so that he could arrange some music for the deceased. Anuj had brought a cassette player too in his jeep. He directed one of his policeman to fetch it, which he did forthwith. No sooner the cassette player was in his hands, he fixed a cassette on to it and turned the play switch on. The cassette player started playing "*Suno Chhoti Si Gudiya Ki Lambi Kahani*" – the song which gave away Gudiya's location to the police – the song which should have filled her ears..., till in a fraction of a second she was no more....she was gone!

Puniya's husband lit the funeral pyre and in a few minutes the final and the only remains of one troubled existence were engulfed in flames.

Anuj kept on playing "*Suno Chhoti Si Gudiya Ki Lambi Kahani*" – again and again, till the cremation was over! The cassette ended the long story of one very fragile Gudiya. Simultaneously, the fire in the 'chita' exhausted whatever remained of the troubled existence of one female – one bandit queen.

Once Gudiya's body had been swallowed by fire, Anuj got up and saluted. Others followed him. Soon everyone was returning to their villages, leaving Gudiya behind – in the wilderness of ravines and the vastness of eternity.

Everyone was sad! Everyone felt that Gudiya should have been spared such a tragic end – at the hands of her own brother

– just prior to her surrender – hers trying to turn a new leaf in her life!

Yet, there was one person who rejoiced this unexpected turn of events. He had lit up his house as if it was 'Deepawali' night. Fireworks and festivities were going on non-stop at his house. And that was Ram Bharose. He was happy at the thought that in the kingdom of 'the king of fair play', it was finally evil which triumphed – a criminal had come out victorious!

* * * * *

Enroute to Gudiya's house, it became dark. Anuj stopped by at Gudiya's house, got down from his jeep, picked up Gudiya's transistor and handed it over to Puniya as a reminder of her sister's great love for music. He thereafter, took leave of Gudiya's parents and got into his jeep. Within few minutes the two jeeps were swallowed by the darkness of the night.

In less than half an hour the two jeeps were on the Ater-Porsa road. Anuj was driving his jeep alright, but his mind was not at all in driving. He was too shaken by his own misfortunes and the 'tragedy'. Something lying by the roadside – wrapped in a bed sheet, jolted him back to reality. He had to brake suddenly to prevent his jeep from running over that object. The jeep skidded about 10 metres on the metalled road, before coming to a halt. The following jeep too came to a halt behind him. Both vehicles had to reverse some 10 metres to arrive at the spot where the object lay. In an effort to light up the road the two jeeps left their head lights on.

Anuj quickly got out of his jeep and went close enough to that strange object lying wrapped in a white bed sheet. Then in one motion he bent down and pulled the sheet from one corner. It was a dead body! Anuj jumped back a few feet, surprised – frightened. It was the dead body of the teacher, the informer – lying stone dead. A small wound on the temple – blood oozing out from one corner of his mouth.

Anuj found his heart undergoing a painful spasm. How many more people would need to die for his one single folly. He remembered the teacher taking leave day before and reciting the funeral chant – no end. He should have anticipated his murder. At least he said so. It took just two days for his premonition to come true. A lucky guy one way. The king of kings in good grace, allowed him the freedom to recite his own funeral chant.

Anuj was too overcome with grief. He did not want to have a second look at the dead body. He therefore entrusted his escort to discharge the unpleasant responsibility of first ferrying the dead body to Police Station Ater and then to the teacher's village. The escort complied with Anuj's instructions by promptly and very respectfully picking up the dead body from the road. As they were placing the dead body on to the rear seat, they noticed a chit tied on to the neck of the deceased. They carefully removed it and handed it over to Anuj – who moved in front of the headlights to read it.

'Chotey Kaptan! A very small gift in your honour. Maharaj – at least now acknowledge that if you are a honest police-wallah, I am also a great 'papi' (sinner) – a big harami and a great criminal. You wanted to get me killed. You did not succeed. You will never succeed. Gudiya was playing tricks with me. She planned to get me killed – with your help. As a rule, baghis don't fire at each other. They certainly don't fire at woman. I also didn't. But look at it – she is dead. You should be sad loosing a sister. I too am sad seeing a fellow baghi killed. But she has gone, as we believe, in the true baghi tradition – as the baghis prefer to go – receiving a police bullet on to their chest'. From one great harami – Rampala D-7.'

Anuj folded the letter and placed it carefully into his shirt pocket. He did not disclose its contents to anyone.

He reached Bhind in less than an hour and went straight to bed-could manage no sleep. The entire night went by – tossing in bed.

First thing in the morning, he rang up the IGP in Bhopal and sought his permission for an interview with him which was promptly granted. He arrived Gwalior that very evening and was in Bhopal the next morning.

* * * * *

4th June 1959: Anuj met the IGP at 10 a.m. – the first visitor in the morning. He had gone to Bhopal ready with his letter of resignation on personal grounds – which he handed over to the IGP. Orally, he admitted his failure in not having been able to fulfil his duties as an upright IPS officer. He went on to add that he has decided to quit due to utter sense of humiliation, defeat and sadness arising from the death of his own 'adopted' sister – at his very own hands – that too just a few days short of her planned surrender. The IGP tried to console and encourage him. He praised Anuj no end and told him that such incidents do occur while dealing with dacoits and seasoned criminals. However, nothing worked. Anuj had taken seriously his failure in being able to protect not only Gudiya but also the teacher and he was not willing to agree to have a rethink on his resignation.

When Anuj finally told the IGP, in no uncertain terms, that he has lost interest in working for the police department and in the context of what had happened – would not be able to do justice to his job, the IGP reluctantly agreed. He told Anuj that he would soon speak to the Chief Minister and the

Union Home Minister and would get his resignation accepted within a month.

Anuj used this opportunity to inform the IGP of his suspicion about foul play in Gudiya's death – a few days prior to her surrender. He said that Gudiya perhaps became a casualty of a well-planned conspiracy, hatched by D-7, who had all along suspected that Gudiya wanted to get him (D-7) killed with the help of police – specially of Anuj – and that the killing was to take place just prior to her own surrender. He added that since dacoits avoid firing at each other, D-7 planted one of his own man, a teacher, as an informer upon Anuj – also upon Ater police. This 'plant' kept on feeding stories to the police about the presence of D-7 in Dau-Bharak, when in effect on the last day, it was only Gudiya's gang which was left in Dau Bharak. D-7, of course had decided to kill the 'plant' too immediately after the police succeeded in liquidating Gudiya – which he did soon enough. To mislead the 'plant' into giving information to the police about presence of D-7, when it was actually Gudiya who was present in Dau-Bharak, he introduced a second person – dacoit Sobarna as a 'cut out'. Sobarna won teacher's confidence by saying that he wanted to settle scores with D-7 (Rampala) and was even willing to share the reward money 50-50 if the teacher passed on information – cooked at Sobarna's end, to Anuj. The chain of information being passed on to Anuj, was therefore not teacher to Anuj – but D-7 to Sobarna to teacher to Anuj – and in effect D-7 was using both Sobarna and teacher to pass on 'misleading information' to both Anuj and to the Ater police."

"However, Sir, these are only my suspicions and it would be quite some time before 'truth' emerged – if at all!"

The IGP was listening to Anuj in rapt attention. He mulled over what Anuj has just said and asked:

'But Anuj, was the teacher so stupid that he could not see the game D-7 was playing?'

'Sir, it appears that the teacher had some reasons to trust Sobarna, blindly – and he could never discover that Sobarna was a mere pawn in D-7's hand. That is why he (teacher) paid for his folly with his life. His getting frightened at the sight of Gudiya's dead body, pointed to his fears. Trusting the information fed to him by Sobarna, the teacher should have genuinely believed that it was the D-7's gang which had been liquidated. Even if the teacher had some inkling of D-7's conspiracy, he was overtaken by events – which were moving at such a brisk pace that he (the teacher) could never get time to think or verify. You can imagine this from the fact that Dau-Bharak was raided thrice in as many days – and in as many days he walked twenty miles to Bhind and back – almost every night.

The IGP had in the meanwhile got out of his chair and moved forward. No sooner Anuj got up from his chair, the IGP held him in a tight embrace – tears in his eyes. Anuj was holding his beret cap in his hands. The IGP patted Anuj in his hair and back – in the manner of a loving father. He blessed Anuj, wishing him a very long and healthy life.

He went on to add: 'I will miss you my boy – greatly. I admired immensely the way you worked – trustingly and fearlessly. Your exit is going to be a great loss – to the police fraternity – personally to me. May God keep you healthy. Let me know if I could ever be any help to you. May God protect you my boy ... ever!'

With one hand on Anuj's shoulder, the IGP unknowingly walked out of his room and into the open verandah of the Police Headquarters. Finding the IGP outside, other officers from the neighbouring cubicles, also started assembling around the – duo. In a few minutes a small crowd had gathered around the IGP and Anuj. No one spoke. The IGP then removed his spects, wiped his tears and started speaking very very gently – emotionally.

'Gentlemen – here bids good bye to the police force – yet another valiant policeman – one who worked more with his heart – one who was willing to stake everything for his principles – for his colleagues. Three cheers for Anuj – Hip, hip hurray! Hip hip hurray! Hip hip hurray! Gentleman, Anuj would ever remain a part of us – part of the police fraternity. Bye-bye- Anuj – Bye!'

The IGP patted Anuj again on his back hugged him again, then did a smart right about turn and disappeared into his room.

Fellow police officers who were left behind in the Police Head Qrs. verandah lifted Anuj up and started singing, 'He is a jolly good fellow – he is a jolly good fellow – he is a jolly good fellow – so say all of us'.

They carried Anuj on to his jeep and then started pulling the jeep out of the Police Head Qrs. Outside the Police Head Qrs. gate they bid him farewell and extended him good wishes for a very bright future.

In a few minutes Anuj was inside the Police Mess situated bang next to the Lower Lake in Bhopal.

Inside the Police Mess, he changed from police uniform into simple pants and shirt and left for the railway station. He was on the train to Gwalior at 8 p.m. enroute to Bhind.

* * * * *

News of Anuj's resignation hit the newspaper headlines next morning. Basic contents were the same. Yet every newspaper had its own story to tell.

Closely following his arrival in Bhind, Anuj applied for one month's leave which was promptly granted. He busied himself in preparing for his departure – destination unknown!

On June 10, he received government orders, accepting his resignation with effect from July 10.

And soon enough, it was July 10. Anuj left Bhind having spent thirty days, attending farewell parties/dinners and taking leave of his colleagues and well-wishers.

During packing, he accidentally discovered the last letter written by Gudiya – received at his residence – soon after his departure for raid on May 31. He went through its contents very carefully, but decided not to take anyone into confidence. He also decided to take this letter as also D-7's letter recovered from the slain teacher's dead body, along with him – as his personal mementos.

* * *

Epilogue

One Year Later

So what happened to D-7 (Rampala)?

He survived another year and added 30 more murders and dozens of other crimes to his score card. People in Bhind and Morena districts started trembling under his fear. Then about a year after Gudiya's death on a similar sizzling afternoon – following one pin-point information from an excellent source, Bhind police, under one new ASP O.N. Shrivastava, succeeded in surrounding him, along with his entire gang, on the top floor of a 2-storied tiled roof construction, in a village within Amayan police station of Bhind district. The ASP kept on requesting him to surrender – avoid bloodshed. But D-7 refused to comply. It had started getting dark and the police officers present on the spot apprehended that if no conclusive action was taken within the next 10-15 minutes, the gang would escape taking cover of darkness. Therefore, an ultimatum 'to surrender within 5 minutes or face imminent death' was conveyed over megaphone. D-7 ignored this time limit too. Finding no alternative, the ASP ordered one LMG (light machine gun) 'burst' to be fired at the upper floor of the house. The house owner had in the meanwhile escaped from the first floor and had confirmed the presence of D-7 along with his entire gang in one room.

D-7 would have perhaps escaped this time too. But his pot of sins had perhaps got filled up to the cracking point. One of the bullets from the LMG burst, hit a kerosene tin kept on the top floor, setting the kerosene on fire. Soon flames became noticeable from outside. In a few minutes the wooden structure of the roof was in flames. A pile of dry grass stacked nearby caught fire too setting the entire house on fire. Three dacoits including Sobarna tried to rush to safety through the back door – but were felled by police bullets. D-7 along with five of his colleagues perished in the fire ... inside the house. One dacoit was subsequently caught, hanging precariously inside a dry well in the neighbour's house. He was captured alive. His presence made the identification of the dead bodies easier.

It was under such dramatic circumstances that D-7's 'king-size life of sin and crime,' came to an end.

* * * * *

Ten Years Later

Nothing happened to **Ram Bharose** till he was seventy. He lived a full life of comfort, intrigue, suppression and oppression till in his seventieth year he passed away – within minutes – in a heart attack. No retribution for sins or crimes.

Twenty Years Later

And what happened to Anuj?

Having resigned from the Indian Police Service, Anuj secured another job with a private company – based in Bombay – now Mumbai. He worked there for almost twenty years. Many believed that the IGP, Madhya Pradesh was behind Anuj getting that job. Then one fine morning he quit this job too – as abruptly as he had quit the police job and settled down into a 2-room cottage in Hershel, enroute to Gangotri. Here he started working with the ISKCON (International Society for Krishna Consciousness) –living the life of a hermit – dressed from head to toe in saffron. The 2-room cottage was so situated that Ma (Mother) Ganga was visible from each room, all the time.

15th April, 1989:

It was Anuj's 55th birthday. Thirty years had elapsed from the date of that fatal encounter with Gudiya.

I was his compatriot in police uniform.

An overpowering urge to meet him and to ascertain his welfare seized me.

Reaching Hershel was no problem. In Hershel too, Anuj was widely known. Everyone knew him since he was composing in Hindi, a condensed commentary on the teachings of Gita – the song celestial. Landing in his cottage, I didn't meet the 'policia Anuj of Bhind!' Instead I met a Sanyasi, all draped in saffron. In 1959 we were contemporaries – he in Bhind and I in Morena. We were therefore meeting after 30 years. He welcomed me – most affectionately.

His eyes misted when during conversation over a hot cup of herbal tea I brought up Gudiya's name. Thirty years had really been a long time for Anuj. The Sanyasi had forgotten almost all details of that day. But he remembered and confirmed in gist all that he had told the IGP in his last meeting with him. On my request he showed me the two letters, which he had saved inside a very antique-looking copy of Ram Charitra Manas – Ramayana – bought according to him from a travelling book-shop in Bhind!

My readers are already aware of the contents of the letter found tied to the informer's (the teacher's) dead body, 48 hours after that fatal encounter.

Regarding the last latter from Gudiya to Anuj…??

Is it possible that, if 'this' letter was received in time by Anuj – i.e. prior to his departure on raid on May 31, 1959 – Gudiya's life would have been saved and, is it also likely that, if Anuj had proceeded on raid that day with a 30 minutes delay, D-7's conspiracy could have been unearthed and foiled – D-7 could have been liquidated, since the information passed on by Gudiya was accurate and pin-pointed – and is it also likely that Gudiya's life would have been saved and she would have got a chance to return to normal life through the process of surrender?

I urge the readers to go through the contents of Gudiya's letter carefully and answer these questions – themselves.

'Chotey Kaptan,

Rampala, these days is very much after me. I don't know his plans. It has been 3 days and he has not allowed me to move out of Dao-Bharak. 10-12 dacoits from his gang, assisted by some gunmen belonging to Ram Bharose are keeping twenty-four hours watch upon me and my gang, and preventing my movements.

Rampala himself came to me last night. He alleged that Sikandara and two of his accomplices did dare to escape from the cordon laid by him (Rampala) and that they have been re-captured near Chombo after a shoot out. Then right in front of me he announced punishment for all the three – got their hands and feet tied with ropes – got them thrown on to the ground face down and then shot them through their temples and hearts. He told me that in their case death was the only appropriate punishment – and since I won't do it – he has done it!

Now the three dead bodies are lying in front of me! How can I move out of this place without giving them – my long time colleagues – a decent cremation?

Bhaiya! Rampala was also alleging that I, in collusion with Chotey Kaptan – and with police help – was conspiring to get him (Rampala) killed. He went on to threaten me that he (Rampala) was an old, crafty, ripened sinner (papi) and that now I should bide my time to enjoy what an old sinner is going to do to me. He went to the extent of saying that Baghis don't fire at each other and at a women – and he would not break any of these traditions. If he did that – he said, the entire dacoit community would spit on his face. He is, however, not going to leave Dau-Bharak, unless he had made appropriate arrangements for dealing with me – he threatened!

Bhaiya! now you alone can save me. I shall be cremating Sikandara and his two associates this evening. After that I am ready to surrender. I am ready to come along with you wherever you want me to surrender. I am ready to surrender right here.

If you do not arrange either, then I would get ready to face Rampala's bullets. But with him, I would not give up – without a fight – without fighting.

We are in Dau-Bharak. ***Rampala is staying at the Mitha Kuan*** *(well containing drinking water) near Barhaiya Khar – exactly between Dau-Bharak and Chombo. He is keeping a watch on me from there itself. I have great faith in you – Bhaiyya! Won't you come to save your sister?*

Your sister, Gudiya".

* * * * *

Reader's would remember that Gudiya got killed just a few days prior to her intended surrender. Readers would also agree that if Gudiya's letter had reached half-an-hour earlier or if Anuj had left for the raid half-an-hour later, not Gudiya, but Rampala would have been killed that very day ... at 'Mitha Kuan'!

But the Gods, resting amidst heavenly comforts had written in black ink – black borders – Gudiya's name against May 31, 1959 and had given licence to veteran sinners like Rampala and Ram Bharose to continue living their life of crime and comfort – of killings, kidnapping and dacoities – without let or hindrance. And has anyone ever won against Gods – against tragedies enacted by that almighty Destiny!! And therefore what are mortals most ordinary – like Gudiya – like Anuj – mere puppets with Them!!!

* * * * *